Light of the Night

Light of the Night

*The Last Eighteen Months
in the Life of Thérèse of Lisieux*

Jean-François Six

UNIVERSITY OF NOTRE DAME PRESS
NOTRE DAME, INDIANA

1998 English Edition published in the U.S.A. by
University of Notre Dame Press
Notre Dame, IN 46556
All Rights Reserved
Manufactured in the United States of America

Translated by John Bowden from the French
Lumière de la Nuit. Les 18 Derniers Mois de Thérèse de Lisieux,
published 1995 by Éditions du Seuil, Paris.

© Éditions du Seuil 1995

Translation © John Bowden 1996

First published in English in 1996 by
SCM Press Ltd
9–17 St Albans Place, London N1 0NX

Typeset at The Spartan Press Ltd
Lymington, Hants, England

Library of Congress Cataloging–in-Publication Data

Six, Jean-François.
    [Lumière de la nuit. English]
    Light of the Night : the last eighteen months in the life of
Thérèse of Lisieux / Jean-François Six : translated by John Bowden.
       p. cm.
    Includes bibliographical references.
    ISBN 0-268-01321-7 (pbk. : alk. paper)
    1. Thérèse, de Lisieux, Saint, 1873–1897. 2. Christian saints—
France—Lisieux—Biography. I. Title.
BX4700.T5S5713 1998
282'.092—dc21   98-9906
[b]

∞ *The paper used in this publication meets the minimum
requirements of the American National Standard for Information Sciences—Permanence of Paper for Printed Library Materials,
ANSI Z39.48-1984.*

Contents

Contents

Contents

Method

For this investigation of the spiritual journey of Thérèse of Lisieux from Easter 1896 until her death on 30 September 1897 I have used only texts which specifically come from Thérèse. This needs some explanation.

In 1950, Mgr Combes was still *persona grata* at the Lisieux Carmel – especially with Mother Agnes, to whom he was bound by a great spiritual friendship – and he hoped to obtain all the truly authentic texts. However, he did not do so and was even to be rejected by the Carmel because of this request. A pioneer in real research into Thérèse and a great theorist on the spiritual life, in a last attempt to reconcile everything he developed a hypothesis to explain the differences that he found between the *Story of a Soul*, the only text then available to the public, and the autobiographical manuscripts of Thérèse, a certain number of fragments of which he had succeeded in getting. These were enormous. His hypothesis was put forward in *Le Problème de l'"histoire d'une âme"*:[1] there are two texts, two originals; Thérèse's autograph is a first draft; the definitive text has been corrected, completed and cut by Pauline (Mother Agnes).

There can be complete agreement on one point: there are two texts, that of Thérèse and that of Pauline. But there is one point on which one cannot follow this hypothesis: the 'definitive' text is not that of Mother Agnes (Pauline), but certainly that of Thérèse. Who would gainsay that today?

Pauline's argument for refusing to publish the true texts of Thérèse was as follows: the *Story of a Soul* had done immense good; it had made Thérèse and her spirituality known, and was an extraordinary success. What more could one want?

I

What would be added by an autograph edition of the true manuscripts?

Why this point of view and this obstinacy? Pauline was persuaded to hold back the truth about Thérèse. She had become Thérèse's 'little mother' when Mme Martin had died. She had been her 'mother prioress' at the Carmel. She sincerely thought that she was the first to have understood the soul of the child Thérèse and that she had been the first to understand the soul of the Carmelite Thérèse. In rewriting the autobiographical manuscripts she had no doubts: she knew Thérèse's thought as well as Thérèse, if not better than Thérèse herself, so she wanted to correct Thérèse and make her accessible to the Carmelites and Catholics of her time. She wanted to become her mother for a third time (or to continue to be her mother) by giving birth to Thérèse for posterity, dedicating herself to bringing Thérèse's spirituality into the world.

'Staging Thérèse's spirituality' would be a better way of putting it.

For half a century Mother Agnes put on a real cinema show (we might remember that the cinema was born in 1895). Thérèse's testimony posed a question for consciences; Mother Agnes and the Lisieux Carmel transformed it into an ordered response, enclosed within four walls, in the same way as at that time charity was transformed into the 'bazaar', a move pioneered by Baroness Staff, who had accommodated the otherness of politeness within worldly rules for society. The language of Mother Agnes, which is the ordinary spiritual language of her time, distorts her sister's text. And as a result, Thérèse's testimony, which is a 'sacrament', i.e. at the same time both symbol and event, presence and absence, cry and question, is basically rejected. This rejection is unconscious: it is required by a vision of the faith, that of Mother Agnes, who regards this testimony as morbid: faith is a knowledge based on the act of seeing and on the certainty which that seems to bring. Mother Agnes keeps her ideas, her themes and her logic; she imposes them as a necessary framework on what to her is an incomprehensible novelty, Thérèse's spiritual revolution. She shamelessly starts from her own spiritual ideology, making a travesty of Thérèse. Happily this travesty is insipid; but what would have happened had Pauline had an incisive thought and style? Her text and her spirituality would certainly have been imposed, for the greater satisfaction of anxious, sensitive and integralist souls – it is all the same. Thérèse's real text would have been 'lost'; indeed, it had to disappear, and almost did disappear. Over the years we can see more and more how Pauline's wineskin was too old for Thérèse's new wine. The 'Thérèse event' as such has thus been long reduced to the level of what preceded it. There has been a subversion of Thérèse. She loves, she wants the other to be, and wants to be with the other, she even wants the impious to exist – she does not eliminate him but wants to receive from him. But this novelty was evaded by Mother Agnes.

So Pauline did not cease to believe, from the death of Thérèse to her own death, not only that she was the authentic interpreter of Thérèse but that she was the one who, literally, was capable of creating her, of giving her to the world. She believed that it was her right to transform; she was only doing her duty. There is precisely nine months between the death of Thérèse and the publication of the *Story of a Soul*, a period of gestation, the period in which Mother Agnes fashioned *her* Thérèse, the Thérèse of the *Story of a Soul*. That is why she allowed the publication of the autobiographical manuscripts only after her death; she only ever wanted to know one Thérèse, the one whom she had brought into the world, the Thérèse of the *Story of a Soul*. For her the other Thérèse, in a way the true Thérèse, did not exist. But in this way she was 'killing a child'.

The *Story of a Soul*, Mother Agnes's Thérèse, has conquered the world like the retouched photographs of Thérèse which also represented Mother Agnes's Thérèse. Scrupulous researcher that he was, Mgr Combes was impressed by the success of the *Story of a Soul*; he called it 'the text which has won souls and given glory to Thérèse all over the world'.

After the publication in 1956 of the authentic manuscripts of Thérèse, a model of honesty and precision, by Fr François de Sainte-Marie and the Carmel (Pauline and Céline having died), unfortunately the argument of the formidable – in the full sense of this adjective – success of the *Story of a Soul* continued to be employed by Lisieux. This success – *vox populi, vox Dei* – canonized the *Story of a Soul* and Mother Agnes.

Here again we can agree on one thing: the Thérèse of the *Story of a Soul* has been canonized by the adherence of millions of readers. We can go even further: it is essentially this Thérèse who was canonized by Rome in 1925, since this canonization mainly came about through the testimonies of Mother Agnes (and the sisters of the Carmel, but Mother Agnes orchestrated them) and the success of the *Story of a Soul*. There was some hesitation about canonizing Thérèse in Rome, but not very much: it had rightly related to this 'crisis' in her faith which Thérèse, it had been noted, had undergone during the last months of her life. This was a canonization through Agnes, which was reinforced by its opponents: if this Thérèse of the *Story of a Soul* had been the laughing-stock of freethinkers and surrealists between 1925 and 1950, these attacks had only reinforced the certainty, of Mother Agnes among others, that she was right.

Certainly, from time to time, some troublemakers like Bernanos had appeared in the Catholic world, reacting against what they called a 'simoniacal' Lisieux: Thérèse, Bernanos wrote, had been 'sold by her sisters'. But he had himself been deeply moved by Thérèse and the fragrance of childhood which he had perceived throughout the *Story of a Soul*.

This has led to an extreme paradox: numerous faithful, simple everyday Christians, priests, religious have succeeded in finding and extracting diamonds, some of extraordinary spiritual richness, from the very text of the *Story of a Soul*, which exasperated some Catholics (Louis Massignon, for example) above all by its idea of the way of childlikeness that was put at the centre of Thérèse's thought by the approved theologians of the time. This is the miracle, the very great and unprecedented miracle, which I believe to have been achieved by Thérèse herself: the Holy Spirit has found the means of bringing out her true thought, despite and through the mists, the indisputable – and thick – mists of the *Story of a Soul*, despite the thousand excessively maternal and suffocating distortions of Mother Agnes. Thérèse's mysticism has found a way of making itself understood by everyday mystics, by hearts in tune with the gospel. Many simple souls who were looking instinctively for a simple spirituality have discovered it in the *Story of a Soul*, despite the wrong signposts and maps falsified and superimposed by Mother Agnes; a track which they have painfully but surely found despite the desertification wrought by Pauline.

I agree, then, with Mgr Combes (whom I knew well and with whom I was able to work) that there are two texts. But we have to follow this logic through to the end and say that there are two spiritualities, that of Mother Agnes and that of Thérèse.

The spirituality of Mother Agnes is a nineteenth-century spirituality – legitimate, certainly, and respectable, a spirituality which corresponds to the sensitivity of the vast majority of the readers of the *Story of a Soul* – and this explains its initial success. Its sensitivity is that of the victim; it is a spirituality of reparation.

If we examine the questions put by Mother Agnes during Thérèse's last months, those which she herself reports in the *Last Conversations*, we can see the point at which they are significant. 31 August: 'If you were to die tomorrow, wouldn't you be afraid? It would be so close!' 5 September: 'If someone told you that you would die suddenly, at this instant, would you be afraid?' On 25 September, Mother Agnes comes to tell her 'what was said in recreation regarding Father Youf [the chaplain, very sick], who had a great fear of death'.

Thus in the last days Mother Agnes expresses to Thérèse, by projection, her own fears of death and the other world. The law of love has not replaced the law of fear in Pauline, whereas the one who is dying, who can hardly speak and yet has to listen to this antiphon, is interested only in the law of love.[2]

In the last year of her life, Thérèse several times took up the same quotation from the Spiritual Canticle of St John of the Cross; she hung on to this thought which she had put forward in her Consecration to the Holy Face, on 6 August 1896; she included it in her letter to Fr Roulland on 19 March 1897; and she put it on each side of the farewell to her sisters in June 1897: 'The smallest movement of pure love is more useful to the Church than all the works that have been achieved.' In the Consecration she had underlined the words *pure love*. And she underlines them again when she quotes this text, this time in an even more significant way, since she is doing so in manuscript B and her hymn to love. Having quoted St John of the Cross, Thérèse adds – and this is a moving question: 'But is *pure love* in my heart?'[3]

Mother Agnes read this quotation form the Spiritual Canticle at least in the farewell souvenir, and doubtless also in what Thérèse wrote to their sister Marie in September; she could not have failed to recall Thérèse's position: 'To satisfy Divine *Justice*, perfect victims were necessary, but the law of Love has succeeded to the law of fear.'[4] Mother Agnes remains under the law of fear, and this is the vital point which distinguishes her spirituality from that of Thérèse: she does not achieve the 'bold abandonment'[5] experienced by Thérèse, the abandonment of which François de Sales was the first to speak and which he conceived of as 'almost like the spirit of childhood'.[6]

One might perhaps recall what François de Sales himself experienced. As a historian has well put it, in a Christianity in which people hardly ever spoke of anything but the other world, is it not 'the very fact of positing an ultimate end, a punishment but also a reward, which arouses fear: not just an excessive or tolerable fear, but fear itself?'[7] Perhaps this fear originates in St Augustine, who conceived of love as 'possession or hope'.[8] 'Now it was by rejecting or twisting this conception of love that the seventeenth-century mystics... attained "indifference"; St François de Sales, overwhelmed by anxiety and tortured by the certainty that he was lost, only found a way out one day at Saint-Étienne-des-Grès by accepting damnation provided that he kept love; this 'desperate' gesture, the renunciation of all recompense, immediately freed him from fear. Hundreds of other mystics made this desperate gesture of true abandonment, an impossible but certainly real presupposition.'[9] And Jacques Le Brun shows well that this is the 'ultimate separation from attachment to the expectation of reward',[10] 'a real inward subversion of Christianity: no more fear, good or bad, no more fear of God or anxiety about God'.[11]

This is precisely the subversion which was also brought about by Thérèse. She never felt fear in the face of her trial after Easter 1896; she never felt damned, and she surpassed the desire for eternal reward, achieving 'indifference' to reward or punishment, the indifference spoken of by François de Sales, which is a manifestation of 'pure love'. What a contrast with Mother Agnes, who complains, up to the last weeks, that Thérèse's trial is going on and who is amazed and even scandalized that Thérèse does not want to see it stop!

Stamped with this mercenary, calculating mentality, in which the question of merits – inherited by Thérèse – was foremost, the spirituality of Mother Agnes is thus at the same time masked by the spirit of fear. Her biographer, J.Vinatier, defines her as 'more an ascetic than a real mystic'. 'Pauline was not Thérèse,' he writes discreetly, and he recalls that Thérèse said to her sister: 'You equivocate too much, little Mother; I see only the graces that I have received from the Good God. You always get it wrong.'

A hesitant and scrupulous soul who subsequently would become all the more assured and authoritarian – an assurance and authority which would also stem from the success of the *Story of a Soul* – Mother Agnes shared in the spirituality universal among the Carmels in nineteenth-century France. This was a spirit that was clearly more ascetical than mystical,[12] in which the emphasis was constantly put on the misdeeds committed against God and the reparation that the Carmelites had to accomplish, 'offering themselves as public victims for the sins of men'.[13]

It is possible to point precisely to a very significant genealogy here. The Lisieux Carmel was founded by two religious from the Carmel of Poitiers, and the links between the two houses had remained very close. Now the key figure of the Poitiers Carmel had been Mother Thérèse of Jesus, who died in 1871 at the age of thirty-three; a grand-daughter of Joseph de Maistre, she had entered the Carmel at the age of twenty. 'Her asceticism is the element which strikes one first. She is inventive in imitating the excessive austerities to be found in the lives of the saints.'[14] What motivated her? 'Her spirituality of reparation',[15] 'a protagonist in a struggle of Jacob with the angel which was not to take place at the level of trust but at that of sacrifice'.[16] Mother Thérèse thought all her life that God remained indifferent to her sacrifices; she put herself among the sinners, but in an opposite way to Thérèse: 'Such a drive to put herself irrevocably on the side of the reprobates could only nurture anxiety and despair in her and make peace ever more remote.'[17] 'Only trust could save me,' she rightly said, but she even prevented herself from asking for it from God. Her directors told her to fight this fear which pursued her, otherwise she would never achieve peace.

In the eyes of Thérèse, Mother Agnes (and she tells her so bluntly) is 'a timid little bird'.[18] In her letter of September 1896 to her sister Marie, Thérèse defined herself as 'a little bird assailed by the storm and dark clouds', but a little bird who 'does not fear'.[19] 'To satisfy divine *Justice*, perfect victims were needed, but the law of Love has succeeded to the law of fear, and Love has chosen me as a holocaust, me, a weak and imperfect creature.' We should re-read this phrase of Thérèse's,[20] who had written to Léonie on 12 July 1896, reminding her of the law of Love: 'I find perfection very easy to practise because I have understood that it is a matter of taking hold of *Jesus by the Heart*.' Moreover Mother Agnes betrays herself without thinking in the *Last Conversations*, when she writes: 'I was speaking to her about certain practices of devotion and perfection counselled by the saints, which were a source of discouragement to me,'[21] or again, 'I was telling her: "Alas, I'll have nothing to offer to God when I die; my hands will be empty, and this saddens me very much."'[22]

Thérèse's spirituality is quite different. Once again – and Mgr Combes has also described her in this way – she is a revolutionary. Hers is a spirituality for the twenty-first century, for the third millennium; it could not be understood all at once, nor accepted in depth by those who during this twentieth century continued to be the heirs of the spirituality of the previous century. They did so in good faith, and moreover it was their perfect right.

In 1973, for the centenary of Thérèse's birth, in a book which is a dialogue with René Laurentin,[23] I reacted vigorously to an assertion by my conversation-partner, who saw *The Story of a Soul* as a necessary stage at a time when all hagiography was retouched. 'Was there not need for a pedagogy, an adaptation, so that Thérèse could be accepted by her time?' What was the argument? 'Thérèse has been travestied and people continue to travesty her. This travesty, this adaptation of someone's message, is a common procedure, but it is very damaging. Unbelievers, Christians who could have profited enormously from the writings of Thérèse, have not been able to do so because good souls have put up this smoke-screen, have created this false spirituality of Thérèse...'

In his customary way, Jean Guitton took up René Laurentin's argument about the *Story of a Soul* very cunningly, as is his wont, in a lecture given in 1971: 'If Port-Royal had not issued a rapid and defective edition of Pascal, the public would not have discovered Pascal.' This is Guitton's adaptation of the *felix culpa* of Augustine!

We cannot follow these exegeses. Even if was a natural thing to do for Mother Agnes who, sure of herself, saw no malignancy in it, the transformation of the texts of Thérèse into the *Story of a Soul* is a fault. What kind of a fault? I said to René Laurentin: 'It is a capital sin and a sin against the Spirit to have wanted to engage in this pedagogy which people are now seeking to justify.' Today I would say rather that this was an original fault. Certainly Mother Agnes did not measure its consequences; she believed that she was doing good. Her intentions were good, but they were among those good intentions with which we know hell to be paved. Mother Agnes succumbed to the temptation to do good.

Given her temperament, her passionate fusion with Thérèse, her fears, her desire to promote the family – the good Fr Piat obtained the authentic texts of Thérèse's letters from the Carmel because he had spoken of his plan to publish *The Story of a Family* (which he did in 1948) – Mother Agnes can certainly be excused. But the fault remains a fault, just as an involuntary homicide remains a homicide.

So in 1956, to blot out the original fault, there was the very precise and incomparable work of Fr François de Sainte-Marie. He restored the whole of the autobiographical manuscripts and even, thanks to financial help from the Carmel ('Render to Caesar'...), produced a very expensive facsimile edition. There is only one mistake, which I have indicated, relating to the lay-out of manuscript B; there are also notes which are still too deferential towards the Carmel and by no means critical enough of the original fault of the *Story of a Soul*.

I was ordained priest that year, and I remember how for me this edition was a ray of light in the greyness of the pontificate of Pius XII, which was coming to an end. It was a light and a great hope.

Disenchantment came in 1973, the centenary of the birth of Thérèse. Although my books published at time that by Les Editions du Seuil, *La Véritable Enfance de Thérèse de Lisieux* and *Thérèse de Lisieux au Carmel,* met with widespread approval, they gave rise to extreme stubborn resistance from Lisieux and die-hard supporters, the kind of opposition which can exist among specialists on spiritual matters and which is as terrible as what one sees, for example, in politics. Going far beyond my book, it was a sign that the guardians of the temple of Thérèse were continuing along the line of Agnes and her nineteenth-century spirituality. Certainly they masked this way of persisting in the original fault by engaging in thousands of lyrical effusions or by a profusion of commentaries which claimed to be scientific, but these came close to being no more than mere compilation, without any real reflection which went to the heart of things.

Thus for almost sixty years the real texts were travestied; and those which finally came down to us forty years ago are drowned in sentimentality and pedanticism by those who have the chief and only hand on publications relating to Thérèse and publicity about her. This is a second scandal after the *Story of a Soul*, a scandal in direct line with the first: after more than a century, Thérèse is truly the object of a monumental spiritual swindle (let us not mince words); and it still continues today.

My original mistake – and it is a mistake for which I have never been forgiven, to the point that my books were excluded from the Carmel library – is said to be that I touched on the Martin parents, that I was 'viciously angry' with the Martin family. The vice-postulator in the cause of the beatification of the Martin parents, a priest from the north, thinking that his cause was going to be at least delayed by *La Véritable Enfance...* immediately wrote a work against my book which was not a critique but a bitter diatribe and a false trial. I confess – 'my mistake' – that I am quite amused at this and that I am even more amused that this pamphlet has been used, not least in the venerable *Dictionnaire de spiritualité*, through the article on Thérèse written by a priest cited several times here, also from the north and as much an adulator as his predecessor.

These devotees are wrong to be so annoyed: I am not at all opposed to the canonization of the Martin parents and indeed of all the Martin family including Mother Agnes, if that is what is wanted. If I have noted imperfections in Agnes and in her parents, how – as a disciple of Thérèse – could I think that imperfections could prevent one from being a saint and even canonized? I read the other day: '850 sanctifications and beatifications at least: John Paul II is much more generous with haloes than his predecessors. Pius XII (55) and Paul VI (52) lag far behind.' The more beatifications there are, the more canonizations there will be and the more one can think that among these 'saints' there will be not only religious and virgin martyrs, but everyday people, good lay people, imperfect people. The fact remains that with the canonization of the Martin family, one must hope that church people will not hold it up as the one and only model of the Christian family – if not, demography and the birth rate, for example, would decline, since the parents, who both thought of the convent, ardently desired all their children to be there. And this in fact happened.

In my dialogue with René Laurentin in 1973, I asked several questions which had been raised for me by the centenary edition, begun in 1971. The Lisieux Carmel had in fact planned a vast programme: to present, after the autobiographical manuscripts, established in 1956 by Fr François de Sainte-Marie, 'all the other writings to the same exact standards', as the (unsigned) preface of the Nouvelle Édition du centenaire (Cerf-DDB, 1992, p.7 of the *Manuscrits autobiographiques*) puts it. Why these questions twenty years later? Because this Édition du centenaire, begun in 1971, had once again started with an original mistake: as the first volumes of this edition it had produced two works entitled *Last Conversations* and *Last Words*. This latter work was presented as a synopsis showing the different versions of the 'last conversations' and 'last words'. Now these 'conversations' are not Thérèse.

In a lecture at Notre-Dame de Paris in 1973, Fr Gaucher recognized this. A note in his published lecture – though this was not said at Notre-Dame – in fact claimed: 'Sound criticism cannot put the words reported by witnesses on the same level as what Thérèse wrote. But one cannot neglect the *Last Conversations*, which offer a certain number of serious guarantees of authenticity.' I am in full agreement with the first phrase, which is a truth of La Palice: the *Last Conversations* and the *Last Words* are not writings of Thérèse but 'reported words'. Better, they are sayings wholly constructed by Mother Agnes.[24]

To provide a basis for the second assertion of Fr Guy Gaucher, 'a certain number of serious guarantees of authenticity', in 1992, for the edition of *Last Conversations* an unprecedented host of proofs was advanced: a general introduction of almost 200 pages, comprising even a 'medical diary' and a mass of notes of all kinds. Now the main text of these *Last Conversations*, which forms the essential part of the *Last Conversations*, is what has been called the 'Yellow Notebook' of Mother Agnes, a text which, we are told, has been taken as a basic text; this text takes up 180 pages (of the 925 pages that the volume comprises).[25]

But what is the history of this Yellow Notebook? In 1904, seven years after the death of her sister, Mother Agnes, took up the notes which she had made during Thérèse's lifetime on loose sheets of paper (and nothing more is left of these notes than a fragment of paper torn from a diary and difficult to read) and transcribed them into a 'Black Notebook'. Then the original notes and the Black Notebook disappeared. In 1910, to prepare for her first deposition to the beatification process, Mother Agnes wrote a certain number of pages in 'Green Notebooks', in which she indicated 'words' of Thérèse. As she wrote to the vice-postulator of the cause, these were 'the most beautiful words that Sister Thérèse so to speak dictated to me during her illness'. This 'so to speak' is, we may agree, marvellous!

Between 1922 and 1924, i.e. a quarter of a century after the death of Thérèse, Mother Agnes re-established these 'last words' in a notebook bound in yellow leather, hence the name 'Yellow Notebook'. The sayings of Thérèse are written in it in black ink and the commentaries by Mother Agnes in red ink. Extracts from the Yellow Notebook in a version which was further elaborated were published by the Central Office of Lisieux in 1926 under the title *Novissima Verba. Last Conversations of St Thérèse of the Child Jesus, May-September 1897*. Mother Agnes also affirmed that she could not understand why historians wanted to know the authentic sayings of Thérèse.

Method

Fr Piat was a friend of the curé of my parish. He often came to see him and I well remember meetings which I had with him at the presbytery when I was still a seminarian: he was absolutely convinced that the *Novissima Verba* of Mother Agnes were the *nec plus ultra* of Thérèse's thought. Here we find once again the extraordinary fascination which Mother Agnes exercised until her death on those men and women, including Cardinal Pacelli, the legate of Pope Pius XI in 1937, who approached her; she appeared to be someone who did not transmit the words of Thérèse but who had raised Thérèse above herself, had so to speak consecrated her by her authority.

Once again, I see nothing at all against saying that one can be disciples of Mother Agnes and her spirituality, like Fr Piat and others. There is an 'Agnesian' corpus: a vast correspondence, for example, of Mother Agnes. Moreover, for me not only are the commentaries which Mother Agnes writes in red ink on the words of Thérèse part of the 'Agnesian' corpus, but also the words which she says and thinks come 'from Thérèse'; these are so stamped by Mother Agnes, are so much the result of a process of osmosis, that they have essentially come to be 'from Mother Agnes'. So beyond question one can put the *Last Conversations* and the *Last Words* in the 'Agnesian corpus' and take spiritual nourishment from them all if one wishes and as one wishes. How could I be so presumptuous as to take exception to them? But all this has to be distinguished from Thérèse.

I demonstrated to René Laurentin, who, having himself published the *Logia of Bernadette,* referred to the composition of the Gospels, that I believe that there was nothing in common between these two processes. We are in the twentieth century, and we have written texts from Thérèse: her autobiographical manuscripts, her poems, her prayers, her sketches and her correspondence. And in addition there are those famous 'words' which are said to have been gathered from her in unfavourable circumstances, words which were taken up again, rearranged and digested for more than twenty-five years by Mother Agnes; if she corrected Thérèse's manuscripts in the way of which we are aware, when she succeeded in transforming what there was in the written manuscripts into the *Story of a Soul – scripta manent –* how can one think that she would have kept to a scrupulous and precise reproduction of spoken words – *verba volant*? The *Last Conversations* and the *Last Words* cannot be included in the corpus of Thérèse, nor can they be counted among her texts – and I am waiting for a serious historian to produce arguments to the contrary. And those who shamelessly want us to believe this, discredit themselves in doing so.

The Nouvelle Édition du centenaire appeared in 1992 (8 volumes, 4,780 pages), along with an edition called *Oeuvres complètes* (a single volume of 1670 pages on India paper). These publications have enormous (what other word could one use?) annotations, the fruit of Benedictine work. Here, it has to be said, one has to pick and choose: alongside excellent criticisms of the text, there are highly dubious commentaries and interpretations.

Le Monde asked me to review these volumes – I did not take the initiative. I began by refusing, but they insisted, and the review was published on 25 December 1992 with a title which was *Le Monde*'s, not mine: 'Thérèse against Lisieux'. In the review I posed what for me is 'the real problem', 'the authorization which Mother Agnes gave herself to market the texts', and I added: 'Thérèse herself is said to have given permission to rework them, but even if this is correct – and there is no proof – did she have the right to do so at this point?' I am still awaiting an answer.

Despite their formal title, these publications contain not only the writings of Thérèse of Lisieux but texts, including the *Last Conversations*, which 'are not certain sayings of Thérèse but reportage, indications and testimonies re-written later'.

In 1898, a year after Thérèse's death, Mother Agnes wrote the *Story of a Soul;* a century later, works which are not Thérèse's are published as though they came from her. One cannot but be disconcerted. Alongside eight volumes containing these additions which one could have considered secondary (the matter is open to discussion), at least only Thérèse's texts could have been included in the India-paper volume. Why the desire to include the *Last Conversations* at all costs? And even leaving aside this text, how can anyone have dared to claim that 'of all the religious in the community, [Mother Agnes] was the best placed to grasp the soul of her sister'? Here we find the original mistake once again: Mother Agnes was persuaded that she was the one who best understood the soul of her sister; she succeeded in persuading her community of this, then the ecclesiastical authorities, and even numerous researchers, including the team which published the *Oeuvres complètes*.

One can only admire such power of persuasion. Will I be forgiven for having resisted it, for not having found that the Yellow Notebook was indispensable to understanding the spiritual journey of Thérèse, and finally, with the support of analyses, for having tried to show this spiritual journey as such, without confusing it with that of Mother Agnes? She survived her sister by more than half a century and built a citadel for her, putting in place its fortified bastions, its compulsory passage-ways, which I have rejected. Will I be forgiven? So great are the peevishness and acts of exclusion which have pursued me since I began to write on Thérèse that I am not certain. Never mind, I shall rise above it and use one of Thérèse's methods, humour. Not to mention patience and time.

That is why in this work devoted to the spiritual career of Thérèse and not that of Mother Agnes I have forbidden myself any quotation from the *Last Conversations*. I would be quite happy for others to engage in this work, which would make possible a better distinction still between the one and the other. That is why in this text I have tried to say nothing about Thérèse's last four months outside the texts of Thérèse herself and the testimony of companions. If only we had at least some letter or writing from Mother Marie de Gonzague during that period! But there is nothing, or rather the Carmel of Lisieux has not supplied us with anything... This is quite amazing: didn't the prioress write anything in these four months? Should we suppose that Mother Agnes destroyed the testimony of Mother Marie de Gonzague?[26] One day we shall know. For the moment, in these four months almost our sole source is the remarks of Mother Agnes: as we have seen, these are to be treated with great caution. We are told (p.4 of the cover of the *Oeuvres complètes*) that in his *Histoire d'une vie* Guy Gaucher 'refused to engage in any romancing'. But his Chapter VII, entitled 'Sickness, Passion, Death (April–30 September 1897)' is entirely based on the *Last Conversations* with, for example, the calumnies against Mother Marie de

Gonzague which have been noted. If this is not a romance, it is a story and imitative complicity.

There are *fioretti* – showers of roses – in what one could irreverently have called the 'Lexovian saga': images and photographs. These have been multiplied, the authentic ones and those which have been retouched, those which have been damaged and those which have been turned into portraits. They can be found in the work *Thérèse et Lisieux*, which provides them in abundance and mixes up true and false images; moreover, carried away by their flood, the book becomes a gigantic sequence of images of Épinal even in its romantic and romanticized commentaries: something to satisfy our contemporaries who have become television viewers. We must not keep silent in the face of this publicity which exalts both the horror of the passing-away of a dying woman and the posthumous triumphs of a 'hurricane of glory'. All the images around Thérèse, and even more those put in the category of the miraculous, do not provide the proofs which people would like to impose on us as irrefutable. How many of these pious images there are in the last conversations of Mother Agnes!

'To Caesar that which is Caesar's.' Let us return to Mother Agnes and what is Mother Agnes's. Here the minimum requirement for a historian is not to confuse his sources, not to attribute to the subject which he is studying, without due consideration, statements which do not truly come from her. I will be told: 'Yes, but this or that saying in the *Last Conversations* sheds real light.' Over the at least twenty-five years that I have been studying all the texts, for all my good will I have not become convinced of this. But it is still possible to convince me; I am in no way blocked on a position. Quite simply, I love the virtue of prudence.

So readers will find in this work devoted to the last eighteen months of the life of Thérèse of Lisieux only texts of Thérèse, authentic, certain texts; at no point will they have to ask themselves whether it is Thérèse who is speaking and expressing herself in the quotations. In these pages there is only 'pure Thérèse'; she is a strong wine – one might think like that offered by Jesus in Cana in Galilee.

Note on the texts used in this work

A. The writings of Thérèse

We now have access to all the known authentic texts of Thérèse of Lisieux. They comprise:

– Three major texts, collected under the title *Manuscrits auto-biographiques*:
- Childhood memoirs, written at the request of Mother Agnes of Jesus, prioress of the Carmel and older sister of Thérèse; these texts were given to Mother Agnes by Thérèse on 20 January 1896 (manuscript A);
- A letter asked for from Thérèse by Sister Marie of the Sacred Heart, another sister of Thérèse, about her spiritual life, written at the beginning of September 1896 (manuscript B);
- A spiritual itinerary asked for from Thérèse by Mother Marie de Gonzague, prioress, written in June and at the beginning of July 1896, unfinished (manuscript C);
– a correspondence (266 letters and notes);
– poems (61 poems);
– pious recreations (8);
– prayers (21);
– various writings.

B. The signs used

1. *Texts of Thérèse*

The three main texts of Thérèse collected in the *Manuscrits autobiographiques* are referred to as A, B and C. They are followed by a number which indicates the original pagination of the manuscript folios of Thérèse herself (e.g. B, 6...). The *Manuscrits autobiographiques* have been published in Paris in the Livre de vie series published by Editions du Seuil, no.8 (last edition 1995). They are also included, with all the other texts of Thérèse, in the *Oeuvres complètes*, Paris: Éditions du Cerf-DDB 1992.

2. Commentaries and other works

French

CJ   *Carnet jaune* (Mother Agnes): published in *DE*.
CV   *Cahiers verts* (Mother Agnes): published in *DE*.
DE   *Derniers Entretiens*, Nouvelle édition du centenaire, Paris: Cerf-DDB 1992
DLTH *Thérèse et Lisieux, Album de photographies*, by H.N. Loose, with commentary by Pierre Descouvemont, Paris: Cerf 1991
DP   *Dernières Paroles*, Nouvelle édition du centenaire, Paris: Cerf-DDB 1992
HA   *Histoire d'une âme* (1898 edition by Mother Agnes), Nouvelle édition du centenaire, Paris: Cerf-DDB 1992
MA   *Commentaires des Manuscrits autobiographiques*, Nouvelle édition du centenaire, Paris: Cerf-DDB 1992
NPPA Notes by the Carmelites preparatory to the apostolic process, unpublished dossier
PA   *Procès apostolique (1915–1917)*, Rome: Édition Teresianum 1976
PO   *Procès de l'ordinaire (1910–1911)*, Rome: Édition Teresianum 1973

Note on English translations

The following translations in the 'Critical Edition of the Complete Works of Saint Thérèse of Lisieux', made by John Clarke, OCD, published by the Institute of Carmelite Studies, Washington DC, have been used in this volume.

GC I *General Correspondence (1877–1890)*, 1982
GC 2 *General Correspondence (1890–1897)*, 1988
LC   *St Thérèse of Lisieux, Her Last Conversations*, 1977
SS   *Story of a Soul, The Autobiography of St Thérèse of Lisieux* (comprises MSS A, B and C), 1975, ²1976

The English reader of Thérèse has one further problem in addition to those discussed in this book, namely that of translation. Translation is never an easy business, and it is all too easy to make mistakes or to distort the meaning. But one has to apply the highest standards to a 'critical edition', and unfortunately the translations listed above are far from being wholly satisfactory.

They have three main weaknesses. First, they are not without simple translation errors, sometimes quite glaring ones. Secondly, the translation of the *Autobiographical Manuscripts* (misleadingly called *Story of a Soul,* which confuses the situation yet further), is often influenced quite strongly by Mother Agnes's text of what can properly be called *Story of a Soul,* to the degree that some of the points made by Fr Six cannot be followed in the English. Thirdly, the translation is often too loose (or too reverential) to be a faithful English rendering of what Thérèse actually wrote; this is particularly the case with capitals and underlining, which play an important part in the following discussion.

Since this is not the place for an extended critical review of the translations, I have contented myself with drawing attention to a few of the most blatant errors or paraphrases by adding comments to the notes. I have consulted the 'Critical Edition' for all passages quoted, but in a number of cases have preferred to make my own translation, in an attempt to keep faithfully to what Thérèse said or wrote.

The problem of reading Thérèse in translation is even greater in other versions; for example, it has been impossible to use the recent edition of her *Poems.* Whatever its literary merits, the choice of rhyming verse gives the translator far too much scope for interpretative paraphrase, which often misses the mark.

For really serious study of Thérèse there seems no real alternative to resorting to the French originals.

John Bowden

1. A Faith on Trial

'The night of nothingness'

In 1896, Easter Day fell on 5 April. Winter had hardly ended in this corner of Normandy, now known world-wide because it was the scene of the Allied invasion of 6 June 1944. After thirteen bombardments, only 300 buildings remained standing in Lisieux, then with a population of 24,000. Most of the marvellous half-timbered Normandy houses had been destroyed; the Carmel, a little convent with red-brick walls in which Thérèse of Lisieux had lived up to her death, had been saved 'by a miracle', as Mother Agnes, prioress of the Carmel and sister of the Saint, put it. So too had the basilica erected in honour of the saint, an enormous domed building which stands to the south-east of the town.

The winter of 1895–1896 was a rough one in Lisieux, not so much because of bitter cold as because of the persistent fine, icy rain in this habitually wet countryside. The religious of the Carmel, built in a particularly damp hollow of land, suffered this winter, all the more so since they fasted strictly during Lent, the forty days preceding Easter. Thérèse of the Child Jesus and the Holy Face, one of these religious, says that she observed the Lenten fast 'in all its rigour'.[1] This meant eating nothing in the morning; having a first meal at 11.30; eating neither eggs nor dairy produce; and taking a collation at six in the evening. That did not prevent her from feeling strong: 'Never had I felt so strong, and this strength remained with me until Easter.'[2]

A night of light

This strength indeed remained until Easter, but in the night of

Thursday 2/Friday 3 April she coughed up blood; a second attack followed on the evening of Friday 3 April.

Thérèse, who had turned twenty-three the previous 2 January, is right to emphasize her 'strength'. A few weeks earlier, in the childhood memoirs which Mother Agnes of Jesus, Prioress of the Carmel and her sister by blood, had ordered her to write, she recounted how she emerged from her childhood and her childish world at Christmas 1886; how God, 'in this *night* of *light*', had made her 'strong': 'Since that blessed night I have never been defeated in any combat,'[3] she added. So at the end of this Lent 1896 she felt stronger than ever, despite these attacks of coughing blood.They did not affect her; on the contrary they gave her an indication that perhaps she was going to die, which was her desire.

This was not a morbid desire. At the end of her childhood memoirs, she tells her sister the essentials: 'And now I have no desire except to *love* Jesus to folly. My childish desires have flown away... Neither do I desire any longer suffering or death..., it is *love* alone that attracts me.'[4] At one moment she had believed that she had 'touched the shores of Heaven';[5] she would be a 'little flower... gathered in the springtime of its life'.[6] She had gone beyond this stage and, seeking only the will of God, wrote at the end of 1896: 'Now, abandonment alone guides me. I have no other compass.'[7]

But there was this coughing blood, a manifest sign. A new birth was in preparation for the one who had been brought up on, and continually nourished by, the thought of the beyond, of death, of Heaven: arrival, at last, on the shores of an eternal love. What was her inner state on Maundy Thursday and Good Friday 1896? She describes it precisely: 'At this time I was enjoying such a clear faith, that the thought of Heaven made up all my happiness.'[8]

Heaven, which she often writes with a capital H, recurs constantly in her writings, since this is the goal, the destination of her life: 'Earth seemed to me to be a place of exile and I could dream only of Heaven.'[9] 'I sighed for the eternal repose of Heaven.'[10] She awaited the 'eternal communion of Heaven'.[11]

Having accepted that Heaven was not an immediate prospect, and having envisaged that she might be sent to the Carmel in Hanoi, which had just been founded in 1895, she recognized these symptoms, which did not deceive her. On that night of Maundy Thursday, 'I had scarcely laid my head on the pillow when I felt something like a bubbling stream mounting to my lips. I didn't know what it was, but I thought that perhaps I was going to die and my soul was flooded with joy.'[12] The next day, Good Friday morning, she noticed that it was blood: 'My soul was filled with a great consolation; I was intimately persuaded that Jesus, on the anniversary of his death, wanted to have me hear a first call.'[13] 'I had the consolation of spending Good Friday just as I desired. Never did the Carmel's austerities seem to me so delightful; the hope of going to Heaven soon transported me with cheerfulness. When the evening of that blessed day arrived, I had to go to my rest; but as on the preceding night, good Jesus gave me the same sign that my entrance into Eternal life was not far off.'[14]

The 'religious souls'

One would be wrong to think, because of her testimony to 'such a clear faith', a faith which led her to derive 'all [her] happiness'[15] from the thought of Heaven, that this faith was naive, childish to the point of being simple, a kind of superhuman and disincarnate faith which was composed only of clear light, without the shadow of a doubt.

She expressed all the truth about herself at the end of the notebook of her memories which she gave to Mother Agnes on 20 January 1896; in it she recalls a retreat preached at the Carmel in October 1891 by a Franciscan, Fr Alexis Prou, a retreat during which she says that she received 'great graces'. She was not expecting anything: 'It seemed to me that the preacher would not be able to understand me since he was supposed to do good to great sinners but not to religious souls.' We should note carefully this distinction between sinners and religious souls; at the end of 1895 and the beginning of 1896 Thérèse did not class herself among the former but among the 'religious souls'.

Thérèse makes – in parenthesis – an enigmatic comment on this preacher: this father 'was appreciated only by me'.[16] Fr Alexis was a famous preacher; he had come to the Carmel because he had been asked for; why was he 'appreciated' only by Thérèse? Did his Franciscan spirituality run contrary to that of the prioress, Mother Marie de Gonzague? Or did she judge haughtily that this father, accustomed to stir the frustrated souls whom he met through the parish missions which he preached in the West, was far from being able to understand contemplative souls?

It was the custom for the Carmelites to make their confession first at the beginning of the retreat and a second time at the end; Mother Marie de Gonzague asked Thérèse,[17] as a matter of obedience, not to return to Fr Alexis to make her confession. Nevertheless, she went: did she defy the irregular prohibition of her prioress? Or was she given permission *in extremis*? We do not know.[18]

At all events, what interests us here is Thérèse's spiritual state and the help that Fr Alexis brought her: 'At that time I was having great interior trials of all kinds (even to the point of sometimes asking myself whether heaven really existed).'[19] This important phrase in brackets has to be emphasized. Fr Alexis did the true work of a spiritual director: this man, the heart of whose spirituality was the abandonment of the child in the hands of God, understood Thérèse and allowed her to advance: 'I felt disposed to say nothing of my inner dispositions since I didn't know how to express them, but I had hardly entered the confessional than I felt my soul expand. After speaking only a few words, I was understood in a marvellous and even *intuitive* way and my soul was like a book in which this priest read better than I did myself. He launched me full sail on the waves of *trust* and *love* which so strongly attracted me, but upon which I did not dare to advance.'[20]

The customary spirituality of the Carmel in the nineteenth century said a great deal about sin and the devil, the victim, and co-operation with redemption; it prevented Thérèse from daring to advance along the way in which trust and love were the essentials. The retreat preachers at the Lisieux Carmel were often very orthodox religious, who were themselves steeped in the spirituality of fear. It took a little Franciscan, who was not thought much of, to be the priest from whom Thérèse finally found confirmation on her way.[21]

We can see Thérèse's confidence some months before Easter 1895; in 1891 she had undergone the trial of asking herself whether there was 'a Heaven'. Her faith, which she declared to be 'so clear and so alive', was 'sometimes' accompanied with moments in which Heaven became indistinct, though without being tarnished or becoming less alive as a result.

On Maundy Thursday and Good Friday 1896, Thérèse was quite clear: the thought of Heaven constituted all her happiness, and the prospect of dying, a sign of which had been given to her, only enhanced this clarity and this happiness. For Thérèse the word 'Heaven' is strictly synonymous with an unfailing hope; for her, human beings are unfinished and do not have a meaning of their own; they are have an openness towards an Other who will give them all their meaning, and that will be Heaven, the Heaven which we receive from God, the luminous manifestation of His tenderness – and not a place that one obtains by oneself, through merits, suffering, resignation and impeccable purity. In hope, and by faith, she was already living out this Heaven on earth.

'I believed that they were actually speaking against their own inner convictions'

Easter 1896 is the most important moment of Thérèse's life. A radical change took place then and one remains flabbergasted by the almost total obliteration of this event, first of all by Mother Agnes, who in the *Story of a Soul* has transformed it from the start. As we have seen, Thérèse spoke of her coughing blood on Maundy Thursday and Good Friday as 'the first call of Jesus'[22] and her 'joy'. At Easter there was a brutal reversal: from then until her death she entered into the darkest night; and she was to say that 'the thought of Heaven',[23] which until then had been 'so sweet', became nothing but 'the cause of struggle and torment for her'.[24] The addition that Mother Agnes makes in her text of the *Story of a Soul* to translate this event falsifies its very content: Mother Agnes makes Thérèse say with reference to Maundy Thursday and Good Friday, 'How happy this memory is to me!',[25] whereas at that point the memory of Heaven had become intolerable to Thérèse. Following Mother Agnes, the majority of biographers and interpreters of the writings of Thérèse have masked the vitally important spiritual event of Easter 1896; they have forgotten it or related it in their own way.[26]

But we have to let Thérèse speak for herself, scrupulously following her text.

First of all the paradox that she introduces: the strength in her of this '*faith*, so clear and so alive' is so great that it completely removes from her mind the idea that there could be beings who do not know this faith; simply because of this '*faith*' which was so clear and alive, 'I was unable to believe,' she says, 'that there were really impious people who had no faith.'[27]

Because it is too clear and too dazzling, Thérèse's faith thus obscures the fact of the unbelief of the 'impious', that unbelief experienced by a certain number of human beings around her. We need to return to this term 'impious' which Thérèse[28] uses in the sense current at the time. The definition of 'impious' in *Le Grand Larousse du XIXe siècle* (1873) is: 'Someone who has no religion, who is opposed to the ideas of religion'; and P.Larousse goes on to specify: '*Impious* is stronger than *irreligious* and that is stronger than *incredulous*.' So *impious* is the height of unbelief, for there is a desire in it to combat God and religion: 'The *impious* takes pleasure in *attacking* religion and even blaspheming against God,' the dictionary adds.

So the term 'impious' which Thérèse uses was in her day a term the rigour of which we can no longer envisage. Now up to Easter 1896 Thérèse, by virtue of her faith, had not come to believe in the impiety of the impious: 'I believed that they were actually speaking against their own inner convictions when they denied the existence of Heaven.'[29] One could say that she was so totally imprisoned in a form of naive faith that she could not arrive at the idea of a real impiety and she denied this reality of impiety by attributing to the impious a deliberate intention: she thought that they were not sincere; for her, they could not be, since Heaven seemed too evident to her and faith certain.

'Jesus made me...'

What happened for her at Easter 1896? Jesus gave her a quite special grace. What? Specifically, to enter into a profound understanding of the extreme point of unbelief, of impiety: 'During those very joyful days of the Easter season, Jesus made me feel that there were really souls who have no faith.'[30] The general tendency at the First Vatican Council, twenty-five years earlier, had been to think that it was difficult, if not impossible, for a human being to be 'impious'; that the only explanations for this position were a lack of reason or immorality. Thérèse shared in this generally accepted view, a view which the youthful freshness of her faith and also her perpetual distancing from the world only reinforced.

Now it was Jesus himself who made Thérèse grasp that the 'impious' existed; in other words, there were beings who rejected this God of love with all their heart, their mind and their reason; they had received enlightenment about this God, and had not lacked graces. As Thérèse puts it, it is precisely through 'the abuse of grace'[31] that they reject faith. So this text is not about feeble or lukewarm souls, all those who live a life in which their way of loving their neighbour is often imperfect or mediocre, but about beings who decide, in full awareness and in profound freedom, to reject God. Is it possible, one will ask, to say no to the Light when one perceives it clearly? Yes, Thérèse tells us; she assures us that she has received from Jesus this understanding of the darkness as it is experienced by these beings who say no.

The sin of these beings has nothing to do with what are habitually called 'sins' and are only peccadilloes, little everyday follies of our human condition. Thérèse often spoke of these sins with a kind of cheerfulness; in the very last lines of manuscript C, some weeks before her death, she would say in a cry: 'Yes, I feel it; even though I had on my conscience all the sins that can be committed, I would go, my heart broken with sorrow, and throw myself into Jesus' arms, for I know how much He loves the prodigal child who returns to Him.'[32] She knows her past imperfections; she is aware of them at the end of her life and she says, 'I expect each day to discover new imperfections in me.'[33] That does not matter very much, 'remembering that Charity covers a multitude of sins'.[34]

But alongside these sins there is real sin: that against the Spirit.

The sin against the Spirit consists in an obstinate rejection of the light. Matthew speaks of this sin in connection with Jesus' cure through exorcism of a person possessed by the devil: 'Blasphemy against the Spirit will not be forgiven.'[35] The Gospel of John emphasizes the opposition between light and darkness to express the drama of sin: the darkness rejects the light. John always maintains the full responsibility of those who refuse to believe in Love, but he is bewildered by the mystery of unbelief which he notes, marked by the drama of the resistance to the Jesus who gives signs and says clearly: 'I have comes as light into the world, that whoever believes in me may not remain in darkness.'[36] God acts within the darkness in which men are and offers the possibility of light. The fundamental sin is not to believe in love – the love of God and others; to condemn Jesus without knowing him or to betray him after having known him. It is a refusal to believe and to hope in the eternal love manifested in Jesus and diffused by the Spirit, which has to spread throughout humanity. Here it is important to emphasize that to sin against the love of men is the same as to sin against the love of God. At Easter 1896 Thérèse sees in a flash that this sin exists; she has encountered it.

Light and darkness

To explain the situation in which she finds herself at that time, after Easter 1896, from one end of her account to the other Thérèse follows the metaphor of 'darkness' and 'light'. At the centre is the very experience of Christ: 'The King of the fatherland of the bright sun actually came and lived for thirty-three years in the land of darkness. Alas! the darkness did not understand that this Divine King was the light of the world.'[37] Thérèse is referring to texts from the Gospel of John, particularly the Prologue. For John, man is originally in an undifferentiated state that can be called darkness; sin consists in preferring the darkness to the irruption of light.[38]

Thérèse now becomes aware that beings today continue to experience what contemporaries of Jesus experienced: they do not recognize the light, and deliberately shut themselves up in the darkness. To that point it was impossible for Thérèse to believe that one could knowingly reject the light. At Easter she accepted this fact: love is truly rejected; some consciously seek the darkness rather than light.

To understand the real experiences of these beings who reject deep within themselves another reality than the human condition and its finitude, these beings who decide that there is nothing beyond death, Thérèse is put by Jesus himself in this darkness. And Jesus only sent her this 'trial' 'the moment,' she says, 'I was capable of bearing it. A little earlier I believe it would have plunged me into a state of discouragement.'[39]

Thérèse constantly uses the word 'trial' to express what she is going through: 'Ah, if the trial that I have been suffering for a year now appeared to the eyes of anyone, what astonishment would be felt!'[40] In April 1897 she simply says: 'This trial was to last not a few days or a few weeks,'[41] it was to last for ever, and it was a trial which robs her of 'all *joy*'[42] in faith. She does not want anyone to be deceived here, and addressing the prioress she declares: 'I may perhaps appear to you to be exaggerating my trial. In fact, if you are judging according to the sentiments I express in my little poems composed this year, I must appear to you as a soul filled with consolations and one for whom the veil of faith is almost torn aside; and yet it is no longer a veil for me, it is a wall which reaches right up to the heavens and covers the starry firmament... When I sing of the happiness of Heaven and of the eternal possession of God, I feel no joy in this, for I sing simply what I *want to believe*.'[43]

It has been noted that, doubtless under the impact of a great upheaval, Thérèse's writing tails off after the writing of the word 'wall', a word which certainly reminded her of a verse from Victor Hugo's' poem 'Antichrist': 'Like a dark wall between heaven and man', a verse which Thérèse knew.[44]

In September 1896, Thérèse writes to her sister Marie, who thinks that she is in the light, that since 'the radiant feast of Easter' she has found a 'dark storm'; 'clouds' are covering her 'Heaven'.[45] The trial is that 'He permitted my soul to be invaded by the thickest darkness, and that the thought of Heaven, up till then so sweet for me, be no longer anything but the cause of struggle and torment.'[46] She finds it very difficult to express what she feels: 'One would have to travel through this dark tunnel to understand its darkness.'[47] She then spends a long time on a 'comparison'[48] to explain her trial; she ends by saying: 'The fog which surrounds me becomes more dense; it penetrates my soul and envelops it in such a way that it is impossible to discover within it the sweet image of my Fatherland; everything has disappeared!'[49]

The 'night of nothingness'

Furthermore: 'When I want to rest my heart fatigued by the darkness which surrounds it by the memory of the luminous country after which I aspire, my torment redoubles.'[50]

Thérèse gives an admirable description of the trial in which she has been plunged, incomparably better than in her little poems, often in the style of someone else. And to make herself even better understood, to the poetic mode she adds the bold figure of the tirade: she makes the darkness which invades her speak personally; the darkness becomes beings who stand before God and speak to her. The effect is compelling: 'The darkness, borrowing the voice of sinners, says mockingly to me: "You are dreaming about the light, about a fatherland embalmed in the sweetest perfumes; you are dreaming about the *eternal* possession of the creator of all these marvels; you believe that one day you will walk out of this fog which surrounds you! Advance, advance; rejoice in death which will give you not what you hope for but a night still more profound, the night of nothingness."'[51]

After these last words, 'the night of nothingness', words like a void into which one sinks indefinitely; after this tirade of an extreme tension when one remembers that it is written by a Carmelite at the heart of her convent to a prioress, Thérèse stops: 'I don't want to write any longer about it; I fear I might blaspheme; I fear even that I have already said too much.'[52]

What she describes is a gigantic struggle which she experiences in her very heart and with all her being: the struggle between darkness and light. The darkness is not a vague emotional blockage or an abstract questioning, but a real existential presence of those who quite deliberately remove the God who is Love from their life. Thérèse does not play with words or practise any exhibitionism: she expresses bluntly and ardently the state in which she finds herself, the trial which she is experiencing.

It would be serious nonsense to see this state purely and simply as atheism. Certainly, the terms that she uses – this 'night of nothingness' – are so strong that some have thought this, like Julien Freund in a text in which he speaks of Thérèse in connection with Chestov, who issues an invitation to another experience than that of knowledge: 'There is faith for Chestov, and reason will never succeed in understanding faith. There is the experience of logic. There is the experience of grace. There are other interiors, other contents. And man is involved with both. There is nothing more terrible than these last texts of St Thérèse of the Child Jesus. This is a real crisis of atheism with the accents of a revolt which I have rarely encountered in other authors. And people have wanted to make her a sweet, happy woman. I believe that there is an absurdity in faith. It is always difficult to live out. It would be so simple if it were enough to say: "Yes, I have faith. Everything is settled." There is a cruelty about faith. Sometimes I am banging my head against the wall.'[53]

Or again Abbé Laurentin. In *Le Figaro* on 3 January 1972 he wrote that at Easter 1896 Thérèse was 'seized within by a radical atheism'.[54] Thérèse certainly no longer knows the joy which is ordinarily attached to the experience of faith; she no longer knows the faith which she had previously; she has left behind the certainty felt where she was, but faith remains.

Let us take Thérèse literally: as we have seen, she constantly speaks of 'trial' and, once only, of 'temptations against the faith'.[55] But in the texts which follow Easter 1896 she never uses the word 'doubts'.[56] 'Trial', 'temptations', are the dynamic terms in which her whole being is engaged. The *Grand Larousse du XIXe siècle* rightly defines the word 'trial' as: 'An experience, whether sought or not, which brings out the solidity or weakness of a character, a virtue or of any quality.' In Thérèse this is not a loss of savour created by doubts, but the raising of all her being by an unprecedented spiritual struggle. The challenge of the darkness leads her to incessant 'acts of faith': 'I think that I have made more acts of faith in the past year than during the whole of my life. On every occasion of struggle, when my enemies come to provoke me, I behave boldly.'

If Thérèse's state is not atheism, it is not a 'dark night of faith' in the sense experienced by St John of the Cross either. In the *Last Conversations*, Mother Agnes did everything possible to get this idea of a 'dark night of faith', experienced by Thérèse like the great Carmelite mystic, accepted.

As Hans Urs von Balthasar quite rightly says, 'if love remains, and if Thérèse knows that it remains, this is not the dark night of the soul'.[57] The theologian adds: 'Thérèse's night remains a kind of "semi-night".'[58] In a letter to a Carmelite,[59] von Balthasar tries to make his thought more precise; he speaks of Thérèse 'in her *subterranean* journey'; he adds that 'a kind of *semi-darkness* is characteristic of Carmelite existence. We must not identify it with St John of the Cross's "dark night", which was a charism typical of the founder, like many of the states which Teresa of Avila describes. These are experiences which people must never try to copy or attain. Here little Thérèse is an indispensable corrective.' Later in his letter he speaks again of the trial of 'semi-darkness' which Thérèse of Lisieux experienced.[60]

Von Balthasar puts this trial in the 'footsteps of Christ (who took upon himself the sins of the world) with its obscuring of God'. The act of faith then appears as a '*suspension* between earth and heaven, like the cross, physically and spiritually'. In this trial, like Christ on the cross, 'we hang in the void'; and von Balthasar immediately puts Thérèse's trial in the whole Carmelite line: 'I am certain that the true Carmelite vocation is to be "suspended" with the Lord, with no verifiable attachment to either earth or heaven.'

The duration

If we refer to the night as a symbol, a symbol common to all spiritual experiences, a universal archetype, it has to be said that night is both immersion in the darkness and the beginning of light: 'The night symbolizes the time of gestations, of germinations, of conspiracies which in the light of day will burst out into manifestations of life. It is rich in all the virtualities of existence. But to enter the night is to return to what is undetermined, where nightmares and monsters, *black ideas* are mixed. It is the image of the unconscious and, in the dream of night, the unconscious is freed. Like all symbols, the night itself has two aspects: that of darkness, in which the future is fermenting; and that of preparation for the day, from which the light of life will spring.'[61]

For Thérèse, the night that she experienced was a 'transforming duration';[62] she was vividly aware of it. When she described her trial on 9 June 1897 it had been going on for more than a year. It had not stopped; it would be there until Thérèse died. It is impossible to emphasize enough that Thérèse's trial lasted from

Easter 1896, over eighteen months, until her death.[63] In its 'transforming duration', she constantly hopes for the end of darkness, but it does not come. She has to pursue her own journey into the depths of night to the end, until her death. Despite the voices of darkness which tell her that the night is everything in itself, a definitive destination, that it is 'the night of nothingness' from which nothing can arise, she resists and does not cease to experience that light is born from the night.[64] Thérèse's text, written between 3 and 9 June 1897,[65] bears witness to this constant struggle over fourteen months, moments of darkness and light which co-exist mysteriously, even if the darkness is the evocative element.

This condition in which, as von Balthasar puts it, one is as it were suspended in the void, is extremely trying for Thérèse: so we can understand all the more the appeal of the void, the attraction of the abyss, of the 'night of nothingness'.

We have seen that Thérèse does not speak of the 'night of faith'; that only Mother Agnes does so, attributing these words to Thérèse, 'I've had a greater desire not to see God and the saints, and to remain in the night of faith, than others desire to see and understand.'[66] Thérèse herself speaks to her sister Marie of 'the night of this life';[67] she refers like this to life in general, the life of all human beings who know a condition of night. One does not know with certainty, one does not see clearly, one does not know where one is going; and there is this wall of death which for many seems like the final night.

Thérèse, who is a solid woman from Normandy, with her feet on the ground, has nothing about her of the angel escaped from this planet: she has always been profoundly aware of this difficulty of living out the human condition, a difficulty common to all beings, which puts them at a loss, which often makes them despair. At Easter 1896 a second awareness comes to be overlaid upon the first: for a certain number of human beings there is not only the night of life with all its darkness, but the rejection of another life, the even more desperate refusal of a light which comes after the darkness of this life. Even if she is in no way involved in the social struggles, she knows that men's work often makes them slaves, that their spirit is fragile – and did not her father have a long stay in a mental hospital? – and that their desire for creativity often comes up against a brick wall. We must note that at the very moment when Thérèse is going through the night of her life, Marx, Nietzsche and Freud are emphasizing this nocturnal situation of the human condition.[68]

Thus Thérèse – all the more since she knows that she is going to die – participates fully in the human condition with its dizzy precariousness. But if up to Easter 1896 this precariousness is full of meaning because it will issue soon in eternal life, the situation changes completely after Easter: faith no longer comes first to bring its light and to give meaning to the night of this life. Thérèse's position is that of those for whom the night of this life opens up, with death, on total night. This confronts her like a wall which gets in the way of all clarity.

Presence of Satan?

Up to the time of Thérèse, all human beings lived in religious belief. The first Christian centuries were confronted with false gods, but the atmosphere was completely religious; John of the Cross found himself in a world in which practically everyone believed in God and saw themselves as infinitely significant in the face of this God. The end of the nineteenth century in which Thérèse lived sees the beginning, for example with Comte and Littré, of an immense agnosticism which sweeps away religious faith and its certainties. We might think of Charles de Foucauld who, between 1874 and 1886, between the age of sixteen and twenty-eight, experienced the agnosticism which took hold of Taine and Renan. During this period, he said, he remained 'denying nothing and believing nothing'. The philosophers of suspicion gradually imposed their thought on people's minds.

Certainly Thérèse had not read them. But she knew the 'impiety' of her age – in the sense which we have seen – this rejection of God and religion. The *Grand Larousse*,[69] which I have already quoted above and which cannot be suspected of benevolence towards Christianity, makes this astounding remark about the impious: 'There is in him something of the spirit which one attributes to Satan; he is the enemy of God; one can be impious even when one believes, if the diabolical spirit with which one is inspired tramples beliefs under foot.' So impiety goes far beyond anticlericalism and denotes a resolute fight against all beliefs.[70]

Thérèse knows this impiety, among other things through an event which stamped her life and which must be analysed more closely: the Diana Vaughan affair.

'It all began on 12 June, when the journal *La Croix* had announced with tears of holy joy: "We learn from an absolutely reliable source that Miss Diana Vaughan is definitively renouncing the palladium and is going to devote the same ardour to fighting the triangles as she deployed in propagating them." The triangles? Clearly the assemblies of Freemasons.'[71]

Diana Vaughan was an American woman, born in 1864 and brought up by her father in the Palladian rite, a Masonic Luciferian spiritism. In 1889 she became high priestess of Palladianism and established herself in New York in 1891; soon she divided her time between the United States and Europe. In France, in 1893, she met two deserters from freemasonry, Dr Bataille and Léo Taxil, and a Catholic figure who painted an ecstatic picture of Diana: 'What a shame that she isn't Catholic!' Diana declared that Satan was the great puppeteer of Freemasonry, and on 1 January 1894 the *Echo de Rome*, taking up the *Osservatore romano*, wrote: 'Freemasonry is *satanic* at every point.'[72]

The atmosphere of the age was that of a vast persecution of the church, which its opponents had stripped of the Papal States in 1870. The Catholics thought of the Pope as a prisoner under constant attack. We can hear this from Brother Simeon, a brother of the Christian Schools and Superior of the College of Saint Joseph, a prominent figure in Rome, where he gave a warm welcome to his compatriots. He had welcomed M.Martin in September 1885 on his return from a journey to Constantinople, and again in November 1887, the time of Thérèse's journey to Rome and her encounter with the Pope. He had written to Thérèse on 31 August 1890: 'Pray for our Holy Father the Pope who is so afflicted and so humiliated in Rome. His enemies are persecuting him in every way; everything is allowed against him here, and the perpetrators are assured of impunity. It is devastating. Hell is triumphing in Rome!'

All over the Catholic world, in parishes and convents, people began to pray for the conversion of Diana, all the more so since there were clashes between her and some hellish Luciferian authorities. Thus *La Croix* of 8 May 1895 reproduced a letter in which readers were asked to pray the venerable Joan of Arc for the conversion of Diana Vaughan. And it was soon related how on 6 June Diana had knelt before a statuette of Joan of Arc. On 12 June *La Croix* announced that Diana 'is definitively renouncing Palladianism' and on 21 June that she had been converted: 'We have just read the proofs of the first chapter of the *Memoirs of an Ex-Palladian*, which Miss Diana Vaughan will be publishing very soon, and we are still in the grip of an unspeakable emotion.'

On 6 July 1895 the journal *Le Normand*, edited by Isidore Guérin, a pharmacist at Lisieux, Thérèse's uncle and a benefactor of the Carmel,[73] told its readers of the imminent appearance of Miss Vaughan's memoirs. A Dominican, Fr Pègues, eulogized her conversion and her work in the *Univers* of 27 April 1896. However, some people asked whether Diana really existed. A Roman commission was charged with investigating whether her conversion was real and her writings were authentic. On 22 January 1897 the commission declared that 'to this day it has found no compelling proof either *for* or *against*'; on 30 January *Le Normand* published this information on its front page.

Miss Vaughan could no longer hide. So she invited friends, religious, journalists and personalities of all kinds to the Geographical Society, Boulevard Saint Germain, Paris, on Easter Monday, 19 April 1897, for a session which was to begin with a speech by Léo Taxil and end with a lecture by her on 'Palladianism Laid Low'. Four hundred people were present; the police were there to ensure the security of the 'convert'.

Projection of the photograph of Thérèse

Throughout Léo Taxil's speech, a picture representing Joan of Arc chained in her prison and consoled by St Catherine was projected on to a large screen. Léo Taxil had announced to his audience that this was a Carmelite disguised as Joan of Arc.

The picture was of Thérèse, playing the role of Joan of Arc, and her sister Céline – in religion, Sister Geneviève – who was playing the role of St Catherine. Thérèse, who was a great admirer of Joan of Arc, had composed a first sketch, 'The Mission of Joan of Arc', which was played at the Carmel on 21 January 1894: in it Joan is responding to her voices. Precisely a year later a second sketch had been performed, 'Joan of Arc accomplishing her Mission', which depicted the rest of Joan's life and above all her death at the stake. Shortly after the second performance, a number of photographs were taken, including the one of Joan of Arc and St Catherine.

Mother Agnes, certainly very excited by the conversion of Diana, asked Thérèse for a piece inspired by this conversion: Thérèse wrote 'The Triumph of Humility', which was performed on 21 June 1896. For this piece she consulted documentation provided by Uncle Guérin.

Thérèse first of all says of Diana in this piece: 'My greatest desire would be, when her mission was finished, to see her united with Jesus in our little Carmel.' Diana a Carmelite at Lisieux: the religious who heard this suggestion were in raptures of delight!

The devil is mentioned: 'He thinks that we are his most mortal enemies,' says Thérèse. The stage directions are explicit: 'Salvoes are fired, heavy chains are dragged, the demons cry and show their chains,' the script notes. Lucifer speaks, and so do Beelzebub and Asmodeus. Lucifer can only achieve 'a complete triumph' 'by destroying the convents', particularly the Carmel, 'the most perfect order of the church'. Lucifer's surest ally is 'pride': 'I know that it is worming its way everywhere', and the Carmelites 'keeping their own will in the depths of their hearts, can obey and desire to command it'. Thérèse's definition of Satan is above all worth remembering: 'The one deprived of love, as our Mother St Teresa called him.'

Then the archangel St Michael arrives with an inscription, 'Humility', and the chorus of demons declare themselves conquered; the angels sing a song the last verse of which is, 'Humility makes hell angry.'

Shortly after this sketch, Mother Agnes suggested to Thérèse that she should write some verses to send to the convert. Thérèse tried, but had no inspiration and told Mother Agnes that she could not. Mother Agnes then retouched the photograph of 'John of Arc and St Catherine' taken the previous year and had the idea of sending it to Diana, 'the new Joan of Arc'. Thérèse added a few words. Miss Vaughan replied with a letter of thanks for this 'symbolic tableau'.

We must be careful here to respect the chronology strictly. On 6 July 1895, *Le Normand* announced the imminent appearance of Diana Vaughan's memoirs after her conversion, memoirs 'unveiling the Mysteries and Satanic Practices of the Luciferian Triangles'. At the end of August 1895, in a convent, Diana Vaughan composed a 'Eucharistic Novena of Reparation', the text of which was published in October. Miss Vaughan wanted to make reparations for nine sins, from unbelief to sectarian profanations.

The Léo Taxil affair and the trial of faith

There has been a great desire to prove that Thérèse did not read any of these texts before what is called 'her trial of doubts against the faith',[74] which began at Easter 1896. Certainly Thérèse only received and read the 'Novena' in July 1896 – and she copied long extracts out of it. But surely we cannot fail to suppose that the Diana Vaughan affair had stirred the Carmel long before? We may remember that *La Croix* of 8 May 1895 had asked its readers to pray to the venerable Joan of Arc[75] for Diana's conversion. Thérèse's uncle I.Guérin had been able to read the proofs of the first chapter of Diana's memoirs in *La Croix* of 21 June. He said that this text left him 'in the grip of an unspeakable emotion'. All the stir around this story, these demonic stories, these fights of Lucifer, Beelzebub and other Asmodeuses against God, the church and souls, made their way through the grilles and walls of the Lisieux Carmel. The distinguished pharmacist M.Guérin, whose daughter was at the Carmel and who was Thérèse's uncle, must have let at least some news slip in. He stigmatized 'the atheistic freemasonry which is governing France' in *Le Normand* of 8 October, in connection with the death of Renan. He demonstrated that 'Jewry and Freemasonry' were 'sister allies' whose aim is 'universal conquest'.[76] From the start they were accomplices in 'these insults and filthy calumnies that the press is spreading about the Catholics'.[77] The *Osservatore romano* had been formal: freemasonry was '*satanic*, making common cause today with Judaism to banish the kingdom of Jesus Christ from this world and substitute the kingdom of Satan for it'.[78] In 1895, in the eyes of the Carmelites Diana Vaughan symbolized the gigantic struggle between God and Satan, which in these years seemed to be a crucial one. Who would win, Heaven or Lucifer? If the freemason Diana Vaughan was converted – and the whole convent had been praying for this – Satan himself would be conquered.

In 1895, Thérèse was also preoccupied with this struggle, which appeared on the public scene as a battle between the angel of God and Lucifer, the fallen angel. Thérèse was certain that this struggle, now brought out into the full light of day, had been always going on in the shadows. In her first manuscript, which she wrote that very year, she speaks of the sickness which affected her at the age of ten: 'I can't describe this strange sickness, but I'm now convinced it was the work of the devil.'[79] She adds: 'I believe the devil had received an *external* power over me.'[80]

On the eve of her religious profession, Sunday 7 September 1890, her religious vocation appeared to her 'as a *dream*, a chimera':[81] 'The devil inspired me with the *assurance* that it wasn't for me.'[82] She feared that if she spoke of it she would be prevented from pronouncing her vows: 'This is an absurdity which shows it was a temptation from the devil.'[83] She was then completely in the dark. She chooses the same word to express this that she was also to use of her trial: 'The darkness was so great that I could see and understand one thing only: I didn't have a *vocation*.'[84] She finally dared to talk about this to her novice mistress, who reassured her: 'The act of humility I had just performed put the devil to flight.'[85]

So the devil exists for her; she has met him. He is at work in the soul but also in society; Thérèse notes this more than ever with the Diana Vaughan affair.

Similarly, at Easter 1896, Thérèse is in the darkness; she no longer sees Heaven, just as at the moment of her profession she no longer saw her vocation. The Diana Vaughan affair shows her that there are beings profoundly plunged into even more profound darkness: the darkness in which one finds oneself when one openly fights God, as Lucifer did – if you like by rejecting God in principle, by refusing to recognize him, by

removing him from one's existence. At Easter 1896 she understands 'that there are really souls who have no faith'.[86] One
cannot doubt that, since she learned from experience, she had
this quite particular awareness as a result of the concrete
existence of these Luciferians who consciously rejected God
with unbounded pride.

The imposture

We know that under the large portrait of Thérèse as Joan of Arc,
Léo Taxil, the impresario, one might say, of Diana Vaughan,
revealed on 19 April 1897 in his speech to the Society of
Geography that Diana Vaughan did not exist, that he had
mounted this immense fraud out of sheer anticlericalism, and
that he was the author of all the Diana texts.[87] *Le Normand* of
24 April 1897 reports 'the claims of Léo Taxil', who is called all
kind of names: 'wretched buffoon', 'disgusting swindler': 'An
enormous, prodigious, somewhat vulgar pride inspires the
master charlatan. Aware of his villainy, he makes a profession of
it.' *Le Normand* in particular notes that there was a projection:
'A photograph representing the appearance of St Catherine to
Joan of Arc, based on a tableau said to have been presented in
honour of Diana Vaughan in a Carmelite convent. What convent? Probably Taxil's house.' Here *Le Normand* is taking up an
article written by Eugène Tavernier in the *Univers*, which reports the session of the Society of Geography; but whereas
Tavernier strongly doubted the veracity of the tableau, did *Le
Normand* – and Guérin – know that the convent in question
was the Lisieux Carmel? Sister Geneviève – the St Catherine of
the tableau which was projected – wrote on 25 April, since the
news arrived at the Carmel very quickly: 'One sees so many
contemptible things, so many defections in the world, that
disgust fills one's soul.'

The commentator of the *Manuscrits autobiographiques* resorts to talking about the obedience which Thérèse customarily
showed,[88] an obedience which, as we shall see, was very strong,
to write this: 'To criticize her superior was to put her will in
place of that of God, and to lose her way. It was enough for
Diana Vaughan to oppose a Roman bishop for Thérèse to

suspect an imposture.' As proof he quotes a phrase from the 'Triumph of Humility': 'It is impossible for this to come from God.' Now at that time Thérèse saw Diana as a real convert, to the point that she was ready to welcome her into the Carmel; and although it is said that she 'guessed'[89] nothing, the commentator on the *Récréations pieuses* writes: 'There is no doubt of the violence of Thérèse's feelings when she learns that she had been duped.'[90] As soon as she learned the news, Thérèse tore up the letter that she had received from Diana Vaughan into little pieces and went to throw them on the manure heap in the garden. 'This must have shaken Thérèse. How could anyone parody religion to the point of playing around with truth and falsehood...?'[91] Thérèse was clearly wounded by this imposture. Beyond the personality of Léo Taxil, who has been described as a 'mythomaniac charlatan',[92] this was parody which she was suffering in the very name of her faith. Particularly at Easter 1896, she saw, despite this derisory hoax on the part of Léo Taxil and beyond it, that there were even more profound blasphemies, those of which Léon Bloy had spoken in 1886 in *Le Désesperé*, in which he wrote: 'Who knows, after all, if the most active form of adoration is not *blasphemy* by love, which would be the prayer of the abandoned?'

The debate of the century

Much emphasis has been put on the fact that 'Thérèse did not discover that she had been tricked until a year and several days after having begun to be tempted in the faith'.[93] There has been a concern to show at any price that the Léo Taxil affair 'was an episode without real significance in Thérèse's life'.[94] It is as if there has been a concern to prove absolutely that Léo Taxil – Diana Vaughan, his game and his imposture, had no influence on Thérèse. By contrast, there are certainly indications of a concern for Thérèse to have been affected by 'the scientists of the time, for they at least were respectable people',[95] and in support of this what Thérèse is claimed to have said is quoted: 'It is the reasoning of the worst materialists which impresses me: in due course, they argue, science, constantly making new progress, will explain everything naturally and there will be an absolute reason for everything which exists and which still remains a problem.'[96] There was a desire for the 'souls which have no faith', of whom Thérèse speaks, to be 'respectable persons', and not ignoble people like Léo Taxil.

In reality Thérèse was hardly up with philosophical texts developing materialist theses (unlike Charles de Foucauld). She had heard talk of the enormous advances of science in this second part of the nineteenth century and the questions that it raised for the church and the Christian faith; she also knew the virulent anticlericalism of her time – Henri Chéron, a former employee at Uncle Guérin's pharmacy, was profoundly anticlerical (he was to become the minister of 'little father' Combes). She was not unaware of the radical atheism which was professed by men who were otherwise very sincere and very straight: thus she could think of René Tostain, acting public prosecutor at Lisieux, who had married a niece of Mme Guérin's in October 1898. After a visit from Mme Tostain to Thérèse, Thérèse writes to her sister Céline on 3 April 1891, saying that it is necessary to pray a great deal for her, as 'she is very exposed'; her faith 'is in great danger'. Thérèse wants her 'to read a book in which she will certainly find the answer to many doubts'. René Tostain is in Thérèse's eyes the very type of the 'souls who have no faith': a man of great moral rectitude who declares himself to be an atheist and who is even leading his wife into his position; she confided to Mother Agnes shortly after Thérèse's death that she had come to 'doubt the existence of a second life' and even to doubt 'yet more', to doubt 'everything'.

After the fraud, to dismiss it, it would be said that Léo Taxil had an infamous air. This trick had the pamphleteering and mocking spirit of Voltaire without his genius. Reading the fury of the Catholic journals after Léo Taxil had unmasked himself and had ridiculed all those who had believed too easily in his staging of a claimed conversion, one has to note that the humiliation to which he was subjected was enormous. To the fore in the apologetic arguments used by the Catholics there were mocking and haughty treatments of their adversaries, who were treated as ignoramuses when they were not dragged in the mud. Passions on both sides were high, and there was no embarrassment about using any means to floor those who had different convictions. Beyond these cries and gesticulations was the very basis of the debate: to believe or not to believe in heaven. Thérèse was familiar with this debate of the century from her childhood. 1895, with among other things Diana Vaughan's fight against Satan, a feigned fight which was nevertheless extremely characteristic of this period, was a year in which the struggle between the two kingdoms and the two standards, those of God and Satan, seemed even more bitter than in the past.[97] What was to arise at Easter 1896 had been preceded by a stronger awareness then ever of this highly topical struggle which was taking place under the eyes of the young Carmelite.

It was a struggle which the Catholics exacerbated. It has to be said that Thérèse was trapped by the positions and struggles of the majority of the Catholics of her time, who felt that they were being persecuted on all sides. Cut to the quick by a political situation to which they were not accustomed, they shut themselves up in their citadel – and it was on this that Léo Taxil was able to build his fraud. There they could cultivate a certain paranoia, and attack on the pretext that the 'other', the adversary, the anticlerical, had attacked them first. And the Catholic Church in France, like Rome itself, shared in a truly pathological hostility to Freemasonry, using it as the explanation for all the setbacks to religion.

Over time we see how, because of their fear, the Catholics mounted an almost complete Masonic plot. But let us leave the description to a historian who in a few lines has given a good account of the real atmosphere of this age in which Thérèse lived:

That such a figure and his pranks had aroused such a prodigious interest in the most varied circles says a lot about this end of a disturbed century with its wavering values and hungry souls. And also about the Catholic Church, a citadel which felt itself to be threatened by the infernal 'Jewish–Masonic plot'. And the church counter–attacked: in 1881 at La Salette, Mgr Fava, Bishop of Grenoble, launched the atoning Crusade of Catholic Freemasons and published a journal, *La Franc–Maçonnerie démasquée*. Books and images proliferated, describing the manifestations of Satan and issuing a summons to the anti–Republican fight.

For their part, the Freemasons of the Great East, who were the most numerous, like those of the Grand Lodge of France, were so linked with Republican power that through their brothers in Parliament they exerted pressure not to pass further measures. They increased in number, growing from around 20,000 in 1890 to 30,000 in 1900, recruiting in the middle classes, among officials, teachers, the liberal professions, furthering careers and keeping an eye on local political life. Their ideal, which abandoned any reference to a supreme Being, can no longer be distinguished from the ardent Republicanism and militant laicism which founded and defended the regime. They were open to social questions, assembled the Republican defence at the time of the Dreyfus affair, and were at the origin of the birth of the Radical Party in 1901 by launching their League of Republican Action, which showed itself for the first time in public on 14 July 1900 without encountering any hostility.

In other words, they cared little about the upsurge of clerical delirium which stigmatized their sect.[98]

Joan at the stake

So Thérèse called what happened from Easter 1896 onwards 'the trial'. It is a word which occurs frequently in her writing, but takes on a far deeper meaning with her 'night': these are no longer trials or such and such a trial, but trial as such. When she speaks of this important moment it is always the word 'trial' that recurs, the trial willed by Jesus: 'A short time before my trial against the faith began, I was saying to myself: Really I have no great exterior trials... what means, then, will Jesus find to try me? The answer was not long in coming, and it showed me that the One whom I love is not at a loss as to the means he uses. Without changing my way he sent me the trial which was to mingle a salutary bitterness with all my joys.'[99]

The word has a strong sense; it is about a fight and about fighting. Thérèse is prepared for this.

For her the emblematic figure of Joan of Arc is a model for

this fight: Joan seems to her like an elder sister in this trial. Here Thérèse parts company with her contemporaries who see Joan in their own way. A parliamentary commission drafted a bill to make 8 May – the date of the deliverance of Orleans – the national festival 'of patriotism', since the defeat of 1870 was always present; revenge had to be taken and the Germans had to be kicked out of Alsace–Lorraine. The Catholics, the majority of whom were still monarchists,[100] sometimes accused of 'cosmopolitanism' because of their bond with the papacy, wanted to show that they would be 'Catholics and French always'; the Republicans and those who had no involvement in Catholicism presented Joan as the one who had kept her head, in her trial, with the ecclesiastical judges, including Cauchon, who was then given the bishopric of Lisieux as a reward for his treason. Joan was also shown to be the one who, though so young, had dared to show courageously the rights of the Protestant conscience; she was a freethinker *avant la lettre*. Guérin expressed the view in *Le Normand* of 5 May 1894 that the Republican plan for a national festival was a manoeuvre by the Freemasons to regain Joan and to desacralize her.

And what about Thérèse? In manuscript A, i.e. in 1895, she relates how enthusiastic she had been about Joan of Arc in her youth; at that time she had had a great desire to imitate her: 'It seemed I felt within me the same burning zeal,'[101] but if she feels, like Joan, 'born for glory',[102] this is not the glory of exploits and 'striking works',[103] but of holiness. Joan's example brings her a grace which she considers one of the greatest in her life: the 'bold confidence of becoming a great saint'.[104] It is the kingdom of holiness that she wants to conquer.

Mother Agnes, prioress of the Carmel since 20 February 1893, asked Thérèse for a dramatic composition to celebrate the first St Agnes' Day of her priorate, on 21 January 1894. Thérèse chose her subject, and at the end of 1893 composed 'The Mission of Joan of Arc', which was indeed performed on 21 January. Thérèse then wrote a poem about Joan for 8 May 1894; at the end of 1894 she composed a new piece on Joan to follow the 'Mission': 'Joan of Arc accomplishing her Mission', which was to be performed on St Agnes' Day 1895. The first part of the text speaks of Joan's 'victories', but we also find in it a prayer of Joan, who wants to make the power of God shine out by driving the English from the kingdom of France and destroying 'the power of Satan, another Goliath who would destroy the faith of the older daughter of the Church'.

Thérèse, who identifies Joan in her mission with herself, knows that the only way of conquering is martyrdom, no longer martyrdom by fire as in the case of Joan, but the martyrdom of love. She makes Joan the captive say: 'Lord, for your love I accept martyrdom... I want no more than to die for your love.'

At her stake Joan sings, 'I am entering eternal life.'

When Thérèse says to Joan, 'You offer yourself as a victim to the God who makes kings', she identifies herself with Joan at her stake, dying as a holocaust; soon, on 9 June 1895, Trinity Sunday, she is going to offer herself 'as a holocaust victim' to God, 'merciful love'; she expresses to God her desire to become a 'Martyr of your Love'.

Thérèse's fight, like that of Joan, is thus a spiritual fight. Up to Easter 1896, the fight is easy for Thérèse; she swims in faith. At the end of 1895, in manuscript A, she writes of her 'joy': 'This year, June 9, the feast of the Holy Trinity, I received the grace to understand more than ever how much Jesus desires to be loved.'[105] Her only suffering is that 'on every side this merciful Love is unknown, rejected',[106] when it 'desires to *set* souls *on fire*'.[107] The only solution is for love to consume the souls which will thus express his 'infinite tenderness' to all. Hence this prayer: 'O my Jesus, let *me* be this happy victim: consume Your holocaust with the fire of your Divine Love.'[108] From this 9 June, 'since that happy day, it seems to me that Love penetrates me and surrounds me... O, how sweet is the way of Love!'[109]

We are understanding all the better how gripping the contrast is between Easter 1896 onwards and what has gone before: to that point Thérèse was experiencing, rightly, great desires, and mainly that of the martyrdom of love; what great lover does not desire to die of love? We have seen the 'tunnel' she found herself in from Easter on.

Strategy

Thérèse's reaction will be to fight, more than ever. But the circumstances have changed completely, and she has to adapt her spiritual fight to this new fact. Paradoxically, her way of fighting it will be flight, and she will think that this method is a deed of valour. She explained this strategy very well: 'At each new occasion of combat, when my enemies come to provoke me, I conduct myself bravely. Knowing it is cowardly to enter into a duel, I turn my back on my enemies without deigning to look them in the face, but I run towards my Jesus. I tell Him I am ready to shed my blood to the last drop to confess that there is a Heaven.'[110]

This text of Thérèse's has been corrected in the *Story of a Soul*: instead of 'when my enemies come to provoke me', Mother Agnes wrote: 'when my enemy wants to provoke me'. The use of the singular – and it is the same, later on, with 'my adversary' – is meant to indicate the devil, whereas Thérèse speaks of the 'darkness', this 'darkness' which is directed at her[111] and which she identifies with the 'unbelievers' whom she names immediately after this passage.[112] Why make her combat, which is not with vague temptations from the devil, so much less concrete? Thérèse is not waging an individual, idealistic, combat against him: she is facing the 'impious', beings of flesh and blood, her contemporaries, who reject God and tell him so.[113]

Does this strategy amount, as has been said, to 'an attitude of prudence in which Thérèse rightly glories'?[114] It is added, in line with Mother Agnes: 'She refuses to reason with the devil.'[115] In fact Thérèse, very cunningly, has understood that to turn her back on her adversaries is the best strategy; for to discuss with the 'impious' and with their ideas would certainly be to get into a muddle, to get tangled up, to get a bit deeper into the tunnel.

The comparison with the duel has to be explained. In Thérèse's time duels were still quite frequent, whereas they hardly exist at all today. They were regarded as forming part of an honour to be defended: to withdraw from a duel often seemed to be real cowardice. The *Grand Dictionnaire Larousse* runs contrary to this current position, by studying at great length in its article 'Duel' of 1870 the moral and philosophical reasons which require the practice of duelling to be abandoned; it calls this practice a 'senseless custom', 'a mania' which always has been and still is the prerogative of a pretentious minority; and it does not allow that one can take revenge oneself. Thérèse, too, and this is a sign of great wisdom, considers that the duel is cowardliness, and she thinks here that if she began to cross swords with the adversaries, the impious, the irreligious, this would not be out of bravery but out of bravado; not out of honour but out of unreflecting pride. Spiritual combat is not, and cannot consist in, firing a broadside of arguments to obliterate the enemy and force him to submit, as the integralists or fundamentalists would have it. Thérèse does not join in this game. Her bravura consists in breaking with what would be only an all too human battle, based on a concern to wipe the other out once and for all. We are far from certain kinds of furious apologetics which have been engaged in regularly in the church and which were particularly virulent in Thérèse's time. She escapes: with finesse, with reason.

Substitution

She even reverses the situation: she is in no way haughty towards the impious who provoke her. She knows their arguments; they are weighty ones and she does not scorn them at all. What she feels from them – for their arguments get to her by virtue of their realism and solidity – is the terrible spiritual combat within her that they provoke. They make life hard for her. And in a way she turns all that back on them: she offers for them her suffering which comes from them. She tells Jesus: 'I tell Him, too, I am happy not to enjoy this beautiful Heaven on earth so that He will open it for all eternity to poor unbelievers.'[116]

Here we find a precise process of substitution. The process appears regularly with Thérèse, and in forms which can be surprising. In one of her last texts, a letter of 21 June 1897 to Abbé Belliere, Thérèse explains to the young seminarian the heart of her spirituality: to throw her faults 'into the devouring fire of Love', because she has understood 'the abysses of love and mercy of the *Heart of Jesus*'. She acts in this way, with 'a loving boldness', like Mary Magdalene; and she is confident that as a result she is not part of the mass 'of saints who spent their life in the practice of astonishing mortifications to expiate their sins'. Have we to conclude from this that she did not practise any mortification? Not at all: 'I have not chosen an austere life to expiate my own faults but those of others.' In offering her suffering for others, Thérèse no longer puts herself in the group of those who think themselves pure and set themselves above sinners: she says more than once that she is of 'the table of sinners', one of them, but that her way is to cast her faults into the divine fire. The fact remains that she suffers for the sins of others, her impious brothers, thus substituting herself for them.

It is not 'redemptive compassion'[117] which will have led her 'to the table of sinners', but a participation in the *infinite mercy* of God, a participation which one can live out here below and also in Heaven. She refers to the 'inexpressible tenderness'[118] of Jesus, a universal tenderness granted to all, of which she speaks in this month of June 1897; Jesus wants people to love others in the same way as he loves them. In her last written text, the letter of 10 August 1897 to Abbé Bellière, Thérèse, who is soon to die, evokes the saints of Heaven who 'have great compassion on our miseries, they remember, being weak and mortal like us, they have committed the same faults, sustained the same combats, and their fraternal tenderness becomes greater than it was when they were on earth'. She herself loves Abbé Bellière with a true 'fraternal tenderness', all the more so since he is weak and fragile, and often returns to his faults and his miseries.

It is in the Pauline writings that the theology of substitution reaches its culminating point: 'Paul does not restrict himself to applying the idea of substitution – of replacement – to the structure of history on a large scale, in the exchange between Jews and pagans, but he also attributes a decisive importance to it for the individual existence of the Christian and in particular the apostle.'[119] Thus the service of substitution achieved by Christ has to extend to the life of each Christian. In her text of September 1896, Thérèse, basing herself on Pauline thought, writes: 'I understood that if the Church had a body composed of different members, the most necessary and most noble of all could not be lacking to it, and so I understood that the Church had a Heart and that this Heart was burning with love.'[120] She adds: 'I understood... that Love was everything, that it embraced all times and places.'[121] In this Heart, there is a 'communion of saints', communion in Love. On 19 March 1897 she quotes John of the Cross to the missionary Fr Roulland: 'The smallest movement of pure love is more useful to the Church than all the works that have been achieved,'[122] and she makes this quite specific: 'Your trials must be profitable to the Church, since it is for the love of Jesus alone that you suffer them *with joy*.' And Thérèse, with a keen sense of the communion of saints, will often repeat that what she has received from Jesus belongs to everyone and that she wants to give it to them.

Thanks to the substitutions, if the 'unbelievers' refuse to enjoy heaven on this earth, at least Heaven may be open to them for eternity in the other life. This is what Thérèse wants for them: and she barters with God, in an admirable exchange, the fact that she no longer enjoys Heaven, that for her henceforth this has been replaced by darkness; she offers this suffering for them. She asks pardon from God for them; she wants God not to refuse to relent towards them; she interposes herself with all her heart between them and Him. Let Him give them Heaven all the same, even if they do not recognize Him here below.

Her brothers

Before God, Thérèse makes common cause with the 'impious' to such a degree that she quite naturally comes to call them her 'brothers';[123] she begs 'pardon for her brothers',[124] she prays 'in the name of her brothers';[125] and there is no commiseration here. A little further on she speaks of the disciples of Jesus: 'They were poor ignorant sinners filled with earthly thoughts. And still Jesus calls them his friends, his brothers.'[126] Thérèse puts herself among the sinners when she makes the prayer, 'Have pity on us, O Lord, for we are poor sinners!'[127] It is 'in his name and in the name of his brothers',[128] indissolubly, that Thérèse says that she will 'accept eating'[129] at the 'table of the sinners' and does not want 'to depart from this table filled with bitterness'[130] before the day that Jesus wills it. For her, it is Jesus who has sent her this trial, and she has accepted it from him; it is not through her own will.[131] In the spirituality of the nineteenth century there is frequently a radical dichotomy between the sinners and the 'pure and spotless victims'. The latter ask of the Lord, 'Have pity on the poor sinners', have pity on the others, those who are sinners. This implicitly indicates, 'We are not. We are ready to sit down, of our own free will, at their table, asking God to turn on us the blows that divine Justice reserves for sinners; we are ready to suffer everything except to suffer being recognized as sinners.'

Thérèse primarily does only one thing with the sinners: Jesus has graciously shown her that in fact she is at this table with everyone; that a spirituality after God's heart cannot be a spirituality in black and white in which some, Pharisees, recognize that they are justified, and the others, publicans, recognize that they are sinners; or in which some are guilty and the others are not.

Thus she indicates to the sinners, her brothers, what it is for a sinner to recognize his sin. Not this abyss of guilt in which according to many preachers he should plunge himself to his very depths, but a trial.

Let us go back to the important passage. Thérèse is well aware of what sin is: she knows it more than ever after Easter 1896. It is the fact of rejecting God freely, in awareness of the reason why, voluntarily. Those sinners persevere in their rejection of the love of God towards them; they accumulate their opposition to God. So this table at which they are seated, the table of denials of God, is as it were 'soiled' by these rejections. Thérèse is aware of this sin as it is, to the point that she is ready to take the place of sinners, so that they need no longer have to eat this bitter bread which is a trial for them; she now understands that she herself is in the trial, is in the darkness. She is ready to take their place, indeed to substitute herself: 'O Jesus! if it is needful that the table soiled by them be purified by a soul who loves You, then I desire to eat this bread of trial at this table alone until it pleases you to bring me into your bright kingdom.'[132]

She speaks of the 'bread of trial';[133] one can get good out of evil; one can get good out of sin, which is an evil, accepting it as a trial, a trial above all to lessen the greatest danger of spiritual life, pride. And we have to recall – it is important here – that at the time when Thérèse is writing these lines, at the beginning of June 1897, she has learned about the trick of Léo Taxil and his imposture, which is literally 'impious'. Thus when she writes manuscript C, when she speaks of the 'impious' who are truly 'darkness' and hide Heaven from her, she knows the ways of the wicked better than ever. These 'unbelievers', these 'sinners' who blaspheme in this way, are in her eyes her 'brothers'; she calls her brothers not only the atheist magistrate René Tostain, a man of great honesty, but also Léo Taxil, whose ignominy she has just discovered.[134] This is the form of an extreme humour – humour is close to humility; is it not the lay name of humility? It prevents her from taking herself too seriously. She makes her enemies brothers. Through this twist we can see at what point the place of Léo Taxil is important for Thérèse's spiritual journey. How, then, can anyone write: 'When all is said and done, the "Léo Taxil affair", put in the context of Thérèse, i.e. reduced to its true proportions, represented only an episode in Thérèse's life without any real significance'?[135] Thérèse has not 'reduced' this affair; she has taken very seriously first of all the false combat between 'Léo Taxil and Diana Vaughan' and then the real combat: the imposture of Léo Taxil. She has taken very seriously the fact that all this history, from one end to the other, expresses the modern incredulity which is beginning to explode in her time, under her eyes.

Heaven, an illusion?

Why this frenzied 'reduction' of the Léo Taxil affair? Is it out of a desire to minimize, in Thérèse, the depth of her trial? 'The point of Léo Taxil's demonstration,' we are told, 'was to reject any objective value to feelings of hope of Heaven and an eternal happiness that one could imagine, taking one's desires as realities.'[136] But by simulating spiritual experiences perfectly in the writings which he composed in the name of Diana Vaughan, as if he had had them himself, Léo Taxil showed that if he had been able to trick others, a religious soul could trick herself. In that case Léo Taxil merely showed, in derisory fashion, what Freud would try to show in a scientific way, namely that religion is illusion. The position of Léo Taxil and that of other more scientific 'impious' of his time converge on this point: that Heaven is an illusion. To write 'We think that Thérèse was not unduly affected by the imposture of this man', because he was 'a person with no respectability', is to leave aside the real place and significance that Léo Taxil assumed for Thérèse. Then all that remains is to put oneself at the level of apologetic, to emphasize that by contrast her sisters *were* affected by the trick – we have seen the sadness expressed by sister Geneviève – and to show that Thérèse supported them with a radical declaration: 'Fifteen days after the incident, on 9 May, we are told, without the customary context, of a reflection of Thérèse which states categorically, for her sisters and for herself, their certainty of faith and the supernatural origin of their enlightenment: "We can say, without any boasting, that we have received very special graces and lights; *we stand in the truth*[137] and see things in their proper light." Such a strong declaration, precisely two weeks after the shock caused by the news of Léo Taxil's trickery, can only be explained as a response to it.'[138]

The quotation which is given to us as authentic, as though it came from Thérèse herself, is in fact a text from the *Last Conversations*, dated 9 May 1897, and thus comes from Mother Agnes. Is it Thérèse's own style to proclaim in this peremptory fashion, 'We stand in the truth'? At this moment when she was in the darkness, could she state the realities in such a triumphalist fashion? We have Thérèse's true text in her letter to her sister, the previous September, when she exclaims: 'Is *pure love* in my heart? Are my measureless desires only a dream, a folly?... Ah, if that be so, Jesus, then enlighten me, for you know I am seeking only the truth...'[139]

Thérèse does not cut back: she recognizes this fundamental question, and experiences it in her flesh, in all her being. And we should not try to get out of this by a distinction which is more mediocre than subtle: 'It is worth recalling that Thérèse's doubts were not about the existence of God but only about the existence of heaven.'[140] So do we have to 'recall' that for Thérèse Heaven is the place of eternal life in God? Heaven, which she evokes very frequently, which most of the time she writes with a capital? How does she react to her first coughing of blood? 'On Good Friday, however, Jesus wished to give me the hope of going to see him soon in Heaven.'[141] If Heaven does not exist, Christ in Heaven does not exist and God does not exist.

For Thérèse, the alternative is either Heaven or 'the night of nothingness'. Before Easter, she only uses the word 'nothingness' once, in manuscript A, but in a relative sense, the word being applied to the 'works' performed by the human being: 'Without love all works are nothing, even the most dazzling.'[142] After Easter 1896, the word is used several times: from now on it denotes 'nothingness' as such. After Easter 1896, Thérèse, at the cost of intense suffering, becomes aware of the 'nothingness'. We shall return to this important point after following the course of her life from Easter to September 1896.

An election at the Carmel

Some days before Easter 1896, on 21 March, the election of the prioress took place. There were two candidates: Thérèse's sister, Mother Agnes, aged thirty-three, who was currently in charge, and Mother Marie de Gonzague, aged sixty-two, who had already had this responsibility several times – sixteen years in all. The climate of the election was very tense between the supporters of the one or the other. Of the twenty-four members of the community, sixteen had the right to vote. The election was difficult; the tension was so great that the secrecy of the voting was not maintained and it took no less than seven scrutinies before finally Mother Marie de Gonzague was elected. Mother Agnes was only a 'counsellor'; it is said that the Martin sisters, the 'four sisters' as they were called in the convent, and also their cousin Guérin, did not have the prioress they wanted, who would have been Agnes.

It was under the priorate of Mother Marie de Gonzague that Thérèse entered the convent; and it was under this priorate of Mother Marie de Gonzague that she experienced Easter 1896 and the last eighteen months of her life. At the process for the beatification of Thérèse, Mother Agnes made accusations against Mother Marie de Gonzague which were strong, even if she made them in an insidious way. Now it is clear that the new prioress was an opportunity for Thérèse's last spiritual journey.

Mother Marie de Gonzague, who in the world was Marie Davy de Virville, came from an old family in Caen: she was a great lady and a strong personality. She was unanimously recognized as having sound judgment; furthermore many priests came to consult her for their spiritual life. She had a sense of organization: in 1874, when she became prioress, she had plans to finish building the Carmel and obtained funds for this. She was a businesswoman; her character was imperious and authoritarian and she had a taste for power and clearly guarded it jealously, since she knew that she could govern her world best. Hers was a lively character: she unhesitatingly showed her anger and her passions.

Having been elected prioress twice in succession, Mother Marie de Gonzague could not be elected again in 1893, and Mother Agnes was. This was to the great displeasure of Mother Marie de Gonzague, since the 'Martin party' got on her nerves; and this election too was not without difficulties.[143]

After the interruption of 1893–1896, Mother Marie de Gonzague could be elected again, and there was a keen struggle. She wanted to show her authority immediately; though it was customary for the former prioress to be nominated novice mistress by the new one – this had been done by Mother Agnes in 1893 for Mother Marie de Gonzague – Mother Marie de Gonzague combined the two responsibilities, prioress and novice mistress, taking Thérèse as an assistant in this task.[144] She thus supplanted Mother Agnes, and made sure that she could not influence the five novices at will. From this election on, Thérèse gathered the five young sisters in the noviciate for half an hour a day, deepening their knowledge of the rule of the Carmel and its constitutions in a simple and lively exchange.

The election had been decided fairly, and Mother Marie de Gonzague felt its bitterness. Thérèse, of whom Mother Agnes was to say later that she was 'stupefied' at the announcement of the election of Mother Marie de Gonzague, in fact received confidences from the new prioress. On 29 June, Thérèse composed for her 'The Legend of a Very Little Lamb', a masterpiece of delicacy and clarity and at the same time a real psychodrama.[145] 'The Legend' shows a Shepherdess – Mother Marie de Gonzague – who loves her flock and is loved by it. The clouds come: 'The Shepherdess became sad; she no longer found any joy in taking care of her flock. And must I say it? The thought of separating herself from it for ever came into her mind.' There was a 'very little lamb' – Thérèse – to whom she confided 'her troubles' and who sought 'vainly in its very little heart the means of consoling her whom it loved *more than itself*'. In this dream, the lamb relives the election and its difficulties; a 'resplendent Shepherd' – Jesus – gives her the key to Mother Marie de Gonzague's suffering: 'Let your Shepherdess be consoled. I am the one who has *not permitted* but *willed* the great trial that has made her suffer so much.' In addition to this *'trial of election'* which Jesus has prepared for the Shepherdess, there is another point, since the lamb indicates to the Pastor 'the greatest sorrow', she says, 'of my Shepherdess': 'You think also that the primitive spirit of our flock is going away...' Thérèse considers that Mother Marie de Gonzague is right: 'I know some sheep who are doing much harm to my Shepherdess with their *mundane* reasoning.' But Thérèse wants the Shepherdess to understand the truth and the significance of her trial: *'her cross'* comes to her from *heaven* and not from earth. 'Yes,' replies the lamb, 'but how,' it tells the Shepherd, 'do you expect her to *understand* the *truth* since she hears only falsehood around her?'

The last question of the lamb to the Shepherd is: 'Why have You chosen the *dear sheep* of my Shepherdess to try her?' One cannot doubt that 'the dear sheep' are Thérèse's elder sisters.

The last argument of the lamb to console the Shepherdess is a word of the 'Good Shepherd': *'Soon*, yes soon, I shall take the Shepherdess and her lamb.' At that moment Mother Marie de Gonzague was in fact having serious health problems, and some weeks before Thérèse had had her two spells of coughing blood and thought that she would die.

This long letter from Thérèse to Mother Marie de Gonzague, in which she expresses herself through a parable, is dated 29 June 1896. The great festival given in honour of the new prioress, some days earlier on 21 June, on the festival of Saint Louis de Gonzague, does not therefore seem to have been enough to soothe her pains and truly restore her to what the sketch 'The Triumph of Humility', performed on that day, calls in its first lines the 'union of hearts' and 'the family spirit'. Thérèse recognizes that there are problems at the Carmel; the essential message of the 'Triumph of Humility', spoken by Thérèse in the sketch, is 'Prevent proud Satan from entering our monasteries.'

Mother Marie de Gonzague

Mother Marie de Gonzague wanted to return to the tradition; she thought that there was unacceptable laxity at the Lisieux Carmel. Could one say that she identified the rule too readily with her person and her views? But this woman had a very high sense of her responsibilities. She was shocked by things which might seem minor but which were not so in her eyes, for example that Mother Agnes as prioress had allowed a camera and all the equipment necessary for developing films into the convent; the rules of the Carmel in force at that time formally prohibited this.[146]

Now we know that Mother Agnes subjected Mother Marie de Gonzague, after her death, to a real purgatory. The notes given in the critical edition of the *Manuscrits autobiographiques* cannot hide it; thus for example this modest note: 'Personal relations between Thérèse and Mother Marie de Gonzague are difficult to evaluate precisely, given the real briefs in the process, of Mother Agnes, Sister Geneviève and Marie of the Trinity against the former prioress, in particular the six-page document ('In what milieu Sister Thérèse of the Child Jesus was sanctified at the Lisieux Carmel'), which Mother Agnes had signed by her sisters Marie of the Angels, Thérèse of St Augustine, Marie of the Sacred Heart, Geneviève of Sainte Thérèse and Marie of the Trinity, in the apostolic process of 1915, ten years after the death of Marie de Gonzague.'[147] Now in manuscript A, asked for by Mother Agnes and intended for her, Thérèse simply says that while Mother Marie de Gonzague was prioress she had been 'VERY SEVERE'[148] towards her and that she thought that this had been an 'inestimable grace': 'What would have become of me if, as worldly people believed, I had been the "pet" of the community?'[149] We should not forget that Thérèse met Mother Marie de Gonzague all by herself, in the parlour of the Carmel, at the age of nine: 'Having listened to my great confidences, this good mother believed in my vocation.'[150] The prioress did not cease to follow Thérèse's career, and she decided to enter the Carmel at the age of fifteen. Thérèse spoke of the '*strong education*'[151] which she had received from Mother Marie de Gonzague and thanked her prioress for not 'sparing' her.[152]

Mother Marie de Gonzague rediscovered in Thérèse the mystical sense and missionary impulse that she had in herself. The prioress held her in high esteem: 'This angel of a child is seventeen and a half and has the mind of a thirty-year-old, the religious perfection of an old dedicated novice and self-possession; she is a perfect religious,' she wrote to the Carmel of Tours the day after Thérèse's profession. Three years later, Mother Marie de Gonzague sent a photograph of Thérèse to the Tours Carmel, on the back of which she gives a description of Thérèse's personality to complete the portrait: 'Big and strong with the air of a child, with a resonant voice and an expression in it which conceals in her a wisdom, a perfection, a perspicacity of someone of fifty. Her soul is always calm and she is completely self- possessed in everything and with everyone. A little "unconscious saint" to whom one would give God without confession, but whose head is full of cunning to do to whoever she will. A mystic, a comic, she is all that. She can make you weep with devotion and equally make you burst out laughing in recreation.'[153]

Thérèse and her prioresses

At the apostolic process, Mother Agnes would say of Mother Marie de Gonzague that it was in Thérèse and 'in her alone that she had confidence'.[154] And Sister Marie of the Trinity affirmed there that Mother Marie de Gonzague had said to her 'several times': 'If a prioress had to be chosen from the whole community, without hesitation Sister Thérèse of the Child Jesus, despite her youth; she is perfect in everything; her sole failing is to have her three sisters with her.'[155]

For her part, Thérèse had great confidence in the judgment of Mother Marie de Gonzague, to the point that she very quickly made known to her her 'trial' of Easter 1896[156] – Mother Agnes was told of it only a year later. Thérèse loved the prioress deeply; Mother Agnes bears witness to that: 'She even asserted that she truly loved Mother Marie de Gonzague and that the appellations "beloved mother", "my dearest" which I would find in her diary expressed the true feelings of her heart.'[157]

So it must not be said too rapidly that 'in the community' it was Mother Agnes who 'knew her sister best'.[158] Pauline, who had become Sister Agnes, was the big sister who, on the death of their mother in 1877, was chosen by Thérèse to be her second mother. When Pauline entered the Carmel in 1882 – Thérèse was not yet ten – henceforth Thérèse's great desire was to join her 'little mother': as we know, she achieved her end when she crossed the threshold of the Carmel on 9 April 1888, at the age of fifteen. Pauline – Sister Agnes – became doubly her mother when in 1893 she was elected prioress of the Carmel – under the name of Mother Agnes.[159] Just as she had corrected her little sister's homework, so she thought that she would be guiding her at the Carmel. Did she 'become unconsciously a spiritual teacher'[160] for Thérèse? Mother Agnes recognized that Thérèse was the one she had seen least during her time as prioress; and when in January 1896 she read the little notebook of memories, manuscript A, which Thérèse wrote at her request in 1895, she was astounded.

It was the oldest of the Martin sisters, Marie of the Sacred Heart, who had suggested to Mother Agnes, the prioress, that she should make Thérèse write memories of her childhood, their childhood. At the beginning of 1895, Mother Agnes had asked Thérèse to put particular emphasis on her childhood and earliest youth. But she only read the manuscript which Thérèse sent her for St Agnes Day, 21 January 1896, after the election of 21 March. On reading it she regretted that Thérèse had not produced pages on her life at the Carmel; but she was no longer prioress and so could no longer ask Thérèse to continue her account; and she did not dare mention this notebook, which she kept in her own possession, to Mother Marie de Gonzague.

What did Mother Agnes think when she read this manuscript A after March 1896? We do not know. An authorized biography of Mother Agnes of Jesus writes this about her: 'Without doubt, at the affective level to the end she was to remain the "little mother", but how many times was Thérèse to have to put her, delicately, on the right way at a spiritual level! Clearly if Mother Agnes shared in Thérèse's sufferings and if she spent herself to the limit of the possible for her, her lack of discernment made her young sister suffer.'[161] We have to conclude that with her character, which was more ascetic than mystical, her rigidity combined with extreme sensitivity, and a certain lack of judgment, Mother Agnes was far from being able to understand and follow Thérèse's spiritual path. The older of the two is not the one one might think, and Mother Marie de Gonzague, who had great discernment, understood well that Thérèse far surpassed her 'little mother'.

'Your word of flame'

Less than a week after Easter 1896, on 11 April, Thérèse wrote to her sister Léonie; speaking of Jesus 'Our Beloved', she evoked Heaven: 'Then we shall understand the price of suffering and the trial.' She is referring to Christ's passion, recalling the words of Christ to the disciples on the Emmaus road, according to which one has to be tried by suffering to attain glory, a text which had been read at the mass on Easter Monday, the day after which she entered on her trial.

Sister Marie of the Trinity had a particular place among Thérèse's novices – we know that in 1893 Mother Agnes had appointed Thérèse official 'sub-mistress' of the novices, under Mother Marie de Gonzague, who was then novice mistress. The thirteenth of a family of nineteen children, born in Calvados, Sister Marie of the Trinity was seventeen when she entered the Carmel in the Avenue de Messine, in Paris; she had to leave it two years later for health reasons. The Lisieux Carmel accepted her on 16 June 1894, and Thérèse was asked to take special care of her – since it was thought to be a problem when someone left another Carmel. This was not an easy task: Sister Marie of the Trinity was sometimes boastful, very dreamy,[162] often critical. But there was something amusing and impulsive about her which Thérèse liked, and their spiritual conversations were carried on at a rapid pace.

On 30 April 1896, some weeks after Easter, Sister Marie of the Trinity pronounced her final vows – we have a photograph taken on the occasion of this profession, a photograph in which we see Sister Marie of the Trinity at the centre of a group of eight Carmelites, kneeling between Mother Marie de Gonzague, who is sitting, and Thérèse, who is standing; Sister Marie of the Trinity has a saucy, quite triumphant smile,[163] which contrasts with Thérèse's grave air. In fact Thérèse is very proud of having brought her novice to the point of profession: 'I felt like John of Arc present at the coronation of Charles VII,'[164] she is said to have remarked.

For this 30 April, Thérèse composed a poem in which she says to Sister Marie of the Trinity:

> You have given life for life
> To Jesus your Beloved.

She recalls that the religious had begun by finding refuge 'in the blessed ark of the Carmel', but in another monastery:

> But alas, poor fugitive,
> you had to go out of the ark
> like the plaintive dove,
> you had to groan for a long time.

On 7 May, Thérèse transcribed some thoughts of St John of the Cross for Sister Marie of the Trinity, who on this day was taking the 'black veil': 'In the evening of this life, you will be examined on love.' On 31 May, the festival of the Holy Trinity, Thérèse offered as a birthday present to the young religious a poem which she entitled 'Song of Sister Marie of the Trinity'. In fact it is Thérèse, speaking for herself, who says to Jesus: 'For you, I want to die.' She says that she is stamped by Jesus:

> Your word of flame
> burns my heart.

She wants to rejoin him, to fly to him, but she has to go through the night, to accept this night in which she is, and she knows it. She asks only one thing: to be more burned by this divine furnace of which the Song of Songs speaks. Here are the last strophes of Thérèse's 'Song':

> I am thirsty for love, fill my hope,
> Increase in me, Lord, your divine fire.
> I am thirsty for Love, my suffering is very great.
> How I long to fly to You, my God.

Your Love is my sole martyrdom.
The more I feel it burn within me
the more my soul desires you...
Jesus, grant that I may expire
of Love for You!! !

Now Sister Marie of the Trinity, who was the infirmarian of Carmel, had immediately told Mother Marie de Gonzague some weeks earlier of Thérèse's two fits of coughing blood. The prioress decided not to mention them to Mother Agnes or to the family. But Thérèse also decided, very sensibly, not to mention them to her 'little mother'. The prioress asked Marie of the Trinity to keep quiet but also to leave her post as infirmarian: she was the 'baby' of the noviciate and the prioress did not want her to risk contagion from tuberculosis. Furthermore a young religious, Sister Marie-Antoinette, was already gravely ill with tuberculosis; she died of it on 4 November 1896. Sister Marie-Antoinette had been porter, and Thérèse had had close contact with her from 1893 to 1896, the period during which she was second porter. Thérèse had minimized the significance of the event, and a physician, Dr La Néele, Thérèse's cousin, also minimized it; he had provided several remedies which in June stopped the dry cough. On 16 July, Thérèse wrote to her aunt, Mme Guérin, who asked her for news of her health (doubtless she had been warned by Dr La Néele, her son-in-law). Thérèse relates humorously, doubtless to play down the incident further, that the official physician of the community has seen her: 'The famous Doctor de Cornières, to whom I had the *distinguished honour* of being presented yesterday in the parlour. This illustrious personage, after having *honoured* me with a look, declared that I looked well!!.'

She adds: 'This *declaration* has not hindered me from thinking that I will soon be allowed to go to Heaven.' Had her state then got worse? She is thinking of death for another reason – but perhaps she gives this reason to her aunt to reassure her. In fact she writes why she envisages 'going to Heaven': 'Not because of my health but because of another declaration made today in the Carmel's chapel.' What was this declaration? A preacher had told them that an era of persecutions was going to begin; and Thérèse thought of martyrdom. Minister Bourgeois, who had finished in April, was renowned for his anticlericalism.

Nine out of eleven of his ministers were Freemasons: was it this event which made the preacher ecstatic? Thérèse's tone would seem to indicate that she did not take him very seriously; and without doubt she used this event to announce the change in her health to her aunt. She took much more seriously the account which Abbé Roger de Teil brought to the Lisieux Carmel at the beginning of September of the approaches he had made towards the canonization of the sixteen Carmelites of Compiègne, martyred a century earlier in 1794. Thérèse enthused over this cause.[165] On 8 September in manuscript B,3, she wrote: 'Martyrdom was the dream of my youth and this dream has grown with me within Carmel's cloisters... When thinking of the torments which will be the lot of Christians at the time of Anti-Christ, I feel my heart leap with joy.'

A young seminarian

On 15 October 1895, a young seminarian of twenty-one, from the diocese of Bayeux, wrote to the prioress of the Lisieux Carmel: 'I shall ask for a religious to be attached particularly to the salvation of my soul and to see that I remain faithful to the vocation that God has given me: that of priest and missionary.'

Mother Agnes turned to Thérèse, who composed a prayer for Abbé Maurice Bellière; she replied to the young abbé, attaching this prayer to the letter and presenting Thérèse as 'a saint, an angel', 'a saint among saints'. 'You are treating me as a son; permit me to consider myself as such,' replied Abbé Bellière, an orphan who had been brought up by an aunt. On 12 November, Abbé Bellière sent a card to Mother Agnes and Sister Thérèse of Jesus (sic) to announce that he was returning to barracks.

Thérèse, who for a long time had had 'a desire which appeared totally unrealizable' to her, 'that of having a *brother priest*',[166] experienced a joy which, she said, 'I can describe only as that of a child'.[167] 'I would really have to go back to my childhood days to recapture once more the memory of joys so great.'[168] This bond with this seminarian, who was a year younger than she, was something very new. But the seminarian soldier did not write again: 'My little brother gave no further sign of life until the following July.'[169]

On 21 July 1896, the Abbé wrote to Mother Agnes from the barracks, not knowing that there had been a change of prioress. It was an appeal for help: 'I am a soldier, Mother, and this time has no value for the seminarian. I have had many a fall, many unheard-of stupidities, in the midst of this world which has taken hold of me again. I have just committed the most beautiful of all... I am plunged into a deplorable situation, and my dear sister, Thérèse of the Child Jesus, must tear me away from it at all costs.' Mother Marie de Gonzague replied to him. He thanked her, on 14 October, for 'the help you have given me in a moment of distress. The storm has passed, calm has returned, and the poor soldier has become again the seminarian of former days.' Mother Marie de Gonzague, who was sick, asked Thérèse to reply to the letter herself. Thérèse did so on 21 October: 'Your letter of July had caused me some sorrow,' she told him. But she saw a sign in these struggles: 'When Jesus calls a soul to direct and to save multitudes of other souls, it is necessary that He have him experience the temptations and trials of life.' What does she ask for him from Jesus? 'That you may be not only a good missionary but a saint all on fire with the love of God and souls; I beg you to obtain also for me this love so that I may help you in your apostolic work.'

We shall return to this text in connection with the letter which Thérèse wrote the previous 17 September to Sister Marie of the Sacred Heart, a letter which constitutes what has been called Manuscript B.

A missionary

Before that, we have to talk about a second brother who was given to Thérèse. He was a seminarian from Calvados, Adolphe Roulland, who entered the seminary of the Foreign Missions of Paris. On 30 May 1896 the Father Abbot of the Premonstratensians of Mondaye, near Caen, wrote to the prioress of the Carmel asking for a religious to be designated to pray specially for this missionary who was soon to be ordained priest, on the following 28 June, and was about to leave for China. Mother Marie de Gonzague, who herself had a great 'apostolic desire',[170] which found an echo in Thérèse's soul,[171] called

Thérèse and suggested that she should be this religious. Mother Marie de Gonzague knew that there was already Maurice Bellière, but he was still very young and had not written again since entering the barracks, and having understood Thérèse's intense missionary dynamism, she wanted to nurture it in Thérèse by giving her this time a solid missionary aged twenty-six, with a proven vocation, already on his way to China. Mother Marie de Gonzague read Thérèse the letter which Fr Roulland had sent her. Thérèse had mixed feelings of joy and fear: was she going to be able to help this missionary? The prioress swept the objections aside: 'One could have several brothers';[172] and Mother Marie de Gonzague made her heart swell by suggesting that 'the zeal of a Carmelite should set the world on fire'.[173] Thérèse told herself that she had to 'pray for all without casting aside simple priests whose mission at times is as difficult to carry out as that of apostles preaching to the infidels'.[174] She accepted, and her prioress asked her not to mention this second brother she was giving her to Mother Agnes; in the eyes of the community Fr Roulland would be 'our Mother's missionary'.[175]

Ordained priest on 28 June, Fr Roulland planned to pass through Lisieux on his way to say good-bye to his family and to celebrate a mass in the chapel of the Carmel. Thérèse then wrote to him and expressed her joy: 'For a long time I wanted to know an Apostle who would pronounce my name at the Holy Altar on the day of his first mass.' What is her desire? 'To ask for me from Jesus... to set me on fire with His Love so that I may enkindle it in hearts.' This is the same theme that she expressed in her letter to Abbé Bellière. She adds: 'I shall be truly happy to work with you for the salvation of souls. It is for this purpose that I became a Carmelite nun; being unable to be an active missionary, I wanted to be one through love.'

On 3 July, Fr Roulland came to say mass at the Carmel; and Mother Marie de Gonzague allowed Thérèse to see him in the parlour; he blessed her before he left. That very day, his cousin, Sister Marie of the Eucharist, wrote to her mother, Mme Guérin, and gave her news of Thérèse: 'She is better but she often does not look well. She no longer has chest pains and has stopped coughing altogether. She is truly better. Our mother

looks after her so well that this is not surprising.' Her sister
Léonie is disturbed about Thérèse's health, while Mother Agnes
does not seem to see anything. Léonie writes to her on 1 July:
'How are you? Dear little sister, on this subject alone I have no
confidence in you, for you always tell me that you are well or
better, and I don't believe any of it. When you write to me, tell
me above all the real truth.' Thérèse replies to her on 12 July,
saying at the end of a long letter: 'I am not coughing any more.
Are you satisfied? This will not prevent God from taking me
when he wills.'[176]

Léonie has an inferiority complex and is full of scruples; she
thinks, as she says in her letter to Thérèse, that she will arrive in
Heaven 'with empty hands', and is tempted by the 'pleasures
and vanities of the world'. Thérèse casually explains to Léonie
her spirituality of abandonment, the opposite of Jansenism: 'I
have understood it is a matter of *taking hold of Jesus by the
Heart*.' She asks her to overcome all fear, referring to a verse in
the Song of Songs: 'How can we fear,' she asks, 'him who allows
himself to be enchained by a *hair* fluttering on our neck!'[177] She
interprets this: 'Let us understand, then, how to hold him
prisoner, this God who becomes the beggar of our love. When
telling us that it is a hair that can effect this prodigy, He is
showing us that the smallest actions done out of love are the
ones which charm His Heart. Ah! if we had to do great things,
how much we would have to be pitied! But how fortunate we
are since Jesus allows himself to be enchained by the smallest.'

Fr Roulland left Paris for Marseilles on 29 July. On that day
he wrote to Thérèse: at mass, in the morning, he said this prayer
for her: 'My God, set my sister on fire with your love'; he
promised to continue praying this all his life.

Thérèse wrote him a long letter on 30 July in which she calls
him 'my brother'. Mother Marie de Gonzague allowed her to
keep a photograph of Fr Roulland: 'This is a *very special*
privilege. A Carmelite does not have even the portraits of her
closest relatives.' She ends her letter, which is essentially a
meditation on passages of Isaiah, by saying: 'If I go to heaven
soon, I will ask Jesus' permission to go to visit you at Su-
Tchuen, and we shall continue our apostolate together.' Mother
Marie de Gonzague adds a word to Thérèse's letter; she says

that she is suffering.[178] 'I am an old worn-out machine, my chest plays tricks with me from time to time.' She tells him, speaking of Thérèse, 'You have a very fervent helper who will neglect nothing for the salvation of souls. The dear little thing is all for God.' She asks him, if he passes by Saigon, to visit the Carmel.

Fr Roulland embarked for China on 2 August.

A Carmel in Saigon

That same day there was a great storm in Thérèse's life: 'Never shall I forget 2 August 1896, the very day of the departure of the missionaries; there was serious consideration of the departure of Mother Agnes of Jesus. Ah! I would not have desired to make any move to prevent her from leaving; I felt, however, a great sadness in my heart, for I found that her very sensitive and delicate soul was not made to live in the midst of souls who could not understand her.'[179]

Had Mother Marie de Gonzague envisaged sending Mother Agnes and 'a few months after this'[180] Sister Geneviève to the Saigon Carmel, which would have removed two of the four Martin sisters from Lisieux? It is almost certain, in fact, that Mother Agnes had herself asked to leave, perhaps because life under the priorate of Mother Marie de Gonzague was 'difficult' for her.[181] But Thérèse herself had also wanted to leave; at that time Mother Marie de Gonzague had told her that 'a very special vocation was necessary to live in foreign Carmels';[182] she had recognized that vocation in her and, Thérèse said, 'only my poor health stood in the way'.[183] What was the reason for this desire in Thérèse? '*Here*,' she tells her superior, 'I am loved by you and all the sisters, and this affection is very sweet to me. This is why I dream of a monastery where I shall be unknown, where I would suffer from poverty, the lack of affection, and finally, the exile of the heart.'[184]

Mother Marie de Gonzague meanwhile decided that Mother Agnes should remain at Lisieux.

Some weeks later, on 31 May, Thérèse dedicated a song which she had composed to her novice Marie de la Trinité, the one who as infirmarian had known about the coughing of blood of

Maundy Thursday and Good Friday. Significant verses run through this poem:

It is late, and the day is already waning.

Thérèse knows that her sister understands. Where is God, this God whom she implores in the night after Easter?

You the Great God whom all Heaven loves,
you live in me, a Prisoner night and day,
your sweet voice implores me at every hour,
you tell me, 'I thirst... thirst for Love!'

I am your prisoner,
And want to repeat in turn
your tender and divine prayer,
'My Beloved, my Brother,
I thirst for Love.'

It will be noted that while the first strophe is addressed to the 'Great God', the second speaks of Jesus the brother. The last strophe reads:

Your Love is my sole martyrdom,
the more I feel it burn in me
the more my soul desires you.
Jesus, make me expire
for Love of You.

'What I want to believe'

This is the moment to recall what she says to her prioress of the period which follows Easter 1896: 'If you are judging according to the sentiments I express in my little poems composed this year, I must appear to you as a soul filled with consolations and one for whom the veil of faith is almost torn aside; and yet... it is no longer a veil for me, it is a wall which reaches right up to the heavens and covers the starry firmament. When I sing of the happiness of Heaven and the eternal possession of God, I feel no joy, for I sing simply *what I want to believe.*'[185]

In another poem, a week later, entitled 'My Heaven for Me', at the beginning and at the end she mentions her 'trial of faith'; in the last verses she twists the situation, as only she can:

> When he wants to hide himself to try my faith,
> to suffer, waiting for Him to look at me again,
> That is my Heaven for me.

And she affirms that his 'sole law' is 'total abandonment'. As she writes in a poem of 12 June 1896, she awaits 'ineffable happiness'. When will it come?

> When I see on your Adorable Face
> the divine glory for the first time.

Thérèse is not speaking here of the Holy Face of Jesus as engraved on Veronica's veil in the course of his way to the cross, but of the face of Christ in Heaven, that Heaven which she no longer sees.

The Holy Face

It is important to study briefly the development of the spirituality of the Holy Face in Thérèse's mind over the course of the years. This spirituality, or this devotion, had begun in the nineteenth century with a religious of the Tours Carmel, Sister Marie de Saint-Pierre. Thérèse had been the first at the Lisieux Carmel to have the appellation 'of the Holy Face' added to her first religious name, 'Sister Thérèse of the Child Jesus'. She received this name the day she took the habit, on 10 January 1889. Over the years Thérèse came to decipher 'the Holy Face' in an increasingly personal way. To begin with, she was certainly influenced by the state of health of M.Martin, her father:[186] some weeks after Thérèse had taken the habit, he had sunk into hallucinations and had had to be transferred to a mental hospital; her father's face then changed, became dark, having lost its light, like the face of Christ on Calvary. Then she spoke of the 'luminous Face of Jesus': 'If in the midst of wounds and tears it is already so beautiful, what will it be, then, when we shall see it in heaven?'[187] However, the image of her father remained, and Mother Agnes, who was particularly adept at this devotion,[188] helped her. When she composed a miniature on parchment for Céline in 1890, Mother Agnes depicted a Holy Face, bleeding, on a Veronica veil surrounded by nine lilies:[189] 'When I was looking at the image of the Holy Face,' Thérèse writes to Céline on 27 April 1890, 'tears came to my eyes; isn't it an image of our family?'

But Thérèse detached herself from this paternal configuration by reading Isaiah and the story of the suffering servant, whose face has 'no form nor beauty', and by plunging herself in the poems of St John of the Cross. And when she speaks of the Holy Face in manuscript A, in 1895, she says that 'the adorable Face [of Jesus] veiled in tears' is her 'Sun'.[190]

In Manuscripts B and C, and thus after Easter 1896, the Holy Face is never mentioned. Always after this date of Easter 1896 she no longer speaks at all of the Holy Face in her correspondence; the only time that the word recurs is to speak of the angels who do not cease 'to see the divine Face'.[191] In her poems there had been a mention of the Holy Face before Easter 1896, for example that of 28 April 1894:

The Face of Jesus showed you his light.

Or in that of 12 August 1895:

Your Face is my sole homeland.

It is not mentioned again after Easter 1896 as the Holy Face, but, as we have seen, as the Divine Face of the Risen Christ. In 'The Angels at Jesus' Cradle' – 25 December 1894 – there is an 'Angel of the Holy Face' who speaks.

Under the priorate of Mother Agnes (1893–1896), the custom became established of celebrating the Holy Face on 6 August, the day of the feast of the Transfiguration.[192] Thérèse undertook to compose a 'Consecration to the Holy Face' for 6 August 1896. She composed it for herself and two of her novices: her sister Céline, in religion Sister Geneviève, but who initially had taken the name of Sister Marie of the Holy Face; and Sister Marie of the Trinity, initially Sister Marie-Agnes of the Holy Face,[193] since she had been very attracted by this devotion from her childhood. All three were to sign the 'Consecration' in red ink.

This Consecration is very important in Thérèse's spiritual career; it is in a direct line with the 'Act of Oblation to Merciful Love' of 9 June 1895. As with the 'Act of Oblation', Thérèse invited Sister Geneviève and Sister Marie of the Trinity to pronounce the Consecration; Marie of the Eucharist, her cousin Marie Guérin, also a novice, who found this devotion truly repugnant, did not take part. But this Consecration is at the same time a text which forms a prelude, in its research and content, to Manuscript B, written a month later, and comprises essential pages of Thérèse. We must study it more closely.

Before the definitive version Thérèse wrote a kind of developed rough copy; it is interesting to go through the two and compare them. On the recto of the definitive version, Thérèse transcribed not only the three names of those who making this Consecration, but also a verse from Psalm 30: 'Lord, hide us in the secret of your Face!' She added five lines, the first two of which had no quotation marks: 'The smallest movement of *Pure Love* is of more use to the church than all other works.' This is in fact a saying of John of the Cross, as we have seen.[194] The last three lines form a conclusion to the preceding ones; they are also from John of the Cross: 'So it is of the utmost importance that our souls practise love much, so that consuming themselves rapidly they scarcely stop here below and promptly come to see *Jesus, Face to Face.*'[195]

Here we immediately find the theme of the face, but as we see, this is 'Face to Face with Jesus in heaven', outside any veil and fog, beyond the night. From Easter 1896 Thérèse thinks intensely of this Face to Face which she hopes for in the blackness in which she finds herself, which she awaits with all her strength; in a way, the crucified face of Jesus and the extreme shadow on it – how is it that Love is not loved, that it can be rejected? – undergo a kind of assumption in the luminous face of the Risen Christ. That is in hope, but really.[196]

The Consecration, written on the verso of the sheet, begins immediately with words which she has underlined:

O Adorable Face of Jesus![197]

Now instead of the face of the Crucified Christ, immediately, put on the lips of Jesus, we have a quotation from the Song of Songs which evokes the dawn after night: 'Open to me, my sisters, my well-beloved spouses, for *my Face* is covered with dew and *my hair* with drops of night.'[198] The text then evokes the face of the Crucified Christ, but speaks of a peaceful, *'sweet'* face: 'We want to wipe your sweet face.' And Thérèse, who, as we have seen, has understood since Easter 1896 that there are really 'impious people', says of them: 'In their eyes you are still as if hidden; they regard you as an object of scorn.' She calls these impious 'our brothers'.[199]

Thérèse and her sisters want to 'console' Jesus for this forgetfulness in which some reject him: 'Our souls understand your language of love.' What is this 'language'? 'From your *Adored Mouth* we have heard *the loving complaint*; the thirst which consumes you is a *thirst for Love*.' They want to quench this thirst, this intense thirst for love which is that of Jesus, a thirst to set hearts on fire with his love.[200] Then comes this cry, 'We need *souls*, above all *souls* of *apostles and martyrs,* so that by them *we* can *set* the multitude of poor sinners *on fire with your love*.' In the original text she had written: 'So that we can convert the multitude of poor sinners to your Love.' She thus changes the perspective radically; she wants, herself and apostles and martyrs with her, to set sinners on fire with the Love of Jesus; she is no longer concerned for 'conversion', but wants this fire of Jesus to pass through her into people's hearts.

The very last phrase of the Consecration shows in a hidden fashion the night in which she finds herself. Her Heaven is no longer luminous, it is veiled; but even when veiled, it is the look of Jesus: 'Your *Veiled Look,* that is our *Heaven, O Jesus*.'

So Thérèse's gaze is fixed obstinately beyond suffering and night, on the *'Veiled Look'* of Jesus. We may remember how on the previous 7 June she had written in the first strophe of a poem entitled 'My Heaven for Me':

The look of my God, his ravishing Smile,
is my Heaven for me.

But the poem ends with a total reversal:

My Heaven is to smile at this God whom I adore
when He wants to hide himself to try my faith,
to suffer, waiting for Him to look at me again,
That is my heaven for me.

From Thérèse we have a brief prayer to the Holy Face composed in summer 1896.[201] There is the same invocation at the beginning, 'O Adorable Face of Jesus'; the last five lines speak discreetly of her trial: 'O my Beloved, for your love I accept not seeing here below the sweetness of your Look, not feeling the inexpressible kiss of your Mouth, but I pray you to set me on fire with your love so that it consumes me rapidly and makes me soon appear before you. Thérèse of the Holy Face' (this name appears as a signature).[202]

2. The Song of Love

'The burning Abyss of Love'

Retreat of 7 to 17 September 1896

We have two major texts of Thérèse from the last eighteen months of her life: one, written in September 1896, has been called Manuscript B in the *Manuscrits autobiographiques*; the other, written in June 1897, constitutes Manuscript C. We have already followed this Manuscript C as far as it relates to the event of Easter 1896; we shall now study it in its chronological context, three months before Thérèse's death.

On the evening of Monday 7 September 1896, Thérèse entered into private retreat – the last that she would make – for ten days; on the next day, 8 September, the festival of the Nativity of Mary, which was a holiday at the Carmel, she celebrated in solitude and silence the sixth anniversary of her profession. It was during these ten days that the pages which form Manuscript B (five sheets recto/verso, B, 1 to 5) were written. But first we encounter a difficulty in establishing the text.

In the first edition of the *Manuscrits autobiographiques* (1956), Fr François de Sainte-Marie had put forward the hypothesis that the text of 8 September was antedated and that it was later than Thérèse's letter of 13 September. In this way he had kept the order established by Mother Agnes in *Story of a Soul*. Now, however, it is certain that the text dated 8 September was written by Thérèse on 8 September and the following days: these are sheets 2 to 5, while sheet 1 was written on Sunday 13.

This is what happened. While Thérèse was already in retreat, Sister Marie of the Sacred Heart, Marie, the oldest of the Martin girls and Thérèse's godmother, asked permission from the prioress – certainly on Sunday 13 – to write to Thérèse to get from her what she had already asked verbally: an explanation in writing, during this retreat which she was in process of making, of her 'little doctrine'. The prioress agreed. So on Sunday 13, Sister Marie of the Sacred Heart sent a letter to Thérèse with this postscript: 'Our mother permits you to reply to me (by return).' The beginning of the letter is explicit: 'I am writing not because I have something to tell you but to get something from you.' As she says, she wants to know better the 'secrets' – a word repeated twice – which Jesus has confided to Thérèse, secrets of which her sister has already spoken to her: 'I would like to hear about them once again,' says Marie. And she asks Thérèse to pray for her: 'Ask Jesus to love me, too, as he does his little Thérèse', so that she, Marie, 'may no longer dream of anything but practising... the art of loving.'

Certainly on the evening of this Sunday 13 September, Thérèse wrote to her sister, and this letter constitutes what has been put as B,1; it is a kind of official letter, allowed by the prioress. But Thérèse had already written what constitutes B, 2 to 5. So text B, 1, the letter to Sister Marie of the Sacred Heart written on 13 September, is an official letter accompanying what Thérèse had already written on the previous days.

Sister Marie of the Sacred Heart received Thérèse's letter and text and reacted immediately with a new letter, written on 16 September, which was delivered to Thérèse. Thérèse, still in retreat, replied to it on the 17th.

So we have an important collection, and we must be aware of its chronology if we are to follow Thérèse's thought:
– Thérèse's text of 8 September and the subsequent days (B, 2 to 5);
– Thérèse's letter to Marie of 13 September (B,1);
– Marie's letter to Thérèse of the 16th;
– Thérèse's reply to Marie of the 17th.

We can only regret keenly that the Nouvelle Édition du centenaire and the India paper *Oeuvres complètes* of Thérèse of Lisieux have both kept the order established by Mother Agnes in *Story of a Soul*.[1]

It would have been so simple and in keeping with reality – and would not have required either great boldness or great financial means –[2] finally to re-establish the texts in their proper order.

This would have given a logical collection which could have been entitled 'Manuscripts B: Retreat of 7 to 17 September 1896', comprising:
– B, 2–5;
– B, 1;
– Thérèse's letter of 17 September.

Marie's letter of 16 September, which is extremely significant because of its failure to understand B,2–5 and B,1, could have been put in this group, in small type, between B,1 and the letter of 17 September.[3] It provoked an important explanation of her texts from Thérèse, namely the letter of 17 September.

The unity of time gives this collection its unity, and we shall now study it chronologically.

A dream in the night

In the text dated 8 September (B, 2–5), Thérèse addresses Jesus, and not her sister: Jesus with whom she finds herself *tête à tête* in this retreat, just the two of them. She begins by addressing Jesus in the formal second person plural, but she soon comes to address him in the more intimate second person singular.

The first paragraph of the text speaks first of all of the central event: Easter, five months earlier. Thérèse says that she is 'in the midst of the darkest storm',[4] a 'storm which', she adds, 'has been raging very strongly' in her soul since 'the radiant feast of Easter'.[5] She then relates that on the evening of Saturday 9 May, 'considering the clouds which were covering her heaven',[6] she began to think 'of the mysterious dreams which are granted at times to certain souls'.[7] And she says that the moment of this consolation had not come for her: she says on the subject of this possible consolation, 'I wasn't asking for it.'[8]

However, in fact she did have a dream that night of 9–10 May: 'I was (in a dream) in a kind of gallery.'[9] Mother Marie de Gonzague was close to her. 'Three Carmelites dressed in their mantles and long veils'[10] arrived: 'What I did understand clearly was that they came from Heaven. In the depths of my heart I cried out, "Oh! how happy I would be if I could see the face of one of these Carmelites!"'[11] The tallest of them advanced towards Thérèse, raised her veil, and covered Thérèse with it:[12] 'Without the least hesitation I recognized Venerable Mother Anne of Jesus, Foundress of the Carmel in France.'[13] Her face was 'suffused with an unspeakably gentle light', 'her face and smile were filled with love'.[14]

Thérèse then asked Mother Anne of Jesus two questions; she dared to do so because she felt that she was recognized by the one who had covered her with her veil: 'Seeing myself so tenderly loved,' she says. The first question that she asked was: 'Will God soon come to get me?' The reply was: 'Yes, soon.' The second question was: 'Tell me further if God is not asking something more of me than my poor actions and my desires. Is he content with me?' 'The saint's face took on an expression incomparably more tender..., she said to me: "God asks no other thing from you. He is content, very content."'[15]

Thérèse was then 'filled with joy';[16] she woke up. She knew it was a dream, but, being in the night as she was, she clung to this dream which she had perhaps prompted herself, since as she went to sleep she had been thinking 'of the mysterious dreams which are granted to certain souls'. Four months after this dream she evokes it at the beginning of her text as a 'ray'[17] of sunlight 'in the midst of the darkest storm'; in this dream, but only in this dream, 'the storm was no longer raging; the sky was calm and serene...,'[18] I *believed*, I *felt* there was a Heaven'. This only confirms how radical was the darkness in her soul; and we must not forget that she was to confess nine months later: 'It is true that at times a very small ray of the sun comes to illuminate my darkness, and then the trial ceases for an instant, but afterwards the memory of this ray, instead of causing me joy, makes my darkness even more dense.'[19] If she reminds Jesus in the first line of her text of this 'ray which he caused to shine' for her, the fact remains that this 'ray' existed only in a dream, and the return to the reality of the night was even harsher.[20]

We may remember that Thérèse was to say in June 1897 that in all these dark months she did not express what she really felt but simply what she wanted to believe.[21] Here she wants to believe that Jesus has caused a ray of his grace to shine on her in this dream, and she expresses her gratitude to him for his 'tenderness', 'his sweetness', which she does not feel, which she no longer feels. For her, to feel is not to 'have a personal experience'[22] but to have an intuitive grasp or to acquire an intimate conviction; and beyond question we have to suppose that the reason why she uses this term so often at this moment in Manuscript B – nineteen times! – is precisely because she does not feel anything, that she no longer has any of her signs or landmarks. So here she is expressing a wish, not an experience.

This not-feeling is a kind of opaqueness thrust on her, what she was to call a 'veil',[23] and more than a veil, a wall of separation. A comparison between different senses of the term 'veil' is interesting. First of all there is the veil which hides in order to display better. When she evokes 'the veil of faith' in 1895,[24] this seems to her to be a veil which displays and does not hide: 'How transparent and light was the veil which concealed Jesus from our glances'; and Thérèse can say that before Easter 1896 her faith is 'clear'. In her dream of 10 May 1896, there is the Carmelite veil of Mother Anne of Jesus; she covers Thérèse with it, so it is a veil of protection and love which also does not hide: 'In spite of the veil,' Thérèse remarks, 'I saw this heavenly face suffused with an unspeakably sweet light.'[25] But on this 10 May, perhaps Thérèse recalled the ceremony which had taken place on 7 May, two days earlier: Sister Marie of the Trinity, newly professed, had taken 'the black veil'. During this ceremony the Carmelite is covered from head to foot by a long black non-transparent veil. So this is a veil which conceals a person from sight, puts them in the dark.

Perfect joy

In this situation, it is not sadness that she comes to feel. On the contrary, paradoxical though it might seem, this black 'veil', this darkness, brings joy. Thérèse describes herself as 'a little bird' which is 'assailed by the storm, and it seems it should believe in the existence of no other thing except the clouds surrounding it'.[26]

In two lines, but in a discreet way so as not to frighten her sister Marie, who is a sensitive soul and is a thousand miles from doubting what she experiences, Thérèse indicates her situation precisely: she is like a bird lost in the clouds who cannot believe in the existence of anything but these clouds. What does Thérèse conclude from this? This is the moment of *'perfect joy* for the *poor* weak *little creature'*.[27]

The reference to Francis of Assisi is explicit. To define perfect joy the Poverello had described the state of a friar minor arriving at his monastery on a cold snowy night. Knocking at the door and not being recognized by the porter, he is cast out into the night. For Thérèse, as she wrote to Abbé Bellière on 26 December 1896, Francis of Assisi 'teaches... the means of finding joy in the midst of the trials and combats of life'.

She makes her joy and her happiness out of her night. First of all there is joy: this moment of becoming aware of what is truly the night, a night which seems to be the only thing that there is, since she is in the dark. Nine months later, in June 1897, she was to speak rightly of the 'night of nothingness': there is nothing but the clouds, so there is nothing beyond the clouds, mists, darkness; there is nothing at the end of the tunnel. This joy is difficult to understand, yet it must be grasped for what it is: to become aware and to be able to express the fact that from henceforth one is in the dark is still an awareness and a certain clarity; it is a moment of joy.

'Remaining there all the same'

There is also happiness; it is no longer, like joy, a matter of 'moment' but a question of 'duration', and we need to pay attention to this second stage after joy for Thérèse.[28]

Happiness is not a flash of lightning given in a sudden moment like joy, a fleeting and ineffable explosion which both fulfils and disturbs. Happiness has to be constructed; it is the fruit of the will and long patience. Thérèse is very precise about this; having spoken of perfect joy, she gives a precise definition of happiness, which can exist in the night: 'happiness' – for the bird, for her – 'of *remaining* there all the same, and gazing at the invisible light which hides itself from her faith'.[29]

In passing, we might note how Mother Agnes has travestied this splendid text in the *Story of a Soul*: 'Should the Star of Love be blotted out by heavy clouds so that nothing but the night of this life seems to exist, then will be the time for *perfect joy*, the moment to push my confidence to the furthest bounds; I shall take good care to stay just where I am, quite certain that beyond the sombre clouds my beloved sun is shining still.'

Clearly Mother Agnes was ill at ease with this text, so she suppressed it, diluted it, robbed it of its force and savour; she wanted to keep 'perfect joy', which she could hardly understand from the perspective of Francis of Assisi, but she makes happiness disappear radically; she remains in 'the moment' and instead of duration speaks of not changing place.

Thérèse is clear: she underlies the verb 'remain'; it is a matter of duration. And it is a matter of remaining there 'all the same'; later in her text she shows clearly all the temptations presented to someone who thus finds himself in the night, in order to avoid remaining in his night. She makes a comparison with a little bird which 'looks for a little meadow on the right or left', which finds 'an attractive flower', all the things that she calls the 'trifles of earth'.[30]

So the condition of happiness which the soul that is in the night knows or can know is duration. Thérèse expresses the content of this happiness in a short and extraordinary definition: 'To gaze on the invisible light which hides itself from its faith.' To gaze: it is still and always a question of duration, of a gaze fixed permanently and persistently on an object: 'A long gaze on the calm of the gods,' the pagan Paul Valéry will say in *Le Cimitière marin*. But what is this object which, gazed at, looked at for a long time, brings true happiness to the one who contemplates it? 'The invisible light hides itself from its faith.'

Faith as such brings light; but here this light conceals itself, makes itself invisible, which is contradictory for light. In this way Thérèse expresses, rightly, the light of the night, and the precise, original, specific happiness of the night.

From Easter 1896 and her 'darkest cloud', which has not ended, Thérèse could derive a happiness which she did not know before, and for good reason. She sees this event as a grace, and above all as the beginning, 'the prelude of the greatest graces'[31] with which Jesus then wanted to fill her.

'My desires which touch on the infinite'

After the preamble, the story of the dream, comes the essential part. For Thérèse it consists in reminding herself, before Jesus, of all the graces that she has received over the past five months; Jesus is the conversation-partner, ceaselessly addressed, ceaselessly and lovingly called to witness.

In her dream, Thérèse had asked Mother Anne of Jesus in particular whether God was content with her desires. That shows clearly that she is asking herself about these 'desires' which have come to her over these five months, since Easter, and which she needs God to recognize. He authenticates them in the dream, and by no less an intermediary than the founder of the Carmel in France; this gives Thérèse a blank cheque to express these desires.

Just as she has spoken of 'small actions', so with desires we find the other extreme, and Thérèse is aware of this. First of all she writes: 'Ah! my Jesus, pardon me if I am unreasonable in wishing to express my desires and hopes which touch on the infinite.'[32] At the same time, she does not shrink from boldness: 'Pardon me and heal my soul by giving it what it hopes for.'[33] She asks Jesus to respond to these desires and 'hopes which touch on the infinite' with a kind of imperious fearlessness, as a childlike heart can do.

It is not enough for her to be a *spouse* of Jesus, a *Carmelite*, a *mother* of souls: 'No doubt these three privileges sum up my vocation', 'and yet, I feel within me other vocations'. And an avalanche of titles comes flooding out: 'Warrior, priest, apostle, doctor, martyr'.[34] She takes up each of these titles in detail, adding others, 'prophet' or 'missionary'. For this last title she says: 'I would like to be a missionary not just for a few years, but I would like to have been one from the creation of the world and to be one until the consummation of the ages.'[35] For the title martyr: 'I would not know how to restrict myself to desiring *one* form of martyrdom. To satisfy me, I would need them *all*.'[36]

She is well aware that her desires are truly infinite: 'Jesus, Jesus, if I wanted to write all my desires, I would have to borrow *your book of life*, in which are reported the actions of all the saints, and I would want to have accomplished them for you.'[37]

The one who spoke to Mother Anne of Jesus of her 'little actions' would like to have performed the greatest and would like to have performed them all! But Thérèse is well aware of the infinite disproportion between her littleness and such desires: 'O my Jesus! what is your answer to all my follies? Is there a soul more *little*, more powerless than mine?'[38]

Thérèse knows what reply she is going to give to Jesus.[39] Why did Jesus want to come to fulfil 'these *desires* that are *greater* than the universe'? 'Precisely because of my weakness,'[40] Thérèse proclaims.

All these desires which invade her heart and mind keep churning around in her, and this inevitably torments her: 'At meditation my desires caused me a veritable martyrdom.' So this person in love who no longer knows what to do with her foolish desires wants to prove her love to the one she loves and show it to him in every possible and imaginable way. But how?

'I have sought, I have found'

'I opened the Epistles of St Paul to find some answers. Chapters 12 and 13 of the First Epistle to the Corinthians fell before my eyes.' At first, however, she did not find reassurance there: 'I read there… that *all* cannot be apostles, prophets, doctors, etc.; that the Church is composed of different members, and the eye should not want *at the same time* to be the hand. The answer was clear, but it did not fulfil my desires and gave me no peace.'[41] It is necessary here to be extremely attentive to what Thérèse says and to grasp the extreme dialectic of her thought. The 'precisely because of my weakness' just before, a very Pauline expression, already points the way; the same paradox, 'weakness – great desires fulfilled', is to be expressed again, but in a much stronger way.

Thérèse begins by referring to Mary Magdalene, a lover in tears next to the tomb of the one she loves: 'Just as Mary Magdalene found what she was seeking by still stooping down and looking into the tomb, so I, abasing myself to the very depths of my nothingness, raised myself so high that I was able to attain my end.'[42] She wrote a few months later: 'It is said in the Gospel that Magdalene, still staying close to the tomb and stooping *several times* to look in, finally saw two angels.'[43]

Thérèse still has the four Gospels with her, and she does not stop reading and re-reading them at every moment. She scrutinizes them almost relentlessly: 'It is said in the Gospel,' she remarks on this passage about Magdalene. Precisely what does the text say? 'Now Mary stood weeping outside the tomb, and as she wept she stooped to look into the tomb; and she saw two angels in white, sitting where the body of Jesus had lain.'[44]

Thérèse has elaborated the text in a way which is very revealing: 'still staying close', 'stooping *several times*'. She thus shows precisely the state that she is in: she has a shy desire to look into the tomb, to repeat and repeat her question about the emptiness that she sees, stubbornly trying to find a way out. She knows that in the end Jesus will show himself, but she knows at the same time that Jesus will show himself only if one seeks him intensely oneself.

The term 'seek' recurs often in her writings. Shortly after the reference to Magdalene, there is a very important passage, which needs to be quoted in all its rhythm, in which we find 'stoop' again: 'Yes, for love to be fully satisfied it is necessary for it to stoop, for it to stoop to nothingness and transform this nothingness into *fire*. O Jesus, I know that love is repaid by love alone, and so I searched and found the way to solace my heart by giving you Love for Love.'[45]

Here is all Thérèse's typical dynamic: those vigorously contrasting verbs: 'I searched, I found'. At the heart of her night she does not cease to seek, resting in all confidence on the saying of Jesus: 'He teaches us that in order to open it is enough to knock and it will be opened, to seek in order to find.'[46] 'You know,' she says to Jesus, still in our text,[47] 'that I am seeking the truth.'

We can see that the emphasis is on incessant movement, on seeking the truth, the truth of the love which constantly hides itself. We are told that this phrase 'I seek the truth' has the sense of a kind of hardened demand for the truth, which must be accepted and followed intransigently: 'A characteristic of Thérèse is the "regular", the "rectilinear": "I never acted like Pilate who refused to hear the truth."'[48] This last phrase is put into the mouth of Thérèse by Mother Agnes on 21 July 1897. The adjectives 'rectilinear' or 'regular' which are attached to Thérèse here show that their author has some concern to correct the texts in the direction of rigidity; along the same line, Mother Agnes made Thérèse say the very day of her death, 'I always sought only the truth',[49] a way of 'internalizing' Thérèse's thought, of making it rough and brittle when it is supple and alive. Her quest comes from love and goes to love. When in her letter of 13 September, seeking to discover what thoughts have come out of the retreat, Sister Marie of the Sacred Heart asks Thérèse to pray that she, Marie, may no longer think of anything but practising the art of loving, Thérèse takes up the term and changes it: 'the science of love', she says, and elaborates: 'I desire only this science. Having given all my riches for it, I esteem it as having given nothing, as did the bride in the sacred Canticles.'[50] This quotation from the Song of Songs[51] recalls another verse of the same text which indicates the whole quest of love: 'I sought the one whom my soul loves. I sought him and did not find him.'[52] In Thérèse there is a passion for seeking and an active way of discovering the truth, a way of being constantly on the look-out, a lively and humble side which is her own and which makes her at the same time both engaging and disturbing – Marie of the Sacred Heart would know something of this while reading what Thérèse had written. This passion and this vivacity are particularly expressed in Manuscript B.

Like Magdalene, who 'finally finds what she sought', Thérèse finds: it is because she is constantly stooping towards the empty tomb, i.e. towards her nothingness, because she is not afraid to stoop over the depth of 'her' nothingness, that Jesus has shown himself.

In the *Story of a Soul*, Mother Agnes puts the second part of this text 'stooping... my goal' between quotation marks and indicates that it is a quotation from John of the Cross. Thérèse does nothing of the sort, so much does she make it her own: she wants to pursue her antithesis to the end. It is right at the end of this part, which, as we shall see, is a hymn to love, that she brings to a strong conclusion the text which has already been quoted and to which we must return: 'Completely satisfied, it must stoop, stoop to the nothingness and transform this nothingness into fire.'[53]

Mother Agnes suppresses the initial capital of Love and only keeps one 'stoop', whereas Thérèse wants to show by the duplication the dynamic of Love which stoops to the very depths of the nothingness.

Love to the nothingness

Let us return to Thérèse's text.

The content of the initial phrase has been completely transformed: it is no longer Mary Magdalene who stoops over the
empty tomb or Thérèse over the depths of her nothingness, but
God himself, 'Love', who 'stoops over the nothingness'. It is God
who acts, who takes the step. The commentator of the *Manuscrits autobiographiques* changes the meaning tremendously here;
keeping only 'I will raise myself so high', and giving her a kind of
superiority, he writes: 'She makes a real leap into God to deny the
nothingness which makes its mark on her.'[54] For Thérèse,
though, it is God who comes to this nothingness where she is, that
she is, and transforms it into fire, i.e. into love. It is as if for the
commentator the essential thing was for Thérèse to appear
victorious over the darkness which 'speaks to her of her
nothingness'.[55] He writes: 'Thérèse triumphs over the trial of
faith (and hope) solely through the love of Jesus.'[56] Now this is
not the 'triumph' of Thérèse; she will continue in the trial to the
end. It is the 'triumph' of Love, which, stooping 'over the
nothingness', transforms it into love.

The answer which Thérèse sought is there: in Love and Love
alone, Love which, out of love, goes 'to the nothingness'. Why
does Thérèse have desires on her which touch on the infinite?
Because Love has set her on fire. And why her? Because she is
'little'. Love has chosen her 'as a holocaust, me a weak and
imperfect creature'.[57] In the spirituality which she does not want,
only the strong were recognized and chosen by God and his
Justice: 'In times past only pure and spotless victims were
accepted by the Strong and Powerful God. To satisfy divine
Justice, perfect victims were necessary.'[58]

At this moment in September 1896, Thérèse sees herself as
'weak', 'imperfect', 'nothing', in the most total darkness. To
recognize this nothing is the act, the only important act: Love, to
fulfil itself, goes 'to the nothingness',[59] and it is because Love is
such that she can make use even of her weakness and give herself,
give this nothingness, to Love: 'I am only a child, powerless and
weak, and yet it is my weakness that gives me the boldness to offer
myself as a victim to your love, O Jesus.'[60]

'It transforms this nothingness into *fire*': Thérèse underlines the fire – a feature which Mother Agnes suppressed; we shall see how much this word, its derivatives like 'hearth' and its synonyms like 'furnace', refers primarily to the last verses of the Song of Songs,[61] in which God is presented as love burning like a furnace.

So the essential thing is this action which Love brings about, which transforms into fire, into love, first of all that which is most alien to it, that which is the greatest nothingness, that which resists it the most. The mystics had often previously used the metaphor of the burning bush. The human being is caught by Love like a piece of wood being caught by the fire. Thérèse herself will speak of a piece of iron consumed by the fire.

We should not forget that Thérèse is writing these lines while remaining plunged into the night, into the void. But she does not allow herself to be overwhelmed by this situation: she looks closely into the void, as Mary Magdalene looked closely into the tomb, to find light and meaning in it. It is at the heart of this night, or rather at the very heart of this night, that she discovers that Love 'stoops to the nothingness' and that it 'transforms this nothingness into *fire*'.

She had ended the last lines of manuscript A, at the end of 1895, with twenty lines on 'the way of Love'[62] and added in an appendix an 'explanation' of her 'armouries' where the 'flaming dart of Love'[63] was. Thérèse says there that she wants 'to give her blood for the One who loves her'. To respond to all the love of Jesus she wants 'to do for him what he has done for her'.

The emphasis in 1895 is on the response that Thérèse wants to make to Jesus: love for love. In September 1896 it is a matter of finding the secret of loving as he loves. And she finds it: 'I have found the secret of possessing your flame', she tells Jesus, whom she calls, in her night 'O luminous Beacon of love'.[64]

There is only one way to possess this fire of the divine Love: to acquiesce in what one is, in one's poor status before God, to accept being set on fire by Love itself instead of wanting to raise oneself up, to allow oneself to be grasped by the very movement of the Love which comes to us, which descends like an eagle. Thérèse has a splendid description of the Incarnation: 'O Divine Word, launching yourself towards the land of exile, you willed to suffer and die in order to *draw* souls to the bosom of the Eternal Hearth of the Blessed Trinity.'[65] Hearth means Fire.

It is Love which does the work: 'Eternal eagle, you desire to nourish me with your Divine substance and yet I am but a poor little thing who would return to nothingness if your divine glance did not give me life from one moment to the next.'[66]

If she does not see Him, she knows in her night that he is looking at her and making her exist. The essential grace, fifteen months earlier, 'on 9 June, the feast of the Holy Trinity', had been to 'understand more than ever how much Jesus desires to be loved',[67] and to offer herself to merciful Love. Today Thérèse, even when she is in the night, no longer thinks of it and simply contemplates Love: 'O Jesus, allow me in the excess of my knowledge, allow me to say to you that your love verges on folly.' Her exuberance here made her first offer herself as victim. Today she hopes that he will take her: '*My folly* is to hope that your Love will accept me as a victim.' The only way in this night is 'trust', 'limitless' trust, abandonment 'with total trust to the infinite mercy'.[68] And the ultimate hope: 'One day, I hope that you, adored Eagle, that you will come to look for your little bird and, rising with it to the Hearth of Love, will plunge it for ever in the burning abyss of this Love.'[69] The abyss of love corresponds to the vertiginous abyss of nothingness. The one calls to the other. Waiting for this moment, Thérèse is ready to remain in the night: 'As long as you desire it, O my Beloved, your little bird will remain without strength and without wings.'[70]

'I shall be Love'

Having got to the end of this text (B, 2–5), let us return to a paragraph which is often quoted but without the overall context which sheds light on everything.

We may remember that to begin with Thérèse wanted to love Jesus with all the love with which all the saints had loved, that she wanted to live out all the vocations and thus satisfy her desire for love which verged on the infinite. Reading the Epistle to the Corinthians helped her to grasp that 'all the most *perfect gifts* are nothing without love'; 'I understood that *Love* comprises all vocations, that Love was everything, that it embraced all times

87

and all places.' Following St Paul and the idea of the church as 'mystical body', she gets to the essence of this 'body', the heart: 'I understood that the Church had a Heart, and that this Heart was burning with love. I understood it was Love alone that made the Church's members act, that if Love were ever quenched, Apostles would no longer preach the Gospel, martyrs would refuse to shed their blood.'[71]

This Heart of the Church, this Love which is everything, is certainly Jesus. The only way of living out all the vocations is to put oneself at the heart, is to love as Jesus loves, with Him. All the rest of the text consists in showing how to appropriate this flame of Love, to be at the centre with Jesus: 'In the excess of my delirious joy, I cried out, "O Jesus, my Love... I have found my vocation at last; it is Love! Yes, I have found my place in the Church, and it is you, O my God, who have given it to me...; in the heart of the Church, my Mother, I shall be Love."'[72]

It is through Jesus that she has been given this 'place'; it is he who has burned her with his flame, as she will say soon afterwards.

After this text of 8 September 1896 with its extraordinary air of folly – she uses the word 'folly' ten times in the short manuscript B, 3–5[73] – which shows the extreme ardour of her quest, there is the letter of 13 September 1896 to Sister Marie of the Sacred Heart, who wants to know 'the secrets from Jesus to Thérèse' and her sister's 'little doctrine'. Thérèse thus addresses her directly. Marie thinks that Thérèse is floating in the highest feelings of spiritual love: 'Do not believe I am swimming in consolations,' Thérèse first replies. 'No, my consolation is to have none on earth.'[74] She recognizes that she has received graces, yes: 'Jesus teaches me in secret', but it is from the night, John of the Cross would say, it is 'without showing himself, without making his voice heard'.[75] She wants only one thing: 'The science of Love.' 'This love is the only good that I aim at.'[76] Then, summing up the essentials of her text of 8 September, what she has arrived at, she tells her sister: 'Jesus is pleased to show me the one way which leads to this divine furnace;[77] this way is the *abandonment* of the little child who goes to sleep in its Father's arms without fear.'[78] 'Jesus does not ask for great deeds,' she says a little further on, 'but only for abandonment and recognition... That is all that Jesus requires of us; there is no need for our works, but only for our love.'[79] Jesus has 'need': 'Jesus did not fear to *beg* a little water from the Samaritan woman. He was thirsty, but when he said, "Give me to drink", it was the love of his young creature that the Creator of the Universe was seeking. He was thirsty for love.' In his Spiritual Canticle, John of the Cross explains in strophe XI that it is the soul which thirsts for the beloved object; here it is Jesus who is thirsty.

Thérèse tells Marie that she is giving her the pages written on 8 September. She points out that 'in writing, it is to Jesus that I am speaking'.[80] She warns her: 'Perhaps you will find my expressions exaggerated. Forgive me, this will have to be put down to my poor style, for I assure you that there is no exaggeration in my *little soul*. Within it all is calm and at rest.'[81] In fact we have seen that in her 'foolish' text of 8 September Thérèse has remained completely mistress of her exuberance, that she has not allowed herself to be carried away by 'a delirious joy' but rather has 'a calm and serene peace'.[82]

Will Sister Marie of the Sacred Heart understand? She begins her letter to Thérèse: 'I have read your pages burning with love for Jesus.' She thanks her for having 'unveiled the secrets of her soul'. But throughout the rest of her letter Sister Marie is turned in on herself; she compares herself with Thérèse and is desolate: 'A certain feeling of sadness came over me in view of your extraordinary desires for martyrdom. That is the proof of your love; yes, you possess love, but I myself! no.'

Manifestly, Sister Marie of the Sacred Heart does not grasp much from the pages which Thérèse has sent her; she has grasped only the vocation of martyrdom desired by Thérèse: 'I dread all that you love', she says on this subject.

Thérèse takes up her pen again on 17 September: she sees clearly that her sister has not understood, and tries to explain again. She immediately gets to the question of martyrdom. 'My desires for martyrdom *are nothing*; they are not what give me the unlimited confidence that I feel in my heart.' And she repeats her thought: 'Understand that to love Jesus, to be his *victim of love*, the weaker one is, without desires or virtues, the more suited one is for the workings of this consuming and transforming Love...

The *desire* to be a victim alone suffices, but we must consent to remain always poor and without strength, and this is the difficulty.' The truly poor must not be sought 'among great souls', but 'in lowliness, in nothingness'. What pleases Jesus is not the desire for martyrdom but *'to see me loving my littleness and my poverty, the blind hope that I have in his mercy'*. Thérèse beseeches her sister: 'Let us love our littleness, let us love to feel nothing, then we shall be poor in spirit, and Jesus will come to look for us, and however *far* we may be, he will transform us into flames of love.'

Thérèse is well aware that all this is difficult for her sister to understand: 'Oh how I would like to be able to make you understand what I feel. It is trust and nothing but trust that must lead us to Love.' The letter ends on a kind or irony which has a great truth, in keeping with all that Thérèse has just written on her retreat, an irony or at least a terrible remark: 'If you do not understand me, it is because you are too great a soul.'

But it seems that Sister Marie of the Sacred Heart did not even grasp this.

The Creed

Fr Godefroid Madelaine[83] preached the community retreat which took place between 8 and 15 October. A Premonstratensian, since 1894 he had been able to regroup the community of which he was prior at Mondaye. He was a friend of Canon Delatroëtte, Curé of Saint-Jacques de Lisieux from 1867 and Superior General of the Carmel from 1870 until his death on 8 October 1895, who had been very vigorously opposed to Thérèse's entering the Carmel because of her youth. Fr Madelaine knew both the Martin and Guérin families; he had been present at the vestings of Marie and Thérèse Martin.

Thérèse was to see him during her retreat and confide in him the trial of her faith. Fr Madelaine counselled her permanently to carry the Creed with her. Thérèse, who constantly had a copy of the four Gospels on her, then wrote the Creed – in her blood – in French on the last page of this volume.

A word needs to be said here about the almoner of the Carmel, Abbé Louis-Auguste Youf. Ordained priest in 1869, he had been appointed assistant priest in the parish of Saint-Jacques de Lisieux and was almoner of the Carmel from July 1873 to his death, which took place eight hours after that of Thérèse. Abbé Youf had wanted the entry of the young Thérèse into the Carmel just as much as Canon Delatroëtte, Curé of Saint-Jacques and superior of the Carmel, had categorically rejected it: 'She is such a charming child,' he said. At that time Abbé Youf allowed the Martin family to by-pass the views of Canon Delatroëtte and go direct to the Bishop of Bayeux. Abbé Youf was the ordinary confessor of the community; a man of austere spirituality; he was a conscientious, meticulous priest, very economical with his time; he steeped himself assiduously in works of piety in order to perform his mission well, and meticulously prepared each of his sermons.

He was not Thérèse's director. She had much affection for him and recognized the part that he had played in her entry to the Carmel. He had a high opinion of her, but this did not prevent him from remonstrating with her over the least peccadillo.[84] Readily promising his penitents hell, this priest was hardly in a position to understand Thérèse when after Easter 1896 she came to confide in him about the darkness in which she found herself and the thoughts which assailed her. Abbé Youf could only tell her: 'Don't dwell on these thoughts! It is very dangerous.' This does not seem to have made much impression on Thérèse; it has to be said that Mother Marie de Gonzague, with her robust good sense, put the almoner in his place and did not take too much notice of some of his suggestions; this must have reassured Thérèse, even if it did not enlighten her.

It will be remembered that a seminarian of the Foreign Missions of Paris, Fr Roulland, had asked Mother Marie de Gonzague on 30 May 1896 for one of her Carmelites to be associated with his missionary apostolate. After she had been designated, Thérèse had written him a first letter on 23 June, some days before his ordination to the priesthood. The missionary had set out for China on 2 August. Fr Roulland wrote a long letter to her from Su-Tchuen in which he described the region of the place where he was, the life and customs of Chinese society, and apostolic work. He quotes 'the expression of a holy missionary' according to whom the missionaries 'splash around in pagan filth'. He relates that he has put on Chinese dress. He also confides in her that his vocation was saved on 8 September 1890.

Thérèse, who replied to him on All Saint's Day, could not fail to note the coincidence of the date: that same day she made her religious profession and 'her sole aim was to save souls, above all the souls of apostles...' This was a sign, given by Jesus, of their brotherhood. 'As I think of you putting on Chinese dress,' she tells him, 'of course I think of the Saviour clothing himself in our poor humanity.' She also thinks that one day he will be a martyr, and she envies him. She asks him for a lock of hair: if he is a martyr, it will be a relic.

A young priest, Théophane Vénard, also from the Foreign Missions of Paris, had been beheaded in Hanoi at the age of thirty-two in 1861, precisely where the Saigon Carmel was to found another Carmel, for which religious were required. In November 1896, Thérèse read a biography of the young martyr. On 2 February 1897, the anniversary of his death, she composed a poem in his honour which she sent to Fr Roulland. She evokes Tonking, 'this infidel plague':

> With happiness I would fly to her
> If God called me one day.

In the month of November 1896, during which she wrote to Fr Roulland, Thérèse knew that her departure for the Hanoi Carmel had been mooted; a novena was held that same month to Théophane Vénard for her complete cure, which would be the sign that she could go there. But actually during the novena she started to cough again.

In February 1897 Thérèse still continued to cherish the dream of joining the Hanoi Carmel, despite this setback in health which happened in December 1896 with the first cold spell. On 19 March 1897, she writes, again to Fr Roulland, that she is still hoping: 'If Jesus doesn't soon come looking for me for the Carmel of heaven, I shall one day leave for that of Hanoi, for now there is a Carmel in that city, the Saigon Carmel recently founded it.'

As a postscript to her letter of 1 November to Fr Roulland she had written: 'I commend to your prayers a young seminarian who would like to be a *missionary*; his vocation has just been shaken by his year of military service.'

We in fact know that she had another missionary 'brother', a young seminarian, also from Calvados, Abbé Bellière. He had left the diocesan seminary, but he wrote to Thérèse on 28 November that without doubt he would soon enter a missionary seminary. For the moment he was waiting among his family, not very far from Lisieux; he needed Thérèse's prayers: 'I have to break myself away from dear and great affections, from sweet and cherished habits of easy living, from a happy and blessed past that still attracts me strongly.'

The chimeras of the night

What about Mother Agnes at the end of this year 1896? She did not know the precise state of Thérèse's health or take account of its gravity. Since the priorate of Mother Marie de Gonzague she had been in charge of the economy of the house, which caused her numerous distractions, and doubtless she sometimes complained about having to carry on 'the little business of the shop', as Thérèse wrote to her on 18 December, adding: 'The Blessed Virgin is so content to have a little donkey and a little servant that she makes them run to the right and the left *for her pleasure*.' On 4 December, Sister Marie of the Eucharist – Marie Guérin – had written to Mother Agnes, her cousin: 'What lessons you are giving now in your little hidden life!' That was without doubt to console her for having been reduced to this subordinate and somewhat ignoble charge.[85] Thérèse also seems to have to console Mother Agnes, writing to her the same day that she 'admires the *humility* of her *Mother*'.

The edition of the General Correspondence[86] gives us a letter from Mother Agnes to her uncle and aunt, M. and Mme Guérin,[87] dated 6 December. It begins like this: 'My dear relatives, Our Mother is allowing me to write to you without my showing her the letter.' Mother Agnes had asked for this permission because she wanted to 'confide a little secret' to the Guérins. This related to a sister, Sister Marie-Madeleine of the Holy Sacrament, who had entered the Carmel as a lay sister in September 1893; Sister Marie-Madeleine had M.Guérin as her godfather and Mother Marie de Gonzague's sister-in-law, Mme de Virville, as her godmother when she took the habit. On this occasion Mme de Virville was received with her daughters by the Guérins, so the latter knew Sister Marie-Madeleine well.

Mother Agnes continued to occupy herself with the direction of the lay sister after the end of her priorate: 'It seemed to me, for several really weighty reasons that she was in need of this.' 'However,' writes Mother Agnes, 'having become aware that she was not profiting enough from this for me to expose me to such great perils, I recently gave it up.' The lay sister then agreed, on the advice of Sister Marie of the Eucharist – Marie Guérin – to see the person who was quasi-novice mistress, Thérèse. Now Mother Agnes recalls that when she was prioress she had compelled the lay sister to meet Thérèse for half an hour each Sunday, an order which was not taken very well: the sister went to hide instead of going to the meeting. Would she accept this time? For Mother Agnes, 'Grappin' – the devil – is at work: 'Night brings on dark counsels and the following morning, alas! the resolution was taken, *unshakeably*, not to go seeking Sister Thérèse of the Child Jesus.' The sister's argument was: 'When our Mother gives her to us openly as mistress, then I will go, but not before.'

This letter from Mother Agnes thus shows both that Thérèse's position – of novice mistress without actually being so – was quite uncomfortable, and that on the other hand she was not accepted so easily – Mother Agnes gives this as a reason for Sister Marie-Madeleine: she felt 'read to the very depths of her soul and, consequently, obliged to wage a real war against her nature'. With the novice Thérèse always continued to maintain a balance, smiling but not very accommodating.[88]

Thérèse sent a lively letter to her aunt, Mme Guérin, on 16 November. She asks her to pray that she may 'grow in wisdom'. 'I am not doing this, I assure you... From day to day I am becoming more wicked, yet it will soon be *nine years* that I have been in the Lord's house. I should, then, be already advanced in the ways of perfection, but I am still at the bottom of the ladder. This does not discourage me, and I am as happy as a cricket.' For her birthday she sent her a poem which she had composed on the sacristans of the Carmel. In fact the poem, dedicated to the sister who made the hosts, is just as much addressed to Mme Guérin who, after the death of her sister-in-law, became a mother to the Martin girls; the little Martin sisters and Marie Guérin form five living 'hosts' which Mme Guérin has offered to the Carmel:

> We are also hosts
> which Jesus wants to change into Him.

In December, Thérèse composed a poem for Sister Marie-Joseph. Sister Marie-Joseph was neurasthenic, with a pronounced cyclical temperament, ups and downs, unpredictable anger and marked changes. The community ostracized her: no one wanted to work with her. Now in March 1896 Thérèse suggested helping her in the linen room. From then on she bore with the changing humour of the sister; the days of ironing were particularly trying. If Sister Marie-Joseph lacked finesse, she was superior to Thérèse at least in having been given a very beautiful voice. Was this deliberate humour? For this sister who saw everything in black, Thérèse composed a poem to the tune of a song 'Where do you go when all is black?' Did this song evoke for Thérèse the night in which she found herself?

In this poem, without a title, but which the sister copied out, giving it the title 'Abandonment', abandonment is indeed the essential point. Jesus – and Thérèse – address the sister as a child:

> Child, you know my name
> and your sweet look calls me.
> It tells me: simple abandonment
> I want to guide your craft.

In a note of December 1896, Thérèse called on her to be 'peaceful', 'not to struggle against the chimeras of the night', 'to abandon herself' and 'to leave far behind the sterile fear of being unfaithful'. Thérèse knows how to understand and guide. She can say, as she wrote to Sister Geneviève on 24 December: 'I know the price of suffering and anguish of heart.'

In January 1897, she wrote to sister Marie-Joseph to thank her for a poem which the sister had composed in her turn. Thérèse confided in her that she was groaning in her corner like 'a poor little sparrow', 'in these days which Jesus is keeping to try our souls'.

Mother Marie de Gonzague made Thérèse have a footwarmer during the winter, which was very rigorous. Sister Genevieve was in charge of looking after it; she also came to rub her, to 'trounce' her as Thérèse puts it, with a horsehair belt, a painful treatment for a skin made sensitive by vesicatories, hot plasters which raised blisters.[89] She needed sleep more than ever, had a bad time waking up, and begged Sister Geneviève to 'drag her gently from her dreams' for the office of the small hours, recited at 7 a.m. in the winter.

Christmas

Christmas 1896. Ten years earlier, Christmas 1886, had been the first great spiritual event in Thérèse's life, what in 1895 she called her *'night* of *light'*.[90] But in her letter of 1 November 1896 to Fr Roulland she said: 'The *night* of Christmas 1886 was, it is true, decisive for my vocation, but to name it more clearly I must call it the night of my conversion. On that blessed night... Jesus... deigned to bring me out of the language and imperfections of childhood. He so transformed me that I no longer recognized myself.' So what did Jesus bring about that Christmas 1886? He 'clothed her with his divine power', he 'armed her for war',[91] she confides to Fr Roulland. The spoilt, egocentric child all at once became humanly and spiritually adult. Ten years later, this Christmas 1896, she was fighting 'arms in hand',[92] face to face with the night.

On the night of Christmas 1896, she wrote to Sister Marie of the Trinity to tell her that Jesus was content with her, signing the letter 'Your little Brother Jesus'. To make herself understood she referred to a trivial little event: the discovery by the novices of a top among the objects received at the Carmel to be sent to mission countries. The sisters did not know this toy, and Sister Marie demonstrated it to them. To make it go, a top needs constantly to be restarted: 'Let your sisters do you this service and recognize that they will be most assiduous in not letting you slow down,' says Thérèse to Sister Marie, putting these words on the lips of Jesus.

The day after Christmas she wrote to Abbé Bellière. He had written to her directly for the first time on 28 November; as we have seen, although it was Advent, Mother Marie de Gonzague allowed Thérèse to know about this letter so that she could pray for the Abbé. Thérèse's reply aims wholly at reassuring her young brother. 'Our Lord never requires of us sacrifice beyond our strength.' She adds – and this applies to herself in the spiritual agony which she is experiencing at this moment: 'Sometimes, it is true, this divine Saviour makes us feel all the bitterness of the chalice that he presents to our soul.' 'But,' she says, 'it is consoling to think that Jesus, the Strong God, has known our weaknesses, that he trembled at the sight of the bitter chalice, this chalice which at another time he had so ardently desired to drink.'

The Abbé had confided to her that he aspired to the happiness of sacrificing his life by martyrdom. 'Martyrdom of the heart is no less fertile than the shedding of blood.' She adds this confidence: 'Our Mother is still suffering.' This bad health is perhaps a mitigating circumstance in excusing the anger of the prioress, an anger which would explode on the evening of 28 December.

Thérèse composed a 'recreation' for the community entitled 'The Aviary of the Child Jesus', to be performed on the evening of this Christmas 1896. At the heart of these fifteen octosyllabic verses, to be sung to a melody by Gounod composed for Lamartine's poem 'To the Nightingale', there is the incarnation: Christmas is the moment when the Son of God becomes man. Thérèse says this in verse:

For us you leave the beautiful Heaven.[93]

So the Son of God is an exile and human beings are 'exiles on earth'; they are like birds in an 'aviary', in a 'cage':

One day, far from the sad earth
when they hear your call,
all the birds of your aviary
will take flight for heaven.

There are many resonances behind this apparently puerile poem: there is the bird to whom God gives sufficient food each day, and whose sole concern is thus to abandon itself to God. There is another evocation, that of the 'weak little bird' to which she compared herself in her text of 8 September: 'The little bird would like *to fly* towards this brilliant sun which charms its eyes;

97

it would like to imitate the eagles, its brothers, which one sees rising to the divine hearth of the Holy Trinity. Alas, all that it can do is to *raise its little wings*; to fly is not within its *little* power.'[94]

The text goes on: 'What will happen to it? Will it die of chagrin seeing itself so impotent? Oh no! The little bird will not even hurt itself. With bold abandonment, it wants to remain fixed to its Divine Sun; nothing can frighten it, neither the wind nor the rain, and if dark clouds come to hide the Star of Love, this little bird will not change its place; it knows that beyond the clouds its Sun is always shining.'[95] The little bird – 'It never sows here below' – has received and will receive what it needs to live; it will abandon itself to Love, which is its sole task.

On 28 December, the Feast of the Holy Innocents, she composed for herself a poem in honour of these children who did nothing in terms of merit and who received 'freely' the immense riches of Paradise. During her retreat in September she had painted a souvenir picture of her four little brothers and sisters who died very young and wrote on the verso, among other things, a passage from Paul (Rom.3.24): 'They are justified by his grace as a gift.' She tells herself that she too has done nothing, or almost nothing, in her short life; but they did not even have to fight.

Without combats you achieved the glory of conquerors;
the Saviour has won the victory for you, charming Conquerors.

The Holy Innocents 'dare to caress his Adorable Face', she says, and again she ends with the Face of Jesus, which the Holy Innocents kiss in Heaven:

Like them, in Heaven I want to kiss your Sweet Face, O my Jesus.

The sisters wanted this new poem to be sung to the community for this 28 December, a festive day at the Carmel. Mother Marie de Gonzague allowed it; but while the sisters were 'under its charm' she broke this charm and stopped the song in a very bad mood. Mother Agnes related the incident in her own way: 'On the evening of 28 December, at recreation, the sisters expressed the desire to hear her beautiful song "To my little brothers of heaven" sung. After giving permission, while the whole community was under its charm, Mother Marie de Gonzague became furiously jealous and said to me going out of recreation, loud enough for Sister Thérèse to hear, "that she was very discontented that people had started singing her poems in community; that could only serve to maintain her pride", and so on. I left very sad at compline, but even more edified than sad, seeing a heavenly expression of peace on the face of the Servant of God. She was too strengthened in humility, and the hour of her death was too near, for her to let herself be troubled by anything.'

This passage from the article 'Humility' in *the Notes for the preparation for the apostolic process* is one of the texts aimed at Mother Marie de Gonzague. The anger – one of the fits of anger on the part of the prioress, who was quick-tempered – was real. How did Thérèse react? She knew the prioress too well and had too much humour to take offence or to be troubled by this outburst, which was not very serious. But perhaps Mother Marie de Gonzague had been annoyed – she well could have been – by the very mawkish tone of this poem, in which the Holy Innocents are 'charming little imps'. As for Mother Agnes, she seems to have forgotten that she herself had similarly interrupted the recreation on 'The Divine Little Christmas Beggar' the previous year, 25 December 1895, when she was prioress.[96]

Certainly, for Thérèse, Christmas did not go smoothly!

'To work in paradise'

2 January 1897 was Thérèse's birthday; she was twenty-four. On 10 January 1897 Sister Genevieve wrote to the venerable Brother Simeon – now eighty-three – with whom the Martin family[97] had remained in touch since their journey to Rome in 1887. She sent him her best wishes for the year, asked him to obtain an apostolic benediction for the fifty years that Sister Saint-Stanislas had been in the religious life, and gave news of everyone. Of Thérèse, a poem of whose entitled 'Live Love' she sent to the brother, she wrote: 'Love consumes her life and her delicate chest gives us serious cause for disquiet.'

On 25 January Brother Simeon replied, sending the apostolic benediction, which he asked not only for Sister Saint-Stanislas but also for Mother Marie de Gonzague, for all the Carmelites, and the 'persons who will be present at the festival'.

Sister Geneviève thanked brother Simeon by a letter dated 17 January. Thérèse adds a word; she tells him in veiled terms that she is quite ill: 'I think that my course here below will not be a long one. When I appear before my Beloved Spouse, I will have only my desires to present to him... The only thing that I beg you to ask for my soul is the grace to *love* Jesus and to *make* him *love* as much as is possible for me.'

The 'festival for the golden wedding' of sister Saint-Stanislas took place on 8 February. Mother Marie de Gonzague asked Thérèse to write a recreation[98] for her: Sister Saint-Stanislas was also doyenne of the community – she was sixty-three. After a few words from Canon Maupas, superior of the Carmel,[99] on the eve of 8 February the novices therefore performed an episode from the life of Saint Stanislas which Thérèse had composed for her. We do not know whether Sister Stanislas heard it properly: she was deaf, but doubtless Thérèse gave her the text. It is the last recreation that she composed before her death. She staged the entry of the young Pole Stanislas Kostka into the noviciate of the Society of Jesus in 1567.[100]

Thérèse used a biography of the saint published in 1845.[101] The life of Stanislas Kostka spoke to her: he was a joyful youth, he entered the noviciate at the age of seventeen and died young, without having done anything – 'with empty hands' as Thérèse wrote to Brother Simeon about herself. Why did Stanislas want to enter the noviciate? 'It is because I want to become a saint,' he says in the playlet. Thérèse takes up precisely what she has already said: 'Tell me,' exclaims Stanislas in a prayer to Marie, 'tell me that the blessed can still work for the salvation of souls. If I cannot work in paradise for the glory of Jesus, I prefer to remain in exile and still fight for him.' To end the piece she makes Stanislas say, in a prayer to Mary, 'Sweet Queen of Heaven, I pray you, when I am near you in the Homeland, allow me to return to earth, in order to protect the holy souls, the souls whose long career here below will complete mine; thus through her, I shall be able to present to the Lord an abundant harvest of merits.'

In reply, the last four verses put on the lips of Mary say:

Dear child, you will protect
souls struggling in this world,
then their harvest will be rich,
and you will shine the more in heaven.

Mother Agnes inverted the last two verses, at the same time inverting the meaning and radically transforming Thérèse's thought on the respective roles of the apostle on earth and the saint in heaven. For Mother Agnes, the more Thérèse shines in Heaven – the more importance is attached to Thérèse's sainthood – the more fertile the work of the apostles on earth will be. Now Thérèse, who knows that she is going to die, and who feels how 'empty' her hands are, does not want to come from on high to supervise the work of the apostles and make them fruitful – Jesus does this; he alone is master of the harvest – but to flow in these apostolic works which will bring as it were a complement to everything that has been lacking in her poor life. She applies the communion of saints and substitution here, but in the precise sense that she counts on the merits of others. Mother Agnes expresses the opposite meaning: Thérèse's merits will help the apostles in their missionary works.

What is Thérèse's dilemma at this moment when she has only a few months to live? She is deeply in love with Jesus; and by the same token with all her strength she wants to make him love: now, while the strength of her heart increases more and more, her physical strength is diminishing. Soon, leaving this earth, she will no longer be able to offer God the outbursts of her heart for those who do not love him. Then she finds two solutions: as we have seen, the first consists in remaining near, after death, to those who are doing concrete work on earth to make Jesus known and loved, to follow from on high 'these holy souls struggling in the world'; then she, Thérèse, in heaven, will be all the more seized by the light of Jesus, the more these 'holy souls' are fruitful and succeed in making Jesus loved. It is this that she wants to obtain from now on as a grace: to be able to continue, in Heaven, making Jesus loved; it is in this sense that between 4 and 12 March she makes a novena to Saint Francis Xavier, the great missionary. The second solution, which follows the same line, is to ensure that those who are going to continue to work after her death will intercede for her constantly. This is an extraordinary reversal; customarily the saints in heaven are seen as interceding for those who toil on earth. Here Thérèse does the opposite: she has made Abbé Bellière promise that he will continue to pray for her after she is dead. She reminds him of this promise on 24 February 1897: 'You have promised to pray for me all your life... you are not allowed to forget your promise. If the Lord soon takes me with Him, I ask you to continue the same little prayer every day, since in Heaven I shall desire the same thing as on earth: to love Jesus and make him loved.'

It is in the same sense that she writes an admirable letter to Fr Roulland on 19 March 1897. However, this important letter needs to be explained. She tells him first that, if Mother Marie de Gonzague has confirmed her in a vocation to leave for Tonking, she does not believe 'my vocation may ever be realized. For this it would be necessary that the sheath be as solid as the sword, and perhaps (our Mother believes) the sheath would have to be cast into the sea before reaching Tonking.' In other words, Thérèse is now so ill that she would not arrive there even if she left.

She is hardly preoccupied with this: 'I am not at all worried about the future; I am sure that God will do his will, it is the only grace I desire. One must not be more kingly than the king.' She would be 'happy to work and to suffer a long time for Him', but her heart experiences deep tranquillity and equanimity of soul; the future is of little importance to her; let it be loving and suffering or 'going to enjoy Him in Heaven'.

It is at this point that she makes a specific request of Fr Roulland, her 'brother' who is a missionary there in China: 'I do not want you to ask God to deliver me from the flames of purgatory; St Teresa said to her daughters when they wanted to pray for her: "What does it matter to me to remain in purgatory until the end of the world if through my prayers I can save a single soul!"[102] These words find an echo in my heart; I would like to save souls and forget myself for them; I would like to save them even after my death. So I would be happy if you were to say then: "My God, allow my sister to make you still loved."'

Thus Thérèse has such a desire to make Jesus loved that she does not want her death to interrupt this possibility; she wants then, in heaven, to continue to make him loved, particularly by his brothers who are most in mission, those who are among the people who do not know or reject Jesus, the people whom Charles de Foucauld called 'those furthest from God'. And without hesitation she makes them promise to continue to pray this intention every day after her death. Through these two brothers whom she has received from God she is asking all 'missionaries' to pray to God that the saints of Heaven continue to make Jesus loved on earth!

Doing good on earth?

Now we have to analyse a famous remark which Thérèse is said to have made, because it originates in this context: 'I want to spend my Heaven doing good on earth.' The witness to this saying is the oldest of the Martin sisters, Marie, Sister Marie of the Sacred Heart. On 10 July 1934, thirty-seven years after the fact, Sister Marie of the Sacred Heart told her infirmarian – Sister Thérèse of the Incarnation – what had happened on 19 March 1897, the day on which Thérèse wrote to Fr Roulland the lines which we have just read. Sister Marie of the Sacred Heart says: 'I also remember that on the day of the festival of St Joseph, I was at his Hermitage, she [Thérèse] had come there, and was very ill. I told her that she would have done better to go straight to her cell than to make this detour. She told me: "I have come to ask St Joseph to obtain for me from God the grace to spend my heaven doing good on earth."'

In the Yellow Notebook, in 1922–1923, Mother Agnes recopied the notes which she had taken on loose leaves by Thérèse's bed from 6 April to her death. This notebook was to be published in 1927, thirty years after Thérèse's death, under the title *Novissima Verba* or *Last Conversations of St Thérèse of the Child Jesus*. The book proved an immense success. Only one of the loose leaves used day by day has ever been found; did Mother Agnes deliberately lose them? In this Yellow Notebook we find the same phrase dated 17 July: 'I feel that I am going to enter into rest... but I feel above all that my mission is going to begin, my mission to make people love God as I love him, to give my little way to souls. If God hears my desire, my Heaven will be spent on earth to the end of the world. Yes, I want to spend my Heaven doing good on earth.'[103]

On 9 March 1910, Mother Agnes had written to Mgr de Teil, vice-postulator of the cause of beatification: 'The saying "I want to spend my Heaven doing good on earth" was said literally to Sister Marie of the Trinity, who bears witness to it on oath.' Abbé Descouvemont states without batting an eyelid that it was 'at two o'clock in the morning'[104] that Thérèse expressed 'her most profound desire': 'I want to spend my heaven doing good on earth.' Others have attested the same saying: thus in 1929 Fr Pichon, who affirms that Thérèse said it to him 'word for word' on several occasions. The commentator of the *Last Conversations* is obliged to admit 'the great improbability of the matter'.[105]

In short, many people claim to have heard the famous saying of Thérèse, one of the most famous, perhaps, the one that was most remembered. Is it authentic? We may doubt it.

What we might suppose, in fact, is this: someone – was it Sister Marie of the Trinity? – had heard Thérèse saying that on 19 March she had expressed her desire to make Love 'still love' after her death. This was translated as 'doing good'! It was recalled that it was said of Fr Prou, who had come to preach a retreat at the Lisieux Carmel, that he could 'do good to great sinners but also to religious souls'.[106] When Thérèse saw Mother Agnes painting, she wanted to do as she did and thus 'also do good to souls'.[107] Now on 19 March, again in the letter to Fr Roulland, she wrote, rightly: 'Jesus does not need anyone to do his work', just as in June 1897 she wrote at the beginning of Manuscript C, 'God does not need anyone... to do good on earth'; or again, 'From afar it would seem to be very rosy to do good to souls.'[108] So it is hard to see Thérèse putting herself in the place of God and declaring that she wants to do good on earth.

In any case, if we are faithful to Thérèse's terms in her letter to Fr Roulland, it cannot be taken in the unfortunate sense which has constantly been attached to it: a Thérèse who, from the height of heaven, would be helping everyone in their daily lives or performing all kinds of little miracles. The meaning that Thérèse gives to Fr Roulland, and which moreover is in line with the great tradition of Teresa of Avila, is Thérèse's great missionary desire:

she wants to spend her life, even in heaven, making Jesus loved. How? Quite specifically by following in a precise way those men and women who devote themselves more particularly to spreading the gospel as far as possible and making Christ's heart loved.

One can regret having to be an iconoclast here, but can one allow a saying attributed to Thérèse still to be used in a superstitious and self-interested way, contrary to her whole message?

A shower of roses

Another quite mythical expression has flowered, which is very much an analogy, in more romantic terms, with 'doing good on earth': 'the shower of roses'.[109] It is certain that the rose was one of Thérèse's favourite flowers; she mentions roses several times in Manuscript A, where she writes, among other things, that 'the world of souls' is 'Jesus' garden. He willed to create great saints who can be compared to lilies and roses.'

Also in Manuscript A she speaks of her childhood and the festivals, which she liked a great deal; she particularly remembers the processions of the Blessed Sacrament in which she threw flowers as high as possible: 'I was never so happy as when I saw my unpetalled roses *touch* the sacred monstrance.'[110]

There is no further mention of roses in Manuscripts B and C. By contrast, on 19 May 1897 she wrote a poem to which she gave the title 'An Unpetalled Rose'. With the month of May, roses had flowered again; the previous year, in the same season, Thérèse's five novices had formed the custom of gathering, after compline, the unpetalled roses at the foot of around twenty rose trees and going with her to throw them at the large crucifix in the garden: 'To see who could throw them the highest,' wrote Marie of the Eucharist on 24 June 1896 to her parents, 'making them touch the face of our Jesus.' On 29 June 1896 Thérèse composed a poem for Mother Agnes's birthday entitled 'Throwing Flowers', in which she speaks of the 'unpetalled rose'.

In the meantime, Mother Henriette, from the Paris Carmel where she had been prioress – Sister Marie of the Trinity had lived there for two years – had proved quite sceptical about the way in which Mother Marie de Gonzague had eulogized Thérèse; and among other things she had asked the prioress of Lisieux for a poem by Thérèse so that she could judge her talent for herself. The poem was 'An Unpetalled Rose'.

Thérèse first of all says that this 'unpetalled rose' is a 'faithful image' of her heart. God, who has taken her at her word, is in process of stripping it. A rose stripped of its petals is not much, compared with a fresh rose: 'The rose in its splendour can embellish your festival, but the unpetalled rose is simply thrown to the winds.'

> *An unpetalled rose* unseekingly gives itself
> *to be no more.*

So what is her profound reaction? Abandonment. Like the unpetalled rose, she says to Jesus,

> With joy I abandon myself to you.

And finally, overwhelming verses in conclusion:

> Jesus, for love of you I have lavished my life,
> my future.
> In mortal eyes a *rose* for ever faded,
> I must *die*.
> *Unpetalling* myself, I want to show that I love you.

We are at the heart of an extreme mystical abandonment. From now on she wants Jesus to throw[111] her life to the flow of days; she abandons herself with a mad prodigality of love 'to each moment'. It will have been noted that, near to what she will call 'the night of nothingness', in this abandonment the unpetalled rose gives itself 'to be no more'.

Over against this extraordinary poem we have the memories of her sisters. In this month of May the readings in the Carmel refectory were a *History of St Louis de Gonzague*, a saint who, like Stanislas, died in the flower of his youth; a passage reported later by Sister Marie of the Sacred Heart[112] relates that a sick person who asked for a cure saw 'a shower of roses falling on his bed'. Thérèse is said to have remarked to her sister at that time, during the following recreation, 'I too, after my death will make roses shower down.' Mother Agnes confirms this in her testimony: 'On 9 August 1897 Sister Marie of the Sacred Heart said to her that we would have much pain after her death. She replied, "Oh no, you'll see... it will be like a shower of roses."'[113] This is a phrase which Mother Agnes reproduces in her Yellow Notebook for that same date.[114]

We know that Sister Marie of the Sacred Heart did not grasp much of the text which Thérèse wrote on 8 September 1896 or even begin to understand it, and that she was quick to build up ideas; she is the one who lies behind the origin of 'doing good on earth' and the 'shower of roses'. Did Thérèse write at least one of these two formulae to one of her correspondents? Did she write one or other in manuscript C which she began precisely on 4 June? There is not a trace.

We might conjecture a simple process: once there was a question of the beatification of Thérèse, people read and re-read her texts. They were polished – just as Mother Agnes immediately did with the *Story of a Soul* – and people were persuaded that Thérèse had spoken this or that saying, or that she would have said this or that. So Thérèse was delivered over to pious and posthumous exploitation by her sisters.

Was there ever any thought of all those men and women who would be put off by the expressions which had been dished out sentimentally to the public, expressions like 'the shower of roses' or others of the same kind? It was said that the important thing was to 'edify' at any price; the salt was robbed of its savour and made into sugar lumps.

'My arms'

On 25 March 1897, Thérèse had the great joy of seeing her last novice, Sister Marie of the Eucharist – her cousin, Marie Guérin – make her profession. We may recall that Marie had entered the Carmel in 1895, at the age of twenty-five. She was to die ten years later, in 1905, of tuberculosis, like Thérèse.

Thérèse's work with this novice had not been easy: even if she showed a great deal of energy and also mischievousness, she was afflicted by scruples, and Thérèse had to work hard to give her confidence. For Marie's profession Thérèse wrote a poem which would be sung on the evening of 25 March to the tune 'Song at the Departure of the Missionaries', 'Depart, heralds of the Good

News', to music by Charles Gounod. The title 'My arms', has two quotations at its head. One is from St Paul, 'Put on the whole armour of God, that you may be able to stand against the wiles of the enemy';[115] the other comes from the Song of Songs: 'The king's spouse is as terrible as an army ranged in battle; she is like a choir of music in an army camp.'

We must not forget these two texts quoted at the head, since they are an important key. Even if she composed this poem for Marie's profession, Thérèse applied it primarily to herself; she was fully engaged in spiritual combat. The tone is ardent, willing, if not voluntarist: she asserts that she wants to die on the battlefield arms in hand – these are the last two lines of the poem. What are these arms?

She tells us in the first verse: they are the arms of God himself, those which He gave her when he made her his bride, the arms which are, for a religious, her three vows. The three following couplets thus speak of poverty, chastity and obedience.

The couplet on poverty contains a quotation from the Gospels which is unexpected for this virtue.

Jesus said: 'It is by violence that they take the kingdom of heaven.'[116]

But already on the previous 2 February, in the poem on the martyr Théophane Vénard which she sent to Fr Roulland on 19 March, Thérèse had launched almost the same war cry:

I want
to assault the kingdom of heaven
for the Lord brought on earth
not peace but the Sword and Fire.[117]

The couplet on chastity also emphasizes the conquering side of this virtue, since chastity is seen as a sword. As for obedience, it is the 'breastplate' of the heart when faced with pride. Two lines must be emphasized which indicate the exact state in which Thérèse finds herself:

I cry in the night of the earth:
'I want always to obey here below.'

These verses correspond to the two preceding ones:

The proud angel at the heart of the light cried out:
'I shall not obey.'

Thus, contrary to Lucifer who, in the light, rejects God, Thérèse, in her night, opens herself to God. This is where her struggle is: to believe in the night.

Abbé Bellière, who received the poem 'My arms', wrote to her[118] that he loved 'the male tones': 'I love to see you speak of the lance, the helmet, the breastplate, the athlete, and I was smiling at the thought of seeing you thus armed.'

She tells him firmly that she is is not the great Carmelite that she seems to him to be: 'I, a poor flower without splendour, find myself in the same garden as the roses (*sic*), my sisters.'[119] She follows both the rhythm of Mary in the Magnificat and that of Mary Magdalene: 'Do not think that it is humility that prevents me from acknowledging the gifts of God. I know He has done great things in me, and I sing of this each day with joy. I remember that the one must love more who has been forgiven more, so I take care to make my life an act of love, and I am no longer disturbed at being a little soul; on the contrary, I take delight in this.' She is not 'ready' and never will be, she says, 'if the Lord does not see fit to transform me'. This transformation that she desires is 'the grace of martyrdom'. What martyrdom? The 'martyrdom of love'.

She confides in him that as a child she dreamed of 'fighting on the battlefield' and what she felt in herself: 'instead of voices from heaven inviting me to combat, I heard in the depths of my soul a gentler and stronger voice'. The voice which called her 'to other exploits' suggested that her 'mission' was 'to make the King of heaven loved'.

Divine Justice

For his part, Fr Roulland replied to her on 29 April by recounting his life as a missionary. He was learning Chinese bit by bit. He was courting some danger and was asking himself a question: if he was killed, would he truly be a martyr? Thérèse's reply on 9 May comes like a thunderbolt: 'I do not understand, Father, how you would seem to doubt your immediate entrance into heaven if the infidels were to take your life. I know one must be very pure to appear before the God of all holiness, but I know, too, that the Lord is infinitely Just; and it is this justice which frightens so many souls that is the object of my joy and confidence.' Thérèse here runs counter to the spirituality which, at the Carmel[120] and elsewhere, put at the pinnacle the divine Justice which claims victim souls to make reparation for the faults of sinners who had attracted the wrath and the vengeance of God. First of all, she puts herself at the heart of this divine Justice to eradicate from it what was only too human and too un-Christian a perspective, the perspective which furthermore had infinitely repelled many men and women of her century and led them to reject this God, made them 'impious': the perspective of an avenging God which inevitably seemed overwhelming to the human being.

Thérèse, putting herself at the very heart of this justice, gives it all its true dimension: 'To be just is not only to exercise severity in order to punish the guilty; it is also to recognize right intentions and to reward virtue.' Hence this astonishing affirmation. 'I expect as much from God's justice as from his mercy.'[121]

And she puts things in their place: it is the justice of God which is the source of his mercy: 'It is because He is just that he is compassionate and filled with gentleness, slow to punish and abundant in mercy.' Thus she presents a God who 'knows our frailty. He remembers we are only dust. As a father has tenderness for his children, so the Lord has compassion on us.' 'This is, Brother,' she concludes, 'what I think of God's justice; my way is all confidence and love. I do not understand souls who fear a Friend so tender.' And she sums up in a page, which needs to be cited, how she dissociates herself from other spiritual ways, those which which I have mentioned:

'At times, when I am reading certain spiritual treatises in which perfection is shown through a thousand obstacles, surrounded by a crowd of illusions my poor little mind quickly tires; I close the learned book that is breaking my head and drying up my heart, and I take up Holy Scripture. Then all seems luminous to me; a single word uncovers infinite horizons for my soul, perfection seems simple to me, I see it is sufficient to recognize one's nothingness and to abandon oneself as a child into God's arms.'

And to make herself understood, to explain better, she repeats what seem to her to be the essentials: 'Leaving to great souls, to great minds, the beautiful books I cannot understand, much less put into practice, I rejoice at being little, since children alone and those who resemble them will be admitted to the heavenly banquet.'

'Great souls, great minds, beautiful books': is there not real humour in this description, a humour which we can find elsewhere in her writing? A humour which expresses itself in what follows, where she wants to show that she is not criticizing these high and complicated ways? But is not the emphasis that she puts on them here another piece of humour, and more devastating? 'I am very happy that there are many mansions in God's kingdom, for if there were only the one whose description and road seems incomprehensible to me, I would not be able to enter there.'

Again with humour, she defines herself as 'the little zero', and tells him: 'What consoles me is to think that at your side I can be useful for something. In fact, zero by itself has no value, but when placed next to a unit it becomes powerful; provided, however, that it is placed on the right side, after and not before... That is where Jesus has placed me, and I hope to remain there always, following you from a distance by prayer and sacrifice.'

Having ended her letter of 9 May to Fr Roulland, Thérèse took it to Mother Marie de Gonzague, who as we know was the only one aware of this comradeship in arms – if one can put it that way – between Thérèse and her correspondent. Mother Marie was evidently aware of the letter. Did she keep a copy? We do not know, but she cannot fail to have been struck by its spiritual depth. Thérèse herself did not take a copy, nor even a make a brief summary as she often did: she wrote these thoughts which were essential for him to see at one sitting.

'To know everything'

On Saturday 3 April, Sister Marie of the Eucharist, writing to her father, M.Guérin, indicated: 'My sister Thérèse of the Child Jesus is not at all well. The vesicatory took very well, but now she has indigestion every day; her meals do not go down at all.' At the end of this letter Thérèse wrote in her own hand: 'This is not true; I have a fever, every day at three o'clock sharp.'

We may remember that Léo Taxil revealed his trick on 19 April, under a large reproduction of Thérèse as Joan of Arc. This trick was to be very humiliating for her when she learned of it at the end of April. Thérèse coughed blood again at this time: while she continued her customary life, she grew increasingly weak.

At this date she had five months to live, and we shall follow this period, not out of a morbid interest in her medical symptoms,[122] but to trace her spiritual journey step by step through this last stage.

As prioress, Mother Marie de Gonzague knew Thérèse's state of health precisely. On 3 April Thérèse tried again to put her uncle on a false scent, but during the month of April she coughed more and more, and was given syrups to conquer the cough; Mother Marie de Gonzague also knew about the blood which appeared again with the coughing at the end of April.

On 23 May Thérèse tried in guarded words to warn Mother Agnes: 'When I am far away from this sad earth where flowers fade...', she says. But at the Carmel it was thought almost snobbery to say that one was going to die soon, a competition between the sisters. This time Mother Agnes took Thérèse at her word; she replied to her the same day: 'Well, die now, I know that up above you will still look after your little Mother. Die quickly so that my heart may no longer have any attachment here below, so that all I love may be up above. Here I am beginning to shed big tears while writing this and I can no longer see... I do not know what is the matter with me today. NEVER had I been so sure of your approaching end.' This is a stronger explosion of sensitivity than is customary with Mother Agnes.

On the evening of Sunday 30 May, before compline, Thérèse told mother Agnes that she had been coughing blood at times for a year now. This time, with things so specific, Mother Agnes had to face the principle of reality. How would she react? There is a reply in a letter of the same day:[123] 'I would have learned these details after your death, and I believe I would never have been consoled.'[124] She adds: 'I have character so strangely formed; it would have always seemed to me that because of my struggles[125] you had hidden yourself away from me, and so I would have always believed that our intimacy, so sweet, so ENTIRE, in my eyes during your life was not to the degree I had supposed it to be. What do you expect? I am not mistress of my sad feelings, this is the weakness of my little character.'[126]

What is more painful for Mother Agnes than anything is not even the imminent death of Thérèse but the fact that she has hidden something from her; she repeats it clearly: 'I want to bear any type of struggle during your life, but afterwards every memory must be sweet to me and I must no longer have anything to *learn*.' She adds: 'Beg that on another occasion they may inform me of everything'; beyond doubt 'they' is Mother Marie de Gonzague.

Mother Agnes returns to the charge a third time, using no more and no less than God for her cause: 'Oh! how I pity God when souls have no trust in him! This is the greatest outrage one can commit against his fatherly tenderness.' And she describes her state after the confidence that Thérèse had shared with her: 'You have a strange little mother. During Compline there was in my heart a kind of real abyss of bitterness, a very special kind, a kind I had never experienced before.'

Thérèse is going to die and Mother Agnes thinks only of herself; she thinks only of the outrage that Thérèse – and Mother Marie de Gonzague – could have done to her by hiding something from her: 'I would not have been able to bear this after the death of my little angel, I would have died of sorrow.' Those are the last words of the letter. Who would not have been stupefied by such a reaction? And this concern to want to 'know everything' about her sister's life! Thérèse replies on 30 May; she knows her sister's concern, her sensitivity and her susceptibility; she takes account of it by making a distinction between her body – an *envelope* – and her soul – the letter, the content of the envelope. She assures Mother Agnes that she has 'never hidden a single line of the *letter*' from her. And she spells this out: 'Oh! little Mother, you know now that it was on Good Friday that Jesus began to tear a little the envelope of *your* little letter.' In a second letter, again on 30 May, again transmitted by the sister in the infirmary, Thérèse emphasizes yet again: 'I really understand your distress. I wanted, more than you perhaps, to hide nothing from you, but it seemed to me that I had to wait. If

I did any wrong, pardon me, and believe that *never* did I fall in my confidence in you.'

The next day, 31 May, saw a new letter from Mother Agnes to Thérèse, somewhat delirious – she even comments on this: 'I do not know what I am saying to you, dear Angel. My heart and my soul, my entire little person is a world this evening.' An essential point for her is: 'Oh what happiness to be your little sister, your little Mother, and to feel that I am *loved* by you.'

But there is something other than Mother Agnes' emotionalism, which is put to a very rough test. We may remember that as prioress she had suggested that Thérèse should write her memories of her childhood and first youth; Thérèse had done this during 1895 in her free time. She had given the notebook to Mother Agnes on 20 January 1896 and Mother Agnes had kept it, not mentioning it to Mother Marie de Gonzague when she had become prioress in 1896.

Mother Agnes, a masterful woman, did not forget this notebook. If Thérèse died, out of obedience she would have to make its existence known to Mother Marie de Gonzague – she should have already done so, out of obedience. But what would the prioress then do? Given this dissimulation on the part of the oldest member of the Martin clan, on reading this notebook which spoke so often of the Martin family, would the prioress become angry and throw it on the fire? This was a possibility which Mother Agnes seriously envisaged. She immediately said so to Thérèse on 31 May, in this letter in which she was just beginning to regain her spirits, and in which she asks for Thérèse to pray that she may 'really begin a new life', in which she tells her that she has understood that nothing is worth 'an act of obedience and renunciation'.

What for her would be the most difficult renunciation? That is quite clear: the notebook: 'Even if our Mother, after your death, were to tear up your little life, it seems to me, if I am as I am this evening, that I shall feel nothing but a more powerful attraction for heaven. I shall fly higher, that is all.' Mother Agnes says that she is ready to transcend the terrible suffering that the destruction of Thérèse's notebook would bring her, this autobiography which she calls her 'little life'.

The letter indicates that on this 31 May there was a conversation between Thérèse and Mother Agnes: Mother Agnes asked Thérèse whether she would agree to continue her autobiography. Thérèse must have replied that the authorization of the prioress was needed for that. Mother Agnes then suggested that Thérèse should ask Mother Marie de Gonzague, even if it met with a refusal. And in her letter of 31 May to Thérèse she adds that she is ready to accept this: 'I do not even want to be sad if our Mother refuses you.'

Why does she want Thérèse to ask the prioress? Because she is afraid of confronting Mother Marie de Gonzague directly, to have to acknowledge to her the existence of the notebook about her childhood memories, but also because Thérèse, so esteemed by the prioress, would be a better intermediary to help her, Mother Agnes, achieve her ends.

Thérèse's reply is that she does not want to continue her autobiography – so she will not ask Mother Marie de Gonzague for anything: 'I prefer to be silent rather than try in vain to sing what is taking place in my little soul.'[127] For Mother Agnes, from now on the only issue is for her to go herself to ask Mother Marie de Gonzague for the authorization for Thérèse to continue her autobiography. If the prioress gives the order to Thérèse she will carry it out.

Feeling that this perspective will hardly please Thérèse, she writes to her on Wednesday 2 June: 'Do not scold me... Is it worth while my asking our Mother for the continuation of your little Life? I fear that if she agrees, this will tire you out, even that it may be impossible for you to do it. Your condition is worsening so much. Then I would perhaps have committed a blunder. You will tell me about this tomorrow.'

That Wednesday 2 June, Thérèse had gone to the parlour with her family, Mother Marie de Gonzague being present. She had hardly looked at Mother Agnes. Suddenly, in the letter of 2 June, Mother Agnes says of the prioress: 'she ignored me completely'. She is suffering from this rejection, but, she tells Thérèse: 'Provided you look after me in Heaven!... When I think that you are about to die.' But she immediately thinks of herself again: 'Ah! I would have been really happy to have something from you this year. I mean the continuation of your little Life. I no longer know what position to take: I would like to let you leave and, at the same time, keep you here.' If that is not possessiveness...

'Something more serious'

Did Thérèse give Mother Agnes her consent? That is not very probable. But Mother Agnes was driven by a kind of inner necessity; as she said, she could not prevent herself from 'attempting the impossible', i.e. getting Mother Marie de Gonzague to ask Thérèse to continue her autobiography. She knew that coming from her, her attempt with the prioress ran a high risk of being brushed off – just as, that morning, in the parlour, she had been ignored. Now after the time in the parlour Mother Marie de Gonzague, doubtless moved at seeing Thérèse in this state, began to cry. Would she be open to Mother Agnes's arguments?

So that very evening of 2 June Mother Agnes went in search of the prioress. After the office, 'towards midnight', she relates: 'Mother, I told her, it is impossible for me to sleep before telling you a secret. While I was prioress, for my pleasure and out of obedience Sister Thérèse wrote some memories of her childhood. I re-read them the other day; they're nice, but you can't get much out of them to help you to write her circular [see below] after her death, since there is almost nothing on her religious life. If you ordered her, she could write something more serious, and I have no doubt that what you had would be incomparably better than what I have.'

Mother Agnes gave this account to the process of the ordinary in 1910, six years after the death of Mother Marie de Gonzague, and the latter has told us nothing of this meeting of 2 June. According to Mother Agnes's own account, so as not to antagonize the prioress, she began, craftily, by minimizing the notebook written by Thérèse: 'It's nice', and she put the emphasis on the obituary that the prioress would have to write and for which the notebook would be insufficient; so it was necessary for Thérèse to write another notebook, more important, in which she would no longer speak of her childhood but of her religious life.

Here we have only Mother Agnes's testimony. It was given more than ten years after the appearance of the *Story of a Soul* and thus with the weight of the immense success of this work. At the same process of the ordinary, Mother Agnes related that on this evening of 2 June she gave Mother Marie de Gonzague another argument than the obituary: we shall see this later.

If it was really used on that evening (but here again there is the whole *Story of a Soul* between the moment of the facts and the moment of the testimony), the argument is much stronger. A prioress like Mother Marie de Gonzague who, if she was not the first founder of the Lisieux Carmel, considered herself to be the one who really organized it, wanted the Carmel to have a great reputation.[128] In her letters addressed to other prioresses of the Carmel across France, she had several times praised Thérèse highly, whom she held in high esteem and whom she loved tenderly – we should recall that she had known her since the age of nine. So she would gladly see herself as the promoter of a biography which made known Thérèse, the Lisieux Carmel, and herself all together.

After the success of *Story of a Soul,* Mother Agnes, the real superior of the Lisieux Carmel, *de facto* and from now on until her death, had to show that if the work existed, it was owing to her initiative. However, Mother Marie de Gonzague was to be elected prioress again in 1899, which proved that her authority was recognized by the community; at the moment when the *Story of a Soul* was published she indicated that she was the one who had been and still was responsible for the work: 'She presided over the publication of the manuscript,' Mother Agnes had to recognize.[129] But at that moment – 2 June 1896 – Mother Agnes knew that the community would hardly want to learn that, to give pleasure to her relatives and friends, eighteen months earlier she had asked her own little sister to write a 'family history' out of obedience; this would have been seen as a form of abuse by the Martin-Guérin clan.

However, on this evening of 2 June, it seems that Mother Marie de Gonzague and Mother Agnes were for once in accord on one point: they should ask Thérèse to write. Each had a different thought and ulterior motive. For Mother Agnes it was that Thérèse should continue to write the history of the family: with her two sisters Marie and Céline she was the only one so far to know the content of the notebook and she was well aware that this was the prime issue. She had always felt herself the head of the family after her mother's death; the family was everything for her and she wanted this family to be known and praised; she felt and knew that Thérèse was the necessary way to this glory. Mother Marie de Gonzague's ulterior motive was that Thérèse should write her way, her thoughts, her spirituality, the depth of which she had been able still to discern in the letter written three weeks earlier to Fr Roulland. Mother Marie de Gonzague wanted the Carmel of Lisieux to be glorified by this. The hostility of Mother Agnes to Mother Marie de Gonzague after her death shows the degree to which she wanted to obliterate her point of view and perspective and enlist Thérèse in her own cause, towards her prime end: the Martin family.

On the next day, June 3, the prioress ordered Thérèse to write. This was to be Manuscript C. She asked her to write with discretion; the community was not to know about it. Mother Agnes was in raptures: she had attained her goal. She wrote, doubtless on 4 June, to Thérèse: 'My poor little Angel, I feel very sorry for having made you undertake[130] you know what; however, it you only knew how much this pleases me!' And she immediately indicates the place that she wants to take, that she is in process of taking: 'Well, I shall be your little herald, I shall proclaim your feats of arms.' It is certain that Mother Agnes had an overflowing affection for Thérèse, the little last member of the family, the sister whom she had had when she was twelve and of whom she felt desperately the mother. Thérèse was to die and now she wanted to give birth to her in glory.

What Mother Agnes had wrung our of the prioress on the evening of 2 June was the continuation of Thérèse's 'memoirs', but also – and all the more – the possibility of her collecting the sayings of her sister: Mother Marie de Gonzague allowed her to be at her bedside and note what she said with a view to the circular, the fine biography which a Carmel wrote on its deceased religious and which was sent to all the Carmels.

We are told that Thérèse had had the idea of her writings being published; there has been a desire to show 'Thérèse's concern, when she was sick, to pass on her message by a means somewhat unusual for a Carmelite'.[131] To support this view, which is thought to be well-founded, and which is claimed as a well-established 'chapter in history',[132] a letter of Thérèse is cited which was written on 6 June to Sister Marie of the Trinity, who had seen her novice-mistress writing and had sent her a word about this: 'I was unable to refrain from laughing when reading the end of your letter,' Thérèse replies. 'Ah! is this how you make fun of me? And who, then, has spoken to you about *my writings*?' Who in fact had spoken to her about this notebook if not Mother Agnes who, armed from head to foot, was learning to fight the battle to establish Thérèse and to be, as she says, her 'herald'. It is along these lines that we have to read the *Last Conversations*; Mother Agnes could say to the process of the ordinary in 1910: 'When the mother prioress ordered her to write about her life at the Carmel, I made her see that this manuscript could serve for the edification of many and that its publication would be a means which God would used to realize her desire to do good after her death, and she accepted this thought very simply.'[133]

In this summer of 1897 Mother Agnes asked questions of herself and gave answers. Thérèse laughed, freely, when Sister Marie spoke to her half-hinting at publication, and this was not a laugh of false humility. She was a thousand miles from thinking of such a publication. At this point she was so far removed from such a thought that she could say to Mother Agnes, who told her that she was arranging her writings, that she could have *carte blanche*, because she was thinking only of her circular and did not imagine that anything would be published. From this moment, the *Story of a Soul* was in gestation in the mind of Mother Agnes.

We cannot follow the position of Fr François de Sainte-Marie, which has been taken up by others: 'Thérèse can die in peace. To this last moment she has worked, sharing personal intuitions and light received about the publication of her writings with the "Little Mother". She leaves Mother Agnes of Jesus charged with the delicate mission of re-reading the manuscripts before printing and editing them at any cost, thwarting manoeuvres which could be opposed to the realization of this very important work "for souls".'[134] How could Thérèse, in her state, in her spiritual behaviour during those moments of summer 1896, 'already be very enlightened on the importance of her writings and their posthumous influence'?[135] All this is no more than a legend carefully maintained by Mother Agnes up to her death.

We have to read all this somewhat disturbing letter[136] of Mother Agnes, on 4 June, in which Thérèse, in her eyes, is already in heaven in the process of rewarding her for having been her 'herald': 'Then you will come and favour me with your caresses, my little Angel, won't you?' She mentions the poem 'To my Little Brothers in Heaven' which Thérèse had composed for the feast of the Holy Innocents on the previous 28 December and which had been sung in the morning by the community. For Mother Agnes, among other things the 'Holy Innocents' are the four children of the Martin family who died at an early age, whom Thérèse is soon to rejoin.

On the Monday after Pentecost, 7 June, Sister Geneviève took a photograph of Thérèse. Thérèse was exhausted, but she obeyed the orders of her sister, who made her pose for a long time. Thérèse sent her a note that same day reminding her that 'all the arts that occupy men under the sun are only "vanity"'. 'The only thing that is not *envied* is the last place.' This is the place that God loves: 'When He sees that we are very much convinced of our nothingness, He extends his hand to us. If we still wish to attempt doing something *great* even under the pretext of zeal, God leaves us alone.' The important thing is 'to bear one's affections with gentleness. That is real sanctity. Let us take each other by the hand, dear sister, and let us run to the last place... no one will come to dispute with us over it.'[137] Thérèse does not want the glory that Mother Agnes dreams of for her, this glory to which Mother Agnes henceforth wants to set up a monument.

'The poor wandering Jew'

So to obey her prioress, Thérèse begins to write, apparently on 3 June. A school exercise book, 19.5 by 15 centimetres in format, with a cardboard cover surfaced with black waxed cotton, was given to her. It consisted of 62 folios; she wrote on 36 of them, and only on the recto of page 37. Exhausted, she ended the last pages in pencil in the first days of July. She wrote either in her cell, or in the afternoon by the side of the avenue of chestnut trees, where they put her in a kind of bath chair: 'The overburdened infirmarians, novices wanting to pass on confidences, lay sisters happy for a chat, came and went there.'[138] Every time, she had to close the exercise book. No one was to know what she was writing.

Sick at this time, she tried to gather her spirits as best she could; she herself relates, in the course of the manuscript and with humour, the ups and downs of writing this exercise book. Addressing Mother Marie de Gonzague, for whom, and for whom alone, we should not forget, it was intended, she writes: 'Dear mother, I would amuse you, I believe, when telling you about all my adventures in the groves of Carmel;[139] I don't know if I have been able to write ten lines without being disturbed; this should not make me laugh nor amuse me.[140] However, for the love of God and my Sisters (so charitable towards me) I take care to appear happy and especially to *be* so. For example, here is a haymaker who is just leaving me after having said very compassionately: "Poor little Sister, it must tire you out writing like that all day long." "Don't worry," I answer, "I appear to be writing very much, but really I'm writing almost nothing." "Very good!" she says, "but just the same, I am very happy that we are doing the haymaking since this always distracts you a little." In fact, it is such a great distraction for me (without taking into account the infirmarians' visits) that I am not telling any lies when I say that I am writing practically nothing. Happily, I'm not easily discouraged.'[141]

And again: 'When I begin to take up my pen, lo and behold a sister passes by, a pitchfork on her shoulder. She believes she will distract me with a little idle chatter: hay, ducks, hens, visits of the doctor, everything is discussed; to tell the truth this doesn't last long, but there is more than one good charitable sister, and all of a sudden another haymaker throws flowers on my lap, perhaps believing that these will inspire me with poetic thoughts. I am not looking for them at the moment and would prefer to see the flowers remain swaying on their stems. Finally, fatigued by opening and shutting this famous exercise book, I open a book (which doesn't want to stay open) and say resolutely that I shall copy out some thoughts from the Psalms and the Gospels for the feast of Our Mother.[142] It's very true, since I'm not being economical with quotations.'

We can see the conditions under which she writes. We can understand how if some passages are well written, others leave much to be desired; it is because she is both tired and in a hurry. She lets her pen run on and hardly seeks any effect. But many passages have a strong flavour, and we can see to what degree she attains a real depth of thought. However, she does not want to produce a literary work – this is neither her task nor her gift.[143]

The question of obedience has been raised in this connection. Thérèse 'lived in a monastery in which the smallest initiatives were ruled by obedience, so she did not seek of her own accord to do the work of a writer... The obedience which has hardly any inspirational virtue for professional writers and the simple mention of which would be enough to freeze all creative force in them is Thérèse's support throughout her work.'[144]

However, Thérèse is not a professional writer. Yes, she writes out of obedience; as she immediately told Mother Agnes on 1 June, she would have preferred to remain silent, and without obedience she would not have written anything. But there is another guiding thread which must not be omitted: Thérèse loved to write – she never jibbed at any order for a poem or a recreation; as a young girl she was particularly keen on history books; and clearly she always loved telling stories. One can say that her accounts have an element of what in painting is called 'primitive art'.[145] They have its freshness; the text has an indisputable spontaneity and truth.

The atmosphere was overheated. Thérèse was going to die, and the family, including Léonie, Thérèse's sister, and the Guérins, who had no direct contact with Thérèse like her three sisters and her cousins, wanted to know her words, her actions and her gestures.[146] Even in the community each of the three sisters and Thérèse's cousin also wanted to collect her last words as a testament.

Mother Agnes had obtained from the prioress – Mother Marie de Gonzague could hardly have refused it – power to ease the task of the infirmarians by looking after Thérèse each evening in her cell. She began on Saturday 5 June, while the community was singing the matins of Pentecost. When Thérèse was transferred to the infirmary on 8 July, Mother Agnes installed herself at the head of the bed during the offices and recreations and when the infirmarians were otherwise occupied.

So Mother Agnes was to be almost constantly with her sister for these roughly four months from 5 June to her death on 30 September.

Did Thérèse allow herself to be infantilized by Mother Agnes during this last period of sickness? I do not think so. She had gained such strength of mind that even when she is exhausted we see her keep this firmness, which had also impressed her sister. In a way it is no longer Mother Agnes who is mother of Thérèse, but Thérèse, more advanced than her in the human mastery of every kind of sensibility, more advanced than her in spiritual rigour.

One of the last letters from Thérèse to Mother Agnes – there would be no more of them, since Mother Agnes was constantly with Thérèse – dates almost certainly from 3 June, and is expressive in its brevity. Contrary to her own will, the prioress has ordered her to write, so she must do so until the end. It is in this sense, it seems, that this short note must be read: 'I must walk right up to my last moment. He will end my torment. Like the poor wandering Jew.'[147] Perhaps at the same time she wants to talk of her 'night', as she will do in her exercise book on subsequent days, of this 'torment' which continues. However, for Thérèse, this exercise book that she has to write is truly, one might say, the galleys.

But there is obedience, and there is also Mother Agnes who is there and who is pressing her. Did she read what her sister wrote day by day? She would not allow herself to: the notebook was intended for Mother Marie de Gonzague and she would be breaking the rule if she read it. Moreover, Thérèse would not have allowed it. So the pages of the exercise book were solely Thérèse's affair.

'Now'

What was Thérèse's plan in writing? Did the prioress give her orders? It does not seem so. Thérèse expresses her thought on the first page of the exercise book: 'To sing the Mercies of the Lord.'[148] She had used the same expression at the beginning of Manuscript A. But she immediately marks the difference from the text written for Mother Agnes, 'the mother entrusted by

God with guiding me in the days of my childhood'. 'Now' is another matter, another time.

'Now that the timid glimmerings of the dawn have given way to the burning heat of noon.' Attention has rightly been drawn to the use of this adverb 'now', which recurs thirteen times in Manuscript C and which 'expresses how much Thérèse is aware of having a threshold which by pure grace has become a point of no return'.[149] The time of Manuscript C is no longer the time of childhood nor that of Manuscript A, when childhood things were being sung. Before Mother Marie de Gonzague – and the change of addressee is very important – Thérèse knows that she is at another stage, the last, that this stage is that of full maturity; before Mother Marie de Gonzague, who is much more mature than Mother Agnes, she dares to speak without hesitation. First of all she writes to her: 'I feel you will allow me to speak to you without considering what is allowed a young religious to say to her Prioress. Perhaps, at times, I shall not keep within the limits prescribed for subjects, but, dear Mother, I make bold to say it, this is your own fault. I am acting with you as a child because you do not act with me as a prioress but as a mother.'[150]

Thérèse feels that she can be open as with a mother, open as a child but a child who has become suddenly adult: throughout the manuscript she speaks both on equal terms and as if to the most intimate friend, to whom one tells everything. First of all, as we have seen, she dares to go back to something that she has already mentioned to the prioress, but which she has not spoken of to anyone else: the darkness which has enveloped her since Easter 1896. In the obedience of this exercise book Thérèse has found someone to talk to.

'In the obedience': the word is never used in Manuscripts A and B, but is used seven times in Manuscript C. First of all to express that it is out of obedience that she is writing: 'I am not writing to produce a literary work, but only through obedience';[151] and in the course of writing she says: 'I can have you listen to nothing but the stammerings of a little child. Unless the words of Jesus were serving me as a support, I would be tempted to ask your permission to lay aside my pen. But no, I must continue through obedience what I have begun through obedience.'[152] Almost at the end, there is a splendid page which one grasps all the better if one remembers the context. Several days earlier, Mother Agnes had communicated to Thérèse her terrible fear of seeing the notebook of Thérèse's childhood memories, which she had asked Thérèse to write and which she had not mentioned to Mother Marie de Gonzaque, confiscated by the prioress when she mentioned it to her and destroyed by her. This possibility, even for the black notebook which she was in process of writing, made Thérèse – one might say – neither hot not cold; she says to Marie de Gonzague – who constantly suffered from the cold! – with a total peace and a marvellous humour which does not deteriorate at all:

> Mother, you have known for a long time what I am thinking and all the unimportant events of my life; I cannot, then, teach you anything new. I can hardly help laughing when I think of how I scrupulously write down so many things you know as well as I. Well, dearest Mother, I am obeying you and if at present you find no interest in reading these pages, perhaps they will distract you in the future and serve to rekindle your fire, and so I will not have wasted my time. But I am only joking by speaking like a child; do not believe, Mother, I am trying to discover what use my poor work can have; since I am doing it under obedience it is enough for me, and if you were to burn it before my eyes without having read it, it would cause me no pain.[153]

If she is speaking about obedience in connection with this notebook that she has been ordered to write, she does so by speaking about her obedience to the current prioress, whom she is also addressing as she writes.

She gives her position above, without equivocation. It is all the more important that there were two rival authorities at the Lisieux Carmel during those years. Mother Agnes, so sensitive, so jealous, even dared to ask Thérèse one day if the signs of affection that she showed towards Mother Marie de Gonzague corresponded to reality. She did not see the depth of Thérèse's obedience: Thérèse made the vow of obedience not a sheer burden but a kind of cheerfulness; she acted as before out of obedience, and turned it into love. But let Thérèse speak for herself. First of all she says what obedience is in her eyes, and makes a happy comparison, that of the compass.

> O Mother, what anxieties the vow of obedience frees us from! How happy are simple religious! Their only compass being their superiors' will, they are always sure of being on the right road; they have nothing to fear from being mistaken even when it seems that their superiors are wrong. But when they cease to look upon the infallible compass, when under the pretext of doing God's will, unclear at times even to his representatives, they wander into arid paths where the water of grace is soon lacking.[154]

Thérèse does not obey her superiors because she thinks that they are infallible, that they cannot be wrong. By their election and function they are 'the infallible compass', even if their persons are fallible; they point to 'the essential way', even if it seems 'certain that they are wrong' in detail.[155] Then she tells Mother Marie de Gonzague what a compass she feels her to be, and how this is so:

> Beloved mother, you are the compass Jesus has given me as a sure guide to the eternal shore. How sweet it is to fix my eyes upon you and thus accomplish the will of the Lord! Since the time He permitted me to suffer temptations against the faith, He has greatly increased the spirit of faith in my heart, which helps me to see in you not only a loving Mother but also Jesus living in your soul and communicating his will to me through you. I know you very well, dear Mother; you are treating me as a feeble soul, a spoiled child, and as a consequence I have no trouble in carrying the burden of obedience, but because of what I feel in my heart, I would not change my attitude towards you, nor would my love decrease if it pleased you to treat me severely. I would see once more that it was the will of Jesus that you were acting in this way for the greater good of my soul.[156]

This is a clear and illuminating text. At its heart are 'the temptations against the faith' which have increased in her 'the spirit of faith': it is from this spirit of increased faith that she has seen that her prioress is not only a bond of affection but a living presence, for her, of Jesus himself. At the heart of the darkness where she no longer sees anything, where Jesus is hidden, there is the prioress who is a compass and who points to Jesus.

The Song of Songs

It has often been noted that Manuscript C is full of biblical quotations; Thérèse confirmed this when the previous May she had written to Fr Roulland: 'I take up Holy Scripture. Then all seems luminous to me; a single word uncovers infinite horizons for my soul.' Throughout the composition of this notebook Thérèse does not cease to nourish herself on the Word, the Old and New Testaments constantly mixed.

And it has to be said that in a way Mother Marie de Gonzague and Scripture were the walls against which she could make her ball bounce, as ramparts which prevented her from being carried away.

Mother Marie de Gonzague has simply expressed a wish to her. Thérèse reminds her: 'You have told me, my dear Mother, of your desire that I finish singing to you the Mercies of the Lord,' she says in the first line of her notebook, and ten lines later she writes: 'It is in answer to your wishes that I shall try.'[157] Now alongside this 'wish', without precise instructions, of Mother Marie de Gonzague there is the continual presence of Mother Agnes, who does have precise intentions. Not only does Mother Agnes want to obtain from Thérèse, day after day, evening after evening, the most intimate confidences, and does not cease to plague her soul,[158] but she has ideas about what Thérèse should write and even would like to tell her, all the more insistently since she cannot read the text. Furthermore, Thérèse, flexible and delicate, does not fail to ask her for her ideas, by way of advice. In a letter of 25 December 1937 Mother Agnes was to write to a religious: 'When she asked me what she should write of her memories I told her, "Speak of the novices, of your missionary brothers, etc."'[159]

Again in this letter of 1937, Mother Agnes writes that Thérèse replied to her: 'I want to, but I have other important things to write, it is about brotherly charity. I have so much light on this subject.' Mother Agnes also bore witness to this at the apostolic process in 1915: 'When Mother Marie de Gonzague asked her to complete the manuscript of her life, she told me: "I am going to speak of brotherly charity. Oh! I want to, because I have received such great light on this subject and I do not want to keep it to myself."'

However, at the ordinary process in 1910 it was quite another matter! It was not Thérèse who wanted to speak of brotherly charity, but Mother Agnes who advised her: 'She even asked me, "On what subject would you like me to write?" I replied: "On charity, on the novices and so on." She did so immediately without any other research.'

Mother Agnes was concerned not only to advise Thérèse – she tells us herself – to write on such and such a theme in her notebook; she also dissuaded her from writing on a particular subject, and that is infinitely more serious.

In a brief article on 'Thérèse and the Song of Songs',[160] Guy Gaucher claims, speaking of Manuscript C: 'An oral tradition relates that Thérèse would have loved to write a commentary on the Song of Songs at that time but that Mother Agnes of Jesus dissuaded her and suggested other subjects (the novices, brotherly charity and so on). She found her sister far too young (twenty-four) to dare to comment on such a biblical subject, following mystics like Gregory of Nyssa, Catherine of Siena, Basil of Caesarea, Augustine, Bernard, François de Sales and above the masters of the Carmel, Teresa of Avila and John of the Cross.'[161] That is corroborated by a testimony, that of Sister Marie of the Trinity: 'If I had time, she told me one day, I would love to comment on[162] the Song of Songs; in this book I have discovered such profound things about the union of the soul with its Beloved.'[163]

So at the moment when she was being asked to write, at the last stage of her life, Thérèse had a profound desire: to comment on the Song of Songs, and she explains why. Mother Agnes dismisses this subject. Now in Manuscript A (the memoirs which she had asked Thérèse to write and which she was the only person to have in her hands) Mother Agnes had not been able to see – since this text has far fewer scriptural quotations than Manuscript C would have – that the Song of Songs is quoted ten times and evoked many more in addition, and that of these ten quotations two only are repeated twice. In 1891, before the coffin of the foundress of the Lisieux Carmel, Mother Geneviève, Thérèse sees herself as if again before her mother's coffin and quotes the Song of Songs without quotation marks: 'Her trials had come to an end and the winter of her soul had passed for ever.'[164] A little later, she says explicitly, 'Contrary to the Spouse of the Song of Songs, I always found my Beloved there.'[165] Or again the 'Lily of the Valley':[166] 'Jesus... hid me first in the crevice of the rock.'[167] The following quotation is between quotation marks: 'Having found us alone, He gave us his kiss, in order that in the future no one could despise us.'[168] Was Mother Agnes so unfamiliar with the Canticle that she did not recognize the origin of this quotation?

Similarly, the next verse is put in quotation marks, twice: 'resting in the shadow of Him whom I desired'.[169] Later, she speaks again of the 'spouse of the Song of Songs' and of a 'chorus in a camp of armies'.[170] Finally, twice we find 'I sleep, but my heart is awake.'[171] Furthermore, Manuscript A ends with words that cannot fail to suggest the Song of Songs: Thérèse tells Mother Agnes that she wants to 'sing eternally with her... the ever New Canticle of Love'.

Even in her correspondence with Mother Agnes, in 1890, the Song of Songs is explicitly evoked: 'The brightness which was diffused around them by the lowered eyes of the Face of my Betrothed'.[172] And Mother Agnes could have heard the numerous quotations of the Song of Songs in the 'pious recreations'[173] or in the prayers,[174] or for her birthday on 21 January 1894. But above all there is a passage from the last long letter which Thérèse wrote to Mother Agnes some days previously on 28 May 1897: she confided to her: 'Jesus does well to hide Himself, to talk to me only from time to time, and "through the lattices" (Song of Songs).' She thus herself indicates where the quotation comes from and what text she is referring to at that moment. Thérèse took up this theme of 'Jesus who hides himself', along the lines of Easter 1896, among other things in 'The Angels at the Cradle' on 25 December 1894, quoting the Song of Songs:[175] 'Like the Dove which hides in the crevice of the rock, so the spouses will seek your face.' And in 'John of Arc accomplishing Her Mission' on 21 January 1895 – for the festival of Mother Agnes's priorate:

Oh! Fly to me, beautiful dove,
come, the winter is past...
In you I still proclaim it
I have seen the flame of love burning.[176]

Two months earlier, on 25 March 1897, Mother Agnes had heard the couplets which Thérèse had composed for the profession of Sister Marie of the Eucharist, a poem which has a verse from the Song of Songs at its head. So when Thérèse wrote to her on 28 May, Mother Agnes should have understood. And when Thérèse, beginning to write her notebook, said that she would have loved to write a commentary on the Song of Songs, Mother Agnes should have immediately taken her up. Instead, however, she found Thérèse too young to write on this subject. Yet quite the contrary, the whole of Manuscript C would show Thérèse's extreme maturity, a spiritual maturity which Mother Marie de Gonzague had certainly seen and which Mother Agnes missed.

All the same, the subject – 'the union of the soul with its Beloved' – is an important one for spirituality, and it was essential for Thérèse. Fr Urs von Balthasar saw this clearly when he said: 'The Song of Songs, which formed as it were a secret sanctuary for John of the Cross and the whole theological tradition of the church, is also a centre of Thérèse's spirituality. She told her sister Marie that she wanted to write a commentary on it.'[177]

Mother Agnes saw nothing,[178] and that is an infinite pity: at the point at which Thérèse was, this summit at which she found herself after Easter 1896, beyond question we would have had a commentary on the Song of Songs equal to the greatest. Mother Agnes's obsession with seeing Thérèse pursuing little memories, but also her own lack of spiritual maturity, prevented her from grasping what such a commentary could have expressed. This commentary was in Thérèse like a child demanding to be born; mother Agnes aborted it – and this is an immense loss to Christians.

'I am entering into life'

For our consolation – and we need some, given this criminal lack of awareness – we shall see that the Song of Songs is present in

Manuscript C on some pages of great beauty. This makes us regret all the more what Thérèse could have contributed if she had used her last strength commenting on the Song of Songs.

Before that, let me draw attention to another trace: a letter of 21 June – the moment when she was writing her notebook – addressed to Abbé Bellière. He had just had his twenty-third birthday and he did not have the maturity of Fr Roulland, a priest and missionary in China. He had written to Thérèse on 7 June; at the beginning of his letter he told her that the day before he had been singing with more enthusiasm than ever 'the first stanza of the Canticle of Love'. At this time the Gospel for this festival was the passage from John 14.23–30 in which Jesus tells the disciples that he will sent them the Holy Spirit and in which he asks them to keep his word. Now the first strophe of the poem 'Living by Love', one of Thérèse's most profound, composed spontaneously in February 1895, takes up this text precisely:

> On the evening of Love, speaking without a parable,
> Jesus said: 'If anyone will love me
> All his life, let him keep my Word,
> My Father and I will come to visit him.'

Abbé Bellière, who had been sent this poem by Thérèse, was happy to tell her that his superiors had confirmed his missionary vocation and that he would be leaving on 1 October next for the noviciate of the White Fathers. Thérèse received this letter on the morning of 9 June, the second anniversary of her Oblation to Love; things were not going at all well, and she wrote to him what in her eyes was to be her last letter to her young brother: 'I am profiting from a moment when the infirmarian is absent to write you a last farewell note. When you receive it, I shall have left the exile.' She tells him that she is 'happy to die', not because she will then be 'delivered from sufferings here below', but, she says, 'because I really feel that such is God's will'.

She tells him that Mother Marie de Gonzague, whom Abbé Bellière knows – he has had quite a frequent correspondence with the prioress – has 'made for Thérèse' a novena of masses to Our Lady of Victories and that she hopes for a miracle. 'But I believe,' adds Thérèse, 'the miracle that she [Our Lady of Victories] will work will be only that of consoling the mother who loves me so tenderly.'[179] She ends by saying: 'I am not dying, I am entering into life.'

On 10 June Thérèse was a little better, and so this letter of 9 June with her farewell to Abbé Bellière was not sent. On 21 June she wrote him another letter which this time was sent; she took up the text of what he had written to her on 7 June. She noted the coincidence of the date: on the feast of Pentecost he has just received confirmation of his missionary vocation: 'It is also on this beautiful feast (ten years ago) that I obtained not from my director but from my father the permission to become an apostle in Carmel.'

Like him, who has confided in her that 'it was the Sacred Heart which converted me', she has understood this Heart: 'When I see Magdalene walking up before the many guests, washing with her tears the feet of her adored Master, whom she is touching for the first time, I feel that *her heart* has understood the abysses of love and mercy of the Heart of Jesus.' And she speaks of herself: 'Ever since I have been given the grace to understand also the love of the Heart of Jesus, I admit that it has expelled all fear from my heart. The remembrance of my faults humbles me, draws me never to depend on my strength which is only weakness, but this remembrance speaks to me of mercy and love even more.' She then clearly refers to the Song of Songs (8.7): 'When we cast our faults with entire filial trust into the devouring fire of love, how would these not be consumed beyond return?'

Some days later, on Friday 2 July, at the end of her strength, she finished the last two folios in pencil and then stopped writing, leaving Manuscript C unfinished. Now the last four folios[180] – or the last seven pages of Manuscript C – are truly a meditation on a passage from the Song of Songs. We have to analyse this last splendid and passionate message closely.

'Draw me'

At the beginning of folio 34, Thérèse quotes a verse from the Song of Songs, a verse on which she is going to comment freely – one could say cheerfully, and in depth – in the following pages: '*Draw me, we shall run* in the fragrance of your perfumes.'[181] We can truly say that despite the reticence of Mother Agnes, Thérèse could not resist: she has to undertake a regular commentary on the Song of Songs, and she begins at the beginning: the very beginning of the Song of Songs, the third verse.

In the middle of these seven pages she takes up this verse again: she wants to be understood as it were a third time, taking Mother Marie de Gonzague as her witness: 'Mother, I think it is necessary to give you more explanation of the passage of the Song of Songs, "Draw me, we shall run", for what I wanted to say seems to me to be difficult to understand'.[182]

During this month of June, when she is writing this unfinished notebook, she obeys Mother Agnes, who has suggested to her – since she sees here a matter of obedience – that she should speak of brotherly charity and novices; she does so at length. But she has not been able to put over to Mother Marie de Gonzague a first essential point: at the beginning of her notebook, what happened at Easter 1896; then, having spoken – at length – of what Mother Agnes wanted, she takes up the second essential point, this commentary on this text, the Song of Songs, which has so to speak crystallized all her research during her darkness. Even more surprising, as she wants to remain in obedience, she introduces this verse through the double 'mission' which has been entrusted to her by Mother Marie de Gonzague: towards her novices and towards her missionary brothers.[183] Thus she continues to be docile towards Mother Agnes and also to be obedient to Mother Marie de Gonzague, indeed even more so.

She stopped at this third verse of the Song of Songs: laid low by the sickness, she could go no further. The last two pages are in pencil because she could no longer hold the pen and the simple act of dipping it in the ink had become impossible; she wrote until she could write no more. On the penultimate page she wants to continue to comment on the text: 'Dearest mother, now I would like to tell you what I understand by the fragrance of the perfumes of the Beloved',[184] and she writes her last fifteen lines.[185]

At the heart of this commentary a word appears which is repeated fourteen times in seven pages, not counting its derivatives, 'draw'.[186] What is the subject and the object of this irresistible 'drawing', 'attraction', that she wants to speak of? Love. With this cry, this key phrase, 'Love draws love'.[187]

There are two loves here: the love which exists in the heart of Jesus, which is immeasurable, and that which lives in Thérèse's heart. The question is that of their union, 'the union of the soul with its Beloved'.[188] Union is what the great lovers sought passionately, beyond words and actions, the foolish encounter of two hearts.[189] Thérèse, on the threshold of death, wants to speak of what alone interests her, love and the union that it provokes, more important than anything in the world.[190]

At the moment when she speaks of the attraction between these two hearts she is keenly aware of the infinite distance between them: one is Love itself, and the other is herself, Thérèse, so imperfect. A heart which loves with an ardour like that of Thérèse takes account of the love which beats in the heart of the other. Because she is a very great lover, Thérèse can measure the love possessed by the heart of this Other, which sets her on fire. She can measure what a profound mystery it is, almost unfathomable: the heart of Jesus loves so much that it can only know this intensity without knowing its degree and its folly.

So what she feels most keenly in her heart is the distance between the one heart and the other, the one which loves and only makes one love, and the other which loves so badly – only those who love can see how badly one loves. Thérèse's trial – the darkness, the tunnel, the night of nothingness – is primarily this perception of the immeasurable distance and the tearing apart to which it leads.

To express these secrets of her heart she uses the same word twice in succession, a word which she uses only once elsewhere in her manuscripts, the word 'abyss'. She is drawn by 'the Abyss of Love' which exists in the Heart of Jesus.

'The Abyss of Love'

We have returned to the beginning of Manuscript C and the description of what took place in Thérèse from Easter 1896 on. She says in three words where she has got to: she describes the three stages of her journey in love with a gripping succinctness: 'Your love has gone before me, and it has grown with me, and now it is an abyss whose depths I cannot fathom.'[191] The joyful days of childhood and then of adult life had all been illuminated by the radiant sun of faith, and a few lines later she gives the reason for this light: her awareness at a very early age of being immensely loved by God.[192] 'Now' is another day: since Easter 1896 there has been the awareness that love is an 'abyss' – it is love that she is speaking of: 'Your love... is an abyss.' It is interesting to note the only other passage in which she uses the word: at the end of Manuscript B, in pages which resemble these. In them she expresses the same dialectic: she asks the 'Beloved' to be, she says, 'the prey of his love', to be plunged by him 'into the burning abyss of this love'.[193]

Love, Abyss with capitals: Love is an Abyss, as she has known intensely since Easter 1896. There is the 'trial': to be torn apart by the awareness of this deep Abyss, to be put by the very fact into 'extreme darkness'.[194]

How can she not lose her footing? How can she not desire to be plunged into 'the night of nothingness' which would assuage this tearing apart?

Thérèse has grasped what one has to call the drama of love: to want union and to see that one loves so little by comparison with the other who loves. Thérèse gives a very good explanation of the outcome of giving 'Love by Love'.[195] First of all she describes the situation, which is impossible: 'Love draws love, and, my Jesus, my love leaps towards you; it wants to fill the abyss which attracts it, but alas! it is not even a drop of dew lost in the ocean!' So what is the solution? 'For me to love you as you love me, I would have to borrow your own love, and then only would I find rest.'

A being who loves cannot not desire to love the other as much as he is loved; and this is Thérèse's sole aim. 'You know, O God, that I have never desired anything but to love you,'[196] she exclaims. As the problem is insoluble in the case of Jesus and Thérèse, Thérèse finds the only way to get out of it: to have trust in the other who loves immeasurably better, to love with his own heart. It is a 'borrowing', a divine borrowing, a sublime borrowing, a solution which could be invented only by those madly in love; and she knows that since He loves, He will agree with this solution. That is the real discovery which she has made and which she passes on to us. Jesus in his love expects only that: that he can be united with her, through her consent, by invading her heart with His love.

Having written this page, Thérèse once again puts her feet on the ground, one might say. She tells Mother Marie de Gonzague: 'My dearest mother, I'm finally coming back to you; I am very much surprised at what I have written, for I had no intention of doing so. But since it is written it must remain.'[197] She who has never experienced ecstasy has found herself here as it were outside herself, so much has she become aware at the depths of her being of her desire for union and of the sole way of reaching it.

The abandonment is there: that it is no longer I who love so poorly, but He who loves in me. Then comes the rest, even if there is darkness, the rest which is the consequence of abandonment.

But soon she returns to the verse from the Song of Songs quoted at the beginning of these seven pages: 'Mother, I think it is necessary to give you more explanation of the passage of the Song of Songs, "Draw me, we shall run"',[198] she adds between the lines, in very small script, doubtless having re-read the passage, 'for what I wanted to say seems to me to be difficult to understand.'

How are we to grasp her thought? She returns to a reference drawn from the Gospel of John: 'No man can come after me, unless *my Father* who sent me draw him', Jesus said.[199] Now, she says, we must ask to be drawn by him; it is simple, but it must be done: 'He teaches us that it is enough to knock and it will be opened, to seek in order to find and to hold out one's hand humbly to receive what is asked for... He also says that everything we ask His Father in His name, He will grant it.'

And she links the two texts: 'No doubt, it is because of this teaching that the Holy Spirit, before Jesus' birth, dictated this prophetic prayer: "Draw me, we shall run."' Thus Mother Marie de Gonzague can grasp beyond the Song of Songs, which may make her hesitate, that the phrase in it is merely announcing, prophetically, the very Word of Jesus.

The essential thing is to understand that God, Love, 'draws' and that he expects only one thing: for one to ask him, with our freedom, to draw us.

The iron and the fire

Having spelt out this point, Thérèse can try to explain what it is to be drawn or, very precisely, 'to ask to be drawn': 'What is it then to ask to be "*Drawn*" if not to be united in an intimate way to the object which captivates our heart?' To explain this she uses a comparison which is different from that employed by several mystics who spoke of a 'burning bush'.[200] The soul, like a piece of wood, is seized by the flame of love and thus becomes united to it. Thérèse, perhaps because she is living in a century of iron, uses a similar comparison, but cites metal. This is perhaps also because while iron resists more than wood, in the end of the day it cannot but be conquered by the fire. Here is the text: 'If fire and iron had the use of reason, and if the latter said to the other "Draw me", would that not prove that it desires to be identified with the fire in such a way that the fire penetrates it and drinks it up with its burning substance and seems to become one with it?'[201] She concludes: 'Beloved mother, this is my prayer. I ask Jesus to draw me into the flames of His love, to unite me so closely to Him that he lives and acts in me.'[202]

At the strongest moment of her desire to be united by Jesus himself most closely with Him, Thérèse keeps her spiritual head: she does not speak of fusion; there is no trace in her of the pantheism into which many religious souls plunge: '*Seems* to become one with it.' She emphasizes this restriction which is so significant; she knows with her utterly ardent and divided heart that the union will never be total identification. He will always be He and she will remain herself; the difference between the iron and the fire is always present. The proof: she adds that she will be no more than a 'poor little piece of iron, useless if I withdraw from the divine furnace'[203] – and the last member of the phrase indicates that even at the strongest point of union she remains a free being: at any moment she can decide to distance herself from 'the divine furnace'.

We are obliged to pause here a moment. Regretfully, since we are forced to leave the summits to enter a kitchen where an insipid mixture has been prepared. This crucial text of Thérèse's has in fact been transformed by Mother Agnes in the *Story of a Soul*. The transformation is this: 'would it not prove...

Thérèse	*Mother Agnes*
that it desires to be identified with the fire	its desire to be
in such a way that the fire penetrates it	identified with the fire
and drinks it up with its burning substance	to the point of sharing
and seems to become one with it?'	in its substance?'

The rhythm of Thérèse's phrase with its three stages, 'penetrates, drinks it up, and seems to become one with it', this ternary rhythm which is so active and alive, which describes the mystical transformation, is broken by Mother Agnes. And at the very depth of the text we see how it loses its important precision: I emphasized the 'seems'. For Mother Agnes, it is a matter of nothing less than sharing the divine 'substance'; this is fully 'fusional',[204] with a pretension which is far removed from Christian truth, a pretension which is proud and ridiculous. Thérèse desires to be set alight by the fire, but she knows that she remains 'iron', that she is not and never will be 'the Fire'. She gives a precise description of the 'way' (a word which Mother Agnes suppresses), i.e. the process by which the Fire will do its work, a process in three stages that the iron accepts and the soul demands. To ask to be '*drawn*', as Thérèse says, is to ask for this process; and her explanation shows well that she knows 'in an intimate way' the process by which the Fire acts, these three stages which Mother Agnes supremely ignores and which she has deleted with a stroke of the pen.

In 1973, the year of the centenary of Thérèse's birth, I had the audacity to present a certain hypothesis about this text arranged by Mother Agnes – but there were those who found this analysis inconvenient, even blasphemous: 'If the corrector transformed this phrase, it is probably because she perceived, unconsciously, the comparison with which the phrase was loaded... "penetrates it", "drinks it up", "seems to be made one with": the imagery in its three phases is at the level of sexual union and we have to note that Thérèse used this strong comparison to express her desire for a loving union with Christ.'[205] The mystics who had recourse to the Song of Songs, which is primarily a profane love song, used this same comparison before Thérèse. Why should we have to blush at it?[206] Literature, including erotic literature, can help us to grasp what goes on in the depths of the mystical life, in the hearts of lovers like Thérèse. At the point at which she has arrived she says clearly: 'I am well aware that I have nothing to fear now.' 'Now' is after Easter 1896. One might think that there was something to fear in this Fire which is going to take you away, fear of being too totally taken and seized by it; on the contrary, the mystic, like the one who is possessed with physical love, no longer has any fear. As we have seen, Sister Geneviève (Thérèse's sister Céline) says that Thérèse is sick with love; her other sister, Marie of the Sacred Heart, on receiving from Thérèse her text of 8 September 1896, cannot find any other way of expressing on 17 September her feeling after having read these 'pages burning with love for Jesus' than to say that 'these lines that are not from earth but an echo from the Heart of God'. She then finds this comparison, which seems to be like a climax for her: 'Do you want me to tell you? Well, you are possessed by God, but what is called... absolutely possessed, just as the wicked are possessed by the devil.'

Since Marie speaks of the devil, are we not allowed to refer to human love which has been created by God himself?

3. Confronted with the Silence of God

'Trust and love'

Fire and perfume

We may remember from the text of September 1896 – Manuscript B – in which Thérèse declares that 'love' is the 'only good' that she 'aims at' that her sole quest is 'the science of love': 'I desire only this science'. Now this science is contained in the 'Book of life'.[1] It is in scrutinizing the Scriptures and thus meditating on them that she discovers something better, after 'the silence and the dryness', namely love.

At the end of her black notebook – its text is now written in pencil – she speaks again of this 'Divine science'.[2] It is a 'science', and on this last page she evokes it speaking, yes... of Archimedes: 'A scholar has said: "Give me a lever and a fulcrum and I will move the world." What Archimedes was not able to obtain... the saints have obtained.' What is this 'fulcrum' that they have obtained? God *'Himself, and Himself alone'*. What is 'the lever'? 'Prayer which sets on fire with a fire of love.'[3]

There is no comma in Thérèse's notebooks between 'prayer' and 'which sets on fire'. The editors have put one in, and this falsifies the sense: Thérèse does not want to assert that it is prayer as such,[4] any kind of prayer, which would be the lever, but the prayer in which the heart demands to be set on fire by the love of Jesus: 'The prayer which sets on fire with a fire of love', this and this alone is the lever. Moreover between the lines Thérèse has added the essential precision, 'which sets on fire with a fire of love',[5] to make her statement quite specific and to emphasize that the lever is the heart burning with love, this heart which is there, without words, to love. She refers to Mary Magdalene: 'At Jesus' feet... she listens to his sweet and burning words.'[6]

In her text of September 1896 she said that she wanted to 'enlighten souls as did the Prophets and the Doctors' and at the same time 'to be an Apostle', to be a 'Martyr'. She then opened the Scriptures and fell upon the First Epistle to the Corinthians: 'I understood that it was Love alone that made the Church's members act.'[7] The lever, the sole lever, is Love.

God, Love, gives himself as the fulcrum, and the lever to transform the world is Love. This is how the saints define themselves: those who have love, and Love alone, as a lever. 'And it is in this way that they have lifted the world; it is in this way that the Saints still militant[8] lift it, and that, until the end of the world, the Saints to come will also lift it.'[9] For Thérèse, the only lever of the church is Love; and this is what the saints put into practice at every moment of history. One day she grasped this lever: 'I understood that the Church had a Heart and that this heart was burning with love.'[10]

Thérèse puts herself at the heart of this church as Jesus has founded it, a church of love; trying to be 'a heart burning with love', she will fulfil her 'vocation'[11] as the church fulfils its by being that. If the church was not that, if it moved away from the 'divine furnace', it would only be a 'poor little piece of useless iron'.

So Thérèse gives us the key to the numerous pages earlier in which she has spoken of the novices, of brotherly charity, of her missionary brothers. Her conviction here is radical: 'The more the fire of love burns my heart, the more I shall say "Draw me," and the more the souls who will approach me (poor little piece of iron, useless if I withdraw from the divine furnace), the more these souls will run swiftly in the fragrance of the perfumes of their Beloved, for a soul that is set on fire with love cannot remain inactive.'[12]

Two pages previously she had thought of the 'treasures' which were hers, those which had been entrusted to her. How did she perform her task towards her novices, towards her missionary brothers? 'For simple souls there must be no complicated ways; as I am of their number, one morning during my thanksgiving, Jesus gave me a *simple* means of accomplishing my mission.'[13] He indicated it to her through the verse of the Song of Songs: 'Draw me, we shall run after you in the fragrance of your perfumes.' 'This simple statement "Draw me" suffices.' From the moment that Thérèse asks Jesus simply to be set on fire by her love, the rest follows: 'I understand, Lord, that when a soul allows herself to be captivated by the intoxicating fragrance of your perfumes, she cannot run alone, all the souls whom she loves follow in her train; this is done without constraint, without effort; it is a natural consequence of her attraction for you.'[14]

The attraction of which she had spoken at the beginning of her last pages is extremely powerful, if not total: it is that with which the fire carries away everything, with its extreme force which leads to the decisive union. Now she comes to speak of it in a different way: as a perfume. The drawing of Jesus, like his word which Mary Magdalene heard, is 'sweet and burning'.[15] So to speak of the sweetness of this attraction again through the Song of Songs, Thérèse resorts to the comparison of the perfume which gives off a fragrance and is followed by its trace, invisible and strong. If Love is a 'divine furnace', the Heaven that she desires is like a perfume. We may remember that at the beginning of the notebook the darkness told her that the Heaven she awaited as a 'fatherland embalmed in the sweetest perfumes'[16] was nothing but a dream.

Thérèse's very last lines are devoted to the second part of the Song of Songs, which speaks of perfumes: 'Dearest mother, now I would like to tell you what I understand by the fragrance of the perfumes of the Beloved.'[17] Earlier she had written, addressing Jesus, 'the intoxicating fragrance of your perfumes'.[18] 'The traces' of Jesus' are 'fragrant'.[19] Where does she find these 'traces' of Jesus himself? In the Gospel. She says this as in a testament: 'I have only to cast a glance at the Gospels and immediately I breathe in the perfumes of Jesus' life and I know where to run.'[20]

So the perfume is Jesus Himself. She wants to be plunged into the fire as Joan of Arc had been, but into the Fire of the 'divine furnace'.

She also wants to be plunged into the 'divine perfume'. She wrote to Sister Geneviève on 22 July, on the 'festival of St Magdalene': 'Oh Jesus, your name is like oil poured out;[21] it is in this divine perfume that I want to bathe myself entirely.'

For her, Jesus is extreme strength and sweetness, fire and perfume.

'Your will is to love in me'

It is because she will be plunged into Him, saturated with his 'substance',[22] saturated with this fire, with this perfume that is Jesus, that she will accomplish the missions which have been entrusted to her: towards the 'impious' of whom she spoke at length at the beginning of her notebook, towards her novices, the sisters of her Carmel, towards the two missionaries who have been given her as brothers: 'O Jesus, the soul who plunges into the faceless ocean of Your Love draws with her all the treasures she possesses... Lord, you know it, I have no other treasures than the souls it has pleased you to unite to mine.'[23]

She who is going to die thinks of all those whom she has met in her life in one way or another and with whom, simply because of this encounter, a link has been made: Pranzini the assassin, the nihilist, or Léo Taxil the blasphemer, just as much as her novices and her missionary brothers. And to express what she feels, she refers without hesitation to Jesus on the 'last evening' of his life: 'It is you,' she tells Jesus in her prayer, 'who entrusted these treasures to me, and so I dare to borrow the words that you addressed to the heavenly Father, the last night which saw you still on our earth as a traveller and a mortal.'[24] She wants to make her own this prayer of Christ at the Last Supper,[25] the prayer in which he entrusts his followers to the Father, since she is at her own 'last evening': 'For me, too, will finally come the last evening, and then I want to be able to say to you, to my God...' There then follows the text of the Gospel which she copies out; it is the longest scriptural quotation in all Thérèse's writings. She copies it out as she customary copied out a quotation from scripture, making her writing bend like italics. But immediately after copying out the text and having reaffirmed, 'Yes, Lord, this is what I would like to repeat after you,' she asks: 'Perhaps this is boldness?' She immediately replies, 'No, for a long time you have permitted me to be bold with you. You have said to me, as the father of the prodigal son said to his older son, "*Everything* that is mine is yours." Your words, O

Jesus, are mine, then, and I can make use of them to draw upon the souls united to me the favours of the Heavenly father.'[26]

She 'borrows' the words of Jesus; as she will say to Jesus, 'I have to borrow your own love.' [27] It is still the same key which she indicated at the beginning of her notebook: the moment of the Last Supper, with the second commandment and the saying of Jesus which indicates to the disciples the source of their mutual love: 'As I have loved you,' in other words his love itself.

She emphasizes the love of Jesus towards them, 'them, poor ignorant sinners filled with earthly thoughts'.[28] 'How did Jesus love his disciples and why did he love them? Ah! It was not their natural qualities which could have attracted him.'[29] So it was a foolish love, totally gratuitous, which transformed their hearts; we may note that Thérèse adds to the Gospel story an indication which is not in the Johannine text; this addition is not just a detail. Here it is: 'At the last Supper, when He knew the hearts of his disciples were burning with a more ardent love for Him who had just given Himself to them in the unspeakable mystery of his Eucharist, this sweet Saviour wished to give them a new commandment. He said to them with inexpressible tenderness: "I give you a new commandment."'[30]

What Thérèse adds, and what she wants to emphasize, is the reciprocity of the love between Jesus and his disciples at the Last Supper, 'the ardent love' which they have towards him[31] in response to his love. It is the atmosphere of the Last Supper: that of the 'sweet savour' of an 'inexpressible tenderness'.

On the last evening of her life, Thérèse wants to love her own, all without exception, with the same Heart, the same Love with which Jesus loved his own on the last evening of his life: that is her great desire. She then uses the Gospel text and draws the logical conclusion from it to arrive at fulfilling her desire. She bases herself on the saying of Jesus: 'It is no longer a question of loving one's neighbour as oneself that he speaks but of loving him as *He, Jesus, has loved him*', and on the fact that this is a 'commandment' from him: 'Ah! Lord, I know that you do not command the impossible. You know better than I do my weakness and imperfection. You know very well that never would I be able to love my sisters as you love them, unless *you yourself*, Jesus, still *loved* them in *me*.'[32] Why did Jesus give a 'new commandment'? Because this commandment, she tells Jesus, 'gives me the assurance that your will is to *love in me* all those you command me to love!'[33] (note the words that she underlines).

The syllogism is incontrovertible: Thérèse has composed it admirably and the theology is impeccable. And it translates her astonishing mystical insights. She can rightly write to Mother Marie de Gonzague: 'This year, dearest Mother, God has given me the grace to understand what charity is.'[34]

Thus the invitation by Mother Agnes, who wanted her to speak of 'brotherly charity' by telling little stories, little edifying accounts in which she would have related how she had tried to make little acts of brotherly charity, is as it were thwarted by Thérèse. She does in fact write this or that story, but there is nothing edifying about them! She bundles them up in anecdotes which are often amusing,[35] sometimes moving, realistic[36] or piquant,[37] but she does not lose her real guideline: to show charity as Love which wants to love in her, and in so doing to suggest a convivial and happy meal in which she offers her sisters 'a spiritual banquet of loving and joyful charity'.[38]

A poor little nothing

Her essential plan throughout the notebook is to indicate ardently that Jesus wants, through his own, to love 'with an inexpressible tenderness' all human beings whatsoever, the religious at the heart of a Carmel or the impious in the world. But she herself, by preference, like Jesus who did not come for the just but for sinners, wants 'to run' to put herself 'in last place', as she says at the end of her notebook, in the place occupied by the Magdalenes, the prodigal sons, the publicans, all those who form 'the table of sinners'. Her own way is to hurtle towards this last place: 'I don't hasten to the first place but to the last';[39] her way, 'trust and love',[40] is not reserved for the pure and the perfect but for those remote from God and those who despise God. She is for all, and more particularly for those who, like her, are 'nothing', since to go to the end of what it is Love goes, rushes, for the last place, and 'transforms this nothing into *fire*'.[41]

We can say that at her keenest perception of what she has not achieved, or more profoundly of her essential lack, Thérèse is aware that there is a void in her, that she is a void, where Love alone can come to the extreme limit, which Love alone can fill. And that has to be understood first on the human level. Theologians have stressed Thérèse's humility 'by which the conviction of being unfulfilled deepened in Thérèse'.[42] But we must not forget that there is a deepening here: in the human equilibrium that she achieved, particularly after Christmas 1886, Thérèse was persuaded that she was, as she often affirmed, 'little'. Today, with Easter 1896, she is *'weakness itself'*.[43]

At the beginning of this black notebook in which she wrote for Mother Marie de Gonzague, she told her in terms which may be poetic but which are truthful, and not just fine words: 'For a year and a half now, Jesus has willed to change the manner of making his little flower grow.'[44] That could evoke Easter 1896 and its night, which the prioress knew: it made Thérèse aware in a completely new way that she was truly 'weak',[45] and she felt, like Francis of Assisi, 'perfect joy'.[46] 'The insipid water of compliments' slips over her, 'the water of praise' does not interest 'the little flower' at all; she does not want to 'add one single drop of false joy to the true joy she experiences in her heart'. Here she sees herself as she is in God's eyes: 'a poor little nothing, no more.'[47] There is nothing by which such a truly loving heart could measure at what point she loves imperfectly and how poor this love is. During her noviciate, 'I made so much fuss over such little things that it makes me laugh now'.[48] 'Now I am no longer astonished at anything. I am not disturbed at seeing myself *as weakness* itself.'[49] For her, the perception of the lack which could be a torment in human terms is on the contrary the starting point of 'trust and love'.

Thus Thérèse's way is aimed primarily at all those who feel the nothingness of their life, its failings, its weaknesses, its voids. Hers is a subversive message. Like the Gospel, it is not addressed to rich hands but to empty hands; not to the strong but to the disabled, to all those who feel excluded from the club of the perfect. Without deliberate provocation, it lends itself to spiritual deviations. One of Thérèse's best exegetes has put it well:

'Little Thérèse plunges all those souls who required from own strength their viaticum of perfection, all those souls who wanted to make so much of their ascetic prowess, or who confused old Stoic themes, old notions of honour in which their subtle pride was masked by the real demands of sainthood, back into their spiritual nothingness.'[50]
Souls which think themselves just would do well to grasp this message.

The bitterness which comes from the Just

On 22 July, Thérèse had sent an important note to her sister Céline – who was occupying a cell next to hers in the infirmary to which Thérèse had been moved down since 8 July. At its head is a passage from Psalm 90:[51] 'Let the just man break me out of compassion for sinners.' She comments on this in the form of a prayer: 'I cannot be broken, tried, except by the just, since all my sisters are pleasing to God. It is less bitter to be broken by a sinner than by a just person; but out of compassion for sinners, in order to obtain their conversion, I ask you, Oh! my God! that I be broken for them by the just souls who surround me.'

A note in the commentary on the *General Correspondence* states: 'We do not know anything about the incident to which Thérèse is making reference in these hidden words.'[52] Is there an incident? What she is evoking is more of a general atmosphere. We find it in the dialectic at the beginning of the black notebook, that of the 'table of the sinners', and in the text of September 1896, where it is by her 'infidelities', her 'wretchedness', that Thérèse wants 'to draw the love of the One who has not come to call the just but the sinners'. She puts herself resolutely on the side of the sinners.

She considers that 'all her sisters are well-pleasing to God'; so she is surrounded by the just and not by sinners. But since she has already completely adopted the cause of sinners, she is ready to be 'broken and tried' by the just who are her sisters of the Carmel, because she has 'compassion' on those who suffer in their solitude where they do not see that Love loves them. This is a prayer addressed to God and a statement: she is already experiencing this situation; she is even obliged to confess that it is 'less bitter to be broken by a sinner than by a just person'.

We find the key word in the second part of the letter in which she writes, again in the form of a prayer to God: 'I ask you, too, that the *oil* of praise so sweet to nature may not weaken my head, that is, my mind, by making me believe I possess virtues that I have hardly practised several times.' It is here that she cites the Song of Songs to say that she wants to plunge herself into Jesus himself, to 'bathe myself entirely' in this 'divine perfume' 'far from the eyes of creatures', she ends.

Since the beginning of June the creatures have been the 'just' who are around her: all the religious and more particularly her sisters by blood, Céline, and above all Mother Agnes, who is constantly at her side, questioning her, wanting to be her 'herald' and thus intent on obtaining from Thérèse as any suggestions and words as possible. That produced the famous *Last Conversations*, which emerged from these continuous interrogations. It is interesting to consult them to see not primarily what Thérèse is thought to have expressed (this is Mother Agnes more than Thérèse) but what Mother Agnes is expressing herself; her words are in italics in the edition of the *Last Conversations* and it is easy to find them. Here is a brief anthology of them: 'I said to her: "The angels will bear you up."'[53] 'Has your trial of faith passed away?'[54] 'How is it that you want to die with your trial against faith that doesn't come to an end?'[55] 'When you are dead, they will place a palm in your hand.'[56] 'Oh, what a feeling I have that you're going to suffer!'[57] 'I begged her to say a few edifying and friendly words to Dr de Cornière.'[58] 'What you have written could very well one day go to the Holy Father.'[59] 'I was speaking to her about the manuscript of her Life, about the good it would do to souls.'[60] 'How God has favoured you! What do you think of this predilection?'[61] 'It's for our sake that you take on this happy mood and say these cheerful things, isn't it?'[62] 'What are you?'[63] 'What would you have done had one of us been sick instead of you?'[64] 'I was always telling her of my fear that she'd have to suffer much more.'[65] 'It's very hard to suffer so much; this must prevent you from thinking?'[66]

'I was telling her that she must have had to struggle a lot in order to become perfect.'[67] 'I was telling her I'd make her virtues valued later on.'[68] 'They told her that she was a saint.'[69] 'They were saying that souls who reached perfect love like her, saw their beauty, and that she was among their number.'[70]

When we remember what Thérèse says in her black notebook, the awareness that she really has of her nothingness before God and the 'true joy' that she knows in this awareness, her concern at the same time to reject 'all false joy' which would come from the 'oil of praise', we can see that the remarks of Mother Agnes must have been a profound trial for her, the trial of which she speaks in the note to Céline, with the prayer to God that her head is not 'weakened' with this 'oil of praise'. However, Mother Agnes should have understood: she had read Manuscript A, the notebook which she had requested from Thérèse and in which, in her childhood memoirs, Thérèse shows how 'vanity slips so easily into the heart';[71] she added that 'the *immense* void of the desires cannot be filled with the praises of an instant'.[72] Mother Agnes should have understood that Thérèse's desires created a void in her, an 'immense void', and that all the praises around her could not in any way fill this void. Quite the contrary; only 'the Lord will be able to fill this void'. He 'will do for us marvels that will infinitely surpass our immense desire', she had written to Mother Agnes on 28 May 1897, some weeks earlier.

Let us dare to recognize that Mother Agnes, whose good will and sincerity are not in question, was a thousand miles from what Thérèse was experiencing at the depths of her being.

If Mother Agnes had finally learned of 'the trial' of Easter 1896, we can see that she did not understand it: did she not ask Thérèse why she wanted to die with this trial? If she had understood it, she would not have asked such a question.[73] In fact, Thérèse did not necessarily want her trial to continue; she wanted only one thing: the will of God. 'I am happy to die because I feel that such is God's will,' she writes to Abbé Bellière on 13 July. In her last letter to her sister Léonie on 17 July she writes: 'God seemed willing to prolong my exile a little. I am not disturbed by it, for I would not want to enter heaven one minute earlier by my own will.' This desire only to fulfil the will of God is also true for what is the end of her trial. Why doesn't Mother Agnes then understand?

In fact, she has so to speak got over the shock of the imminent death of Thérèse in advance. She has transformed it into an exaltation which we can see constantly in her remarks in the *Last Conversations*. The thought of making herself the 'herald'[74] of her little sister, of publishing her life, already puts her beyond Thérèse's death. This allows her to accept this death in a way of which Thérèse also speaks in a letter of 18 July to Abbé Bellière: 'Ah! how happy I would be if you were to welcome my death as Mother Agnes of Jesus welcomes it. Undoubtedly, you do not know that she is my sister twice over[75] and that she has served me as mother in my childhood. *Our good Mother*[76] feared very much that her sensitive nature and her very great affection for me would make my departure very bitter for her; the contrary has happened. She speaks of my death as a celebration.'[77]

What a contrast with the experience of Mother Marie de Gonzague! On 13 July Thérèse had written to the same Abbé Bellière: 'Pray very much for me, prayers are so necessary for me at this moment; *but above all* pray *for our Mother*. She would have liked to hold me back here below for a long time yet.' As we have seen already, Mother Marie de Gonzague did not get over Thérèse's imminent death. On 8 July, Sister Marie of the Eucharist had written to her father, Thérèse's uncle, that Mother Agnes 'is to be admired for her courage and resignation', while Mother Marie de Gonzague 'is in the midst of the greatest of pains, for Sister Thérèse of the Child Jesus was her greatest treasure'. In a letter which Mother Marie de Gonzague writes on 12 July, this cry is unmistakable: 'If Jesus would be touched and left us this treasure for a few more years, how happy I would be; but now I am going to live in anxiety for this angel.' One can prefer this suffering of the prioress to the exaltation of Mother Agnes.[78] This exaltation could only make her more formidable in her questions and remarks to Thérèse, and unaware of what she was subjecting Thérèse to. Thérèse was exhausted and on the threshold of death; and she left God alone to count the minutes which separated her from it.

Ready for a joke

This trial 'by the just', which came to double her profound trial, did not get in the way of Thérèse's joy. Quite the contrary. As we have seen, on 8 July her cousin Sister Marie of the Eucharist had written to her father telling him of Thérèse's state, and how she was constantly coughing blood.[79] She tells him: 'When we visit her, we find her very much changed, very emaciated, but she's always calm, always ready for a joke'.[80] She writes again to her father on 9 July: 'If you were to see our dear little patient, you wouldn't be able to stop laughing. She always has to be saying something amusing. Ever since she has believed that she is dying, she has been as happy as a lark. It's amusing to see her laugh and her mischievous look.' She ends her letter by repeating that Thérèse is 'a very amusing patient; she only knows how to make us laugh; but she is forbidden to talk so as not to tire her'.

The next day, 10 July, Sister Marie writes at length, this time to her mother, about Thérèse: 'For food, two or three cups of milk a day... But as for morale, it's always the same, she is cheerfulness itself, making all those who come near her laugh and happily talking about the thief (God) who will soon be coming.' Thérèse is 'always very cheerful', she writes to her father on 12 July,[81] and she will say to him on 31 July: 'She amuses us by talking about all the things that will happen after her death. Because of the way in which she does this, where we should be weeping, we burst out laughing because she is so amusing... She reviews everything; that is her happiness; she shares it with us in terms which make us laugh. I believe that she will die laughing because she is so cheerful.'

Thérèse herself writes on 16 July to her uncle and aunt; she asks to be excused 'a trembling hand'. 'My sisters, I know, have spoken to you about my cheerfulness. It is true that I am happy as a lark except when I have a fever; fortunately, it usually comes to visit me only at night during the hour when larks sleep, their heads hidden beneath their wings. I would not be as cheerful as I am were not God showing me that the only joy on earth is to accomplish his will.'

For Thérèse, the will of God in these last weeks is abandonment to each day as it comes, an abandonment which she experiences in this cheerfulness of which she herself speaks and which makes her witty and realistic at the same time. 'One day, I believe that I am at the door of heaven because of the puzzled look of M.de C.,[82] and the next day he goes off very happy, saying: "Here you are on the road to recovery." What I think (the little *milk baby*)[83] is that I shall not be cured, but that I could *drag on* for a long time still.'[84] Clearly Thérèse experiences the continual highs and lows which are so trying with a great serenity, as her daily bread: 'The only happiness on earth,' she writes on 16 July to Léonie, 'is to apply oneself in always finding delightful the lot that Jesus is giving us.'

In her own way, in her borrowed style, Sister Marie of the Sacred Heart writes to her cousin Jeanne on 11 July: 'I will not give you any details of her patience, her cheerfulness, her holiness. I shall refrain from doing so because it is untranslatable; it is a ravishing abandonment, the trust of a child who feels its parents' favourite, a trust without limits.'

On 20 July, Sister Marie of the Eucharist wrote to her cousin Céline – a childhood friend of Thérèse – to give her news: 'She gets thinner day by day; she can still go on like this for some weeks, perhaps some months.' And she, who was a novice trained by Thérèse, precisely defines Thérèse's spirituality: 'It is not an extraordinary sanctity, it is not a love of extraordinary penances; no, it is the *Love* of God. Ordinary people can imitate her sanctity, since she has studied only to do everything for love and to accept all the little hindrances, all the little sacrifices which happen at every moment as coming from the hand of God. She saw God in everything and performed all her actions as perfectly as possible... Always duty before all, and pleasure; she knew how to sanctify everything by tasting it.' For Thérèse, it was a matter of 'seeing' God in all 'circumstances'.[85]

The circumstances. Tuberculosis and nursing

For her the 'circumstances', 'now', are tuberculosis, that progressive suffocation, and the anguish in which this girl of twenty-four, solid and resisting, is plunged:[86] she will take a long time to die, from a death over a low fire.

In *Thérèse de Lisieux au Carmel*[87] I demonstrated at length that tuberculosis was a social illness: in the nineteenth century it was considered to be either an illness of the poor,[88] or an illness of the marginal: poets, artists, actresses or courtesans like Marie Duplessis, 'La Dame aux camélias', who died at twenty-three of 'galloping consumption'.[89] Country people and the middle class regarded the illness with repugnance. Was it for this reason that even on 7 July 1897, Doctor de Cornière said that 'it's not tuberculosis, but an accident which happened to the lungs, a real pulmonary congestion'?[90] Sister Marie of the Eucharist did not use the word 'tuberculosis' until 17 August in a letter to her father, and then only because her brother-in-law, Dr Francis La Néele, who had visited Thérèse on that day, had dared to use the tabu word: he said that 'the tuberculosis had got to the final stage'. Dr La Néele told his father in law, M.Guérin, on 26 August how he had listened to Thérèse's chest: 'The right lung is totally lost, full of tubercles in the process of softening.'[91]

Why did Doctor de Cornière, who had had in his possession the symptoms which would have allowed him to make the diagnosis of 'tuberculosis', continue to speak of 'congestion' for so long? Had he perhaps he told the truth to Mother Marie de Gonzague? The prioress was capable of taking it, not the family. Besides, at a very early stage[92] she had removed the novices and the young Carmelites on the pretext of not tiring Thérèse, but doubtless really to avoid contagion. It was Dr La Néele, the son-in-law of M.Guérin, who in fact announced to his family that it was tuberculosis. Be this it may, Doctor de Cornière was not deceived – and did not deceive anyone[93] – about the gravity of the illness; he declared to the prioress on 7 July: 'In her present state, the chances of survival are about two out of a hundred. If she could take food, this could be extended, but a cure is impossible.'[94] As for Thérèse, when she had first started coughing blood in April 1897, seventeen months earlier, and promptly thought of death, she doubtless immediately understood what she had. But the whole of society was reluctant to speak of the illness clearly, as is often still the case with AIDS, and Thérèse was surrounded with the same kind of avoidance of the word.

What was the position of Mother Marie de Gonzague? On the basis of Sister Geneviève's statement to the apostolic process that 'Mother Marie de Gonzague left the invalid without a doctor',[95] the biographies have put the prioress vigorously on trial. When Sister Geneviève was preparing her deposition for the ordinary process she went even further: 'At the end of her illness she remained a whole month without a doctor. The community doctor, who had left for the South, entrusted his little invalid to Dr La Néele, our cousin by marriage, but the prioress forbade him to enter all that time. The family protested, and Dr La Néele went once, but afterwards there was such a scene that one would not believe the details if one heard them.'[96] What is the truth?

An imbroglio

Dr de Cornière left on 9 August to join his wife, who was taking a cure at Plombières; before he went, he met his friends the Guérins and suggested a doctor in Lisieux to replace him in looking after Thérèse. On 1 September Mme Guérin wrote to her daughter, Jeanne La Néele: 'He said that the little remedies that he indicated were enough for the moment. I had my doubts about that. I know the sweet way of M.de Cornière.' Dr de Cornière was to send a prescription from Plombieres around 25 August; while he was away, Dr La Néele visited Thérèse four times: on 17, 30, 31 August and 5 September.[97] What Sister Geneviève said in 1908 and 1910 does not fit well with what was said by close witnesses who were writing at the time of the events: the Guérins, for example, and their daughter Sister Marie of the Eucharist. She had written to her father on 8 July, 'She is being looked after admirably', and the Guérins constantly kept thanking Mother Marie de Gonzague.

The problem seems to revolve around Dr La Néele. Despite what Sister Geneviève says, he was not indicated by Doctor de Cornière as his replacement during his absence. The regular doctor had noted a stationary condition before his departure.[98] There was clear aggravation from 15 August on, and Mother Marie de Gonzague allowed Dr La Néele to enter the infirmary on the 17th. He thought her 'very bad and gave her barely two weeks before leaving for Heaven':[99] 'The tuberculosis has reached the last stage.'[100] Sister Marie of the Eucharist adds: 'He found our little patient admirably cared for and he said that with all the care that M.de Cornière has given her, if she was not restored to health, it was because God willed to take her for Himself in spite of everything.'[101]

It has been said that Mother Marie de Gonzague had omitted to summon the replacement for Doctor de Cornière. It seems that he was away.[102] At any rate, on 17 August she allowed Dr Francis La Néele to see Thérèse. She even thought ahead. The doctor had to leave on a pilgrimage to Lourdes with his wife and Léonie; she wondered whether he should take the tickets: 'We are were very much at a loss, seeing her state get worse,' wrote Sister Marie of the Eucharist to her father on 17 August. 'Then our Mother was so good as to suggest to Francis to come and see for himself if it was inconvenient to leave on pilgrimage.' La Néele left for Lourdes, where he was to be from 19 to 25 August.

On 24 August, Mother Agnes wrote to the Guérins: 'We are giving her peptone, but she doesn't like that because it is very expensive and our Mother was obliged to console her this morning.' After twelve days of extremely painful suffering an unexpected respite came after the evening of Friday 27 August.

When Dr La Néele had seen Thérèse on 17 August, at the invitation of the prioress, Mother Marie de Gonzague was certainly present, along with Sister Geneviève. He had kissed Thérèse, doubtless on the forehead, but this was a gesture which must have offended Mother Marie de Gonzague. She had introduced him as a doctor, and he was only Thérèse's cousin by marriage; how could he have allowed himself this gesture of familiarity, when in the Carmel parlour the curtain was drawn back only for the father, mother and brothers and sisters of a religious? Before going to the infirmary, Francis Le Néele had not been able to see but only to 'hear' his sister-in-law, Marie of the Eucharist, as he himself remarked in his letter of 26 August to M.Guérin. Now in this letter the doctor showed his awareness of his provocative gesture: 'I kissed our little saint on the forehead for you and mother and all the family. I had asked permission as a matter of form from Mother Prioress, and without waiting for the answer that perhaps the rule forbade it, I took what was your due.' So in giving this kiss, Francis Le Néele considered that he was doing a service for the whole family and emphasized what seemed to him to be 'due'. 'I kissed her again as I left', he says at the end of his letter. He wanted to go again on 18 August, but Sister Marie of the Sacred Heart and Mother Agnes 'didn't dare to ask Mother Marie de Gonzague's permission for me to enter a second time'. All the same he made Céline – who was the infirmarian – get permission to see him so as to give her 'some advice'.

How could Mother Marie de Gonzague not have found the young Dr La Néele[103] somewhat cavalier? Mme Guérin understood the situation and wrote to her daughter on 27 August giving precise information about Thérèse's state, so that the husband could give advice: 'But,' she says, 'above all, dear children, do not write direct but to me, since I must present the advice that you give me as my own. There are susceptibilities to watch out for.' The allusion is clear: it is to Mother Marie de Gonzague, in whose eyes Dr La Néele, who had a tendency to overstep the mark, has become *persona non grata*. She adds: 'At the same time I recommend that dear Francis does not ask to see Thérèse. If he is offered a visit, fine, but otherwise don't ask. That does not prevent him giving me the bit of advice I want from him.' Now Dr La Néele was to go to see Thérèse on the evening of 30 August by the 7.00 p.m. train. He found Thérèse 'relatively well, no fever, and less oppressed than last time'.[104] 'She still has her beautiful blue eyes. She smiled when the doctor told her that she would soon be going above. She is very pale, but her eyes are not dead.'[105] Mme Guérin wrote to her husband 'while Francis is finishing dinner', she said – Dr La Néele having just come back from the Carmel.

Two days later, on Wednesday 1 September, Mme Guérin wrote to her daughter and told her: 'I hope that Frances is no longer worked up, as he was the other day.'[106] The rest of the letter shows that Dr La Néele had been 'worked up' about the prioress on the evening of the 30th.

Mme Guérin tells her daughter that she had gone to the Carmel the day before: 'Mother Prioress sent him a picture of our little Thérèse on her bed of pain to make up for disturbing

him on Monday.' She adds: 'I think that my husband would like
to write a kind word to thank her, or if he will not I know that
you would, but his father would like him to do it.' The explanation of this is that M.Guérin, having returned the previous
evening and having been told everything by his wife, also
thought, like his wife, that Francis should send a kind word.
What had happened? 'A real imbroglio', says Mme Guérin to
her daughter, and she explains what has happened. On Monday
morning at 6 a.m. the extern sister of the Carmel was sent by the
prioress to the Guérins to ask for Dr La Néele to come to see
Thérèse. 'They thought,' says Mme Guérin, 'that you had slept
at home. Alex did not tell me. Thus Alexandre Mariette, who
worked for the Guérins, had not passed on to his employer what
the extern sister had said: 'He didn't tell me so as not to frighten
me. Isn't that stupid? So the good mother was desolate.' In fact
the prioress had waited for Dr La Néele all that Monday 30
August; when she saw that he was not coming, 'she was sure
that he was offended'. She wept and said, 'But I didn't say
anything that could hurt him.'

What did the prioress say? Did she perhaps show her disap-
proval on his visit on 17 August when she saw him kiss Thérèse
and he was offended at that? The tone of the Doctor's letter to
his father-in-law on 26 August could allow this hypothesis. Be
this as it may, at the end of the afternoon of Monday 30, 'after
hesitating, the prioress decided to ask me to send a telegram.
What made her hesitate was the disturbance that it would cause
you.' Thus it was the prioress who asked Mme Guérin to call Dr
La Néele; and so it was that Dr La Néele immediately came
from Caen to Lisieux on 30 August in the evening.

Given his reactions, not to say his brusqueness, perhaps even
his words, the prioress understood that the doctor was cool
towards her: 'She felt this very much and wept after the visit.
She said, "I wondered whether he was offended, but now I am
certain of it. The situation is clear; I like that better."'

Mme Guérin concludes: 'You can see, my dear little Jeanne,
that there's a real imbroglio in all this...' Fortunately Dr La
Néele visited Thérèse again – a visit at least asked for by the
prioress – on the morning of 31 August:[107] 'The morning visit
remedied everything,' added Mme Guérin.

Mme Guérin then gives us her husband's opinion:[108] 'Your father thinks that if the mother was wrong,[109] it doesn't matter; he doesn't really blame her.'[110] And in the same letter she asks her daughter: 'So be our interpreter... to dear Francis and ask him always to be kind to her if he is called. You can tell him that they have every confidence in him. He told me: "I am certain that they are not carrying out all my instructions." They have done everything and the compresses of water have been applied. I asked Céline to do this.'[111]

A calumny

I wanted to set out this incident, what Mme Guérin, a very precise witness whom one cannot doubt, calls this 'imbroglio', as precisely as possible. Mme Guérin is a member of the family, and she would certainly have come to the defence of Thérèse had Thérèse, who in a way had become her child since being orphaned at the age of five, not been well looked after. Furthermore, her testimony, written at the very time of the events, is reported by her daughter Jeanne, the doctor's wife. She is at the heart of the event and one has to find the report that she gives of it authentic.

The only thing is that this testimony disqualifies that of Sister Geneviève. And it also disqualifies another more important testimony, written by Mother Agnes in 1909. Here it is : 'She had no doctor: I ran to our Mother and besought her to summon Dr La Néele from Caen since she did not want any other doctor from Lisieux to enter during the absence of Dr de Cornière. She knew the day before that Dr La Néele was at Lisieux but she had taken no account of this. She decided to send him a telegram. He was so cross that he said some very hard things to her: "You should know, Mother, that this poor little sister is suffering a real martyrdom and that in her state she should be seeing a doctor every day. Moreover I was in Lisieux yesterday. Why didn't you call me?"'[112]

How could Mother Agnes not have known, the very moment it happened, of the 'imbroglio' that Mme Guérin had immediately wanted to denounce? And how, in 1908, could she have forgotten it? One is astounded at such a distortion of the facts, the sole aim of which seem to be a desire to discredit the prioress, who in 1909 was no longer in a position to defend herself.

How, moreover, can we accept Mother Agnes's testimony when again in 1909 she describes a 'scene' which is said to have taken place on the evening of this Monday 30 August before Dr La Néele's departure? 'When he had gone, the poor mother prioress made a scene, became irritated, and cried out against the patient's family, and also against the patient. But Thérèse kept calm: "You have done your duty," she told me, "don't be disturbed. The doctor is right: when one is as sick as I am, with complications at every moment, a doctor should come every day. Otherwise one exposes the poor patients to a lack of patience."'[113]

Who, through internal criticism, could think that this text, put into Thérèse's mouth, could come from Thérèse? Her obedience to the prioress alone would have prevented her from taking sides in this way and telling Mother Agnes that she was right. The text sounds all wrong: the persistent concern to get at the prioress, without even hesitating to use pseudo sayings of Thérèse to do so. We have to say no to such texts[114] and, by the same token, cast considerable doubt on all the *Last Conversations* as Mother Agnes has transcribed them.

Do I need to quote the few words with which Mother Agnes concludes her testimony and the pseudo-words of Thérèse? 'However, her spirit of faith never left her. She remained submissive, even affectionate towards our Mother.' Is this unconscious hypocrisy? The reader can judge.

While I do not want to defend the prioress, a certain number of points have to be made. This woman, who wanted her monastery to respect the rule, granted numerous permissions which were unusual in the Carmel. Thus she allowed Mother Agnes to be constantly by Thérèse; Sister Genevieve to become Thérèse's infirmarian by replacing the titular sister infirmarian; Sister Marie of the Eucharist to write often – almost every day – to her relatives to give them news; and the Guérins to make exceptional visits to the parlour. Mother Agnes assures us[115] that the prioress prevented Dr de Cornière from injecting morphine at the beginning of September; now at that time, as Sister Geneviève would point out, these tranquillizers which

Mother Marie de Gonzague was to refuse in 1904 when she had reached the last stage of her cancer, were 'prohibited as shameful'. However, Mother Marie de Gonzague did allow Thérèse to take ether: 'She is continually breathing ether,' writes Sister Marie of the Eucharist to her father on 30 July.

Finally, the prioress allowed Dr La Néele to visit Thérèse again on 5 September. Jeanne La Néele wrote to Thérèse on that day: 'The good Mother Prioress has sent Francis your photograph as a token of thanks,' she said. 'But I believe that the roles were changed; it is for us to thank this good Mother who has so much kindness and goodness, and to thank her from the bottom of our hearts.' In connection with the 'imbroglio' Mme Guérin writes to her daughter on 1 September: 'Each one had his or her own little bit of suffering, yet everything could easily have been explained.'

The fact remains – and the noise by her bedside almost makes one forget this – that there is Thérèse, suffering physically, who cannot fail to suffer morally from the dissensions around her, because of her, while she is in process of dying.

The circumstances. Noise

The circumstances were the days which continued at the Carmel. Sister Geneviève looked after Thérèse, but while she was doing so, no time could be lost; Sister Geneviève was occupied in work which helped the community to survive: making artificial flowers with coloured paper which a Paris shop sent them. Thérèse was so weak that she could not take any more. Sister Marie of the Eucharist writes to M.Guérin on 27 August that 'she is weaker and weaker, can no longer bear the slightest noise around her, not even the rustling of paper, or a few words spoken in a whisper'. Sister Geneviève was quite unaware of the weariness that she was causing. So was Mother Agnes, who indefatigably plied Thérèse with questions.[116] And there was the noise caused by the visits and the incessant conversations of the three Martin sisters which clashed with one another: 'There was too much talking when all three found themselves together next to her; it tired her, because they were asking too many questions all at once. "What would you like us to talk about today?" "It would be good to say nothing at all, because truth to tell there is nothing to be said,"[117] replied Thérèse.

Not to mention the continual compliments; there has been talk of the danger which threatened her: 'That of being canonized alive by her sisters. She was almost completely out of reach of this danger; she was beyond such temptation. She responded to it only by a superior humour.'[118] But it is these little things which are the most painful.

The circumstances were also the great moments. On Friday 30 July, when it was thought that she was going to die because she was choking so much,[119] she was given the sacrament of extreme unction and communion: 'It was very touching, I assure you,' writes Sister Marie of the Eucharist next day to her father, 'to see our little patient with such a calm and pure aspect; when she begged forgiveness from the whole community, more than one broke down in tears.'

Another great moment was the communion on 19 August. This was Thérèse's last communion, but she did not know it, far less those around her – moreover it was to be a profound suffering for her to be deprived of the eucharist until her death.[120] For this event of 19 August, the testimony of Sister Marie of the Eucharist is once more particularly valuable: 'To prove her illness is becoming worse, I will tell you that she's obliged to deprive herself of the happiness of receiving communion. She was receiving every two or three days, but at present, if she is able, it will be once a week. When Father brings her communion the whole community enter chanting the Miserere; and the last time,[121] she was so weak that just hearing us got on her nerves. She is suffering martyrdom.' As a postscript she adds that Thérèse is suffering even more this afternoon of the 22nd. 'She can't bear to hear anyone talk or make a move around her.' We can understand how hearing the Miserere chanted by all the community at her bedside must have been a trial, not to mention the noise which had preceded that of the preparation of the ceremony, nor the ritual of this period, which was long and solemn.

September came. The great pain had stopped on 28 August. On 2 September she wanted roast meat and mashed potatoes;

she ate a chocolate éclair – which she asked for from Sister Geneviève. The latter had passed on this wish to Mme Guérin, writing Thérèse's words: 'I'd love to have something, but only Aunt or Léonie would be able to get it for me. Since I'm eating now, I'd really love to have a little chocolate cake, soft inside.' Sister Geneviève then mentioned a chocolate puff to her: 'Oh! no, it's much better; it's long, narrow; I believe that it's called an éclair.'[122] 'But only one,' she said.[123]

At the beginning of September 1897 the weather in Lisieux was more than grey: 'Your father is finding our Lisieux very damp', Mme Guérin wrote to her daughter Jeanne on 3 September. 'You could imagine that we were in the month of November, the weather is so bad.'

Seeing, the appearance, the torch

When Thérèse died, Mother Agnes wrote to M. and Mme Guérin to give them the news: 'She had just lifted her eyes to heaven; what was she seeing!!!' At the end of her Yellow Notebook she wrote that the sisters, kneeling by Thérèse's bed, 'witnessed the ecstasy of the little dying saint... This ecstasy lasted around the space of a Creed, and she sighed for the last time.'[124] A few days after Thérèse's death, Sister Geneviève would also say that she seemed to be 'in ecstasy': 'Then she caught a glimpse of a little corner of Paradise.'

When one reads these testimonies by Thérèse's three sisters to the process of beatification and canonization, one is struck by the way in which they particularly emphasize the 'seeing', the external aspect, and more especially Thérèse's 'angelic' aspect, from her early childhood right to her death; along with them, other witnesses also affirmed to the process that she seemed to be 'more of Heaven than on earth', that she had 'Heaven in her eyes'.[125] More realistic witnesses who have spoken elsewhere have noted her 'quite prominent chin' and said that Thérèse was 'not particularly beautiful', despite her 'marvellous blonde hair'.[126]

Thérèse's sisters had been disappointed by the photographs of her, and Mother Agnes even had a tendency to 'lose' them. Rather than rediscovering them, they began to retouch them for publication. So it is that, as Fr François de Sainte-Marie tells us,[127] in the eighth edition of *Story of a Soul,* 'for the first time the official presentation of Thérèse's face' appears.

Thus, discontented with the photographic documents, the sisters retouched them.[128] Better still, thinking that photography was only a 'brutal reproduction of mechanical procedures',[129] Sister Geneviève, under the long continuous priorate of mother Agnes,[130] at the invitation of her prioress resorted to the art of portraiture,[131] giving herself an 'iconographic mission',[132] while Mother Agnes gave herself the 'mission of historian and editor of Thérèse's manuscripts'.[133] Sister Geneviève would herself say: 'The eye of the painter is not deceived, above all when it is a sisterly eye.'[134]

Why this retouching of both Thérèse's texts and her face? Fr François de Saint-Martin gives this explanation:

'It was "to do good to souls" that Mother Agnes of Jesus largely corrected Thérèse's manuscripts so as to adapt them better to the public taste of her time... It was similarly for the incontestable good of which the portraits of saints were to become the instrument.'[135] He writes on the retouching of the photographs done by Sister Geneviève: 'Thérèse was only concerned with being... By contrast, through her retouching Céline put the emphasis on "appearing"... By this retouching she made her sister an official saint. One need only think of the difference between the document in which Thérèse appears as sacristan and the interpretation which Céline has given of it. In the document, Thérèse is sad. We are in November 1896; lucid, she feels lost, and spiritual darkness haunts her. By contrast, under Céline's pencil she will take on the face of a saint who is miniature perfection. Her mouth, the gateway for earthly food,[136] is made smaller, her chin is made less prominent, while her eyes are very much enlarged. She has become so celestial that one cannot understand how she is still on earth.'[137] Fr François de Sainte-Marie is obliged to comment that 'these remarks bear less on Sister Geneviève than on the state of mind of a spirit which, through sacrificing to idealism, to the super-terrestrial, turned its back on true incarnation and settled down in artificial incarnation'.[138]

Because these false texts and these false portraits came from the saint's sister, they were thought to be truer than nature, authentic and genuine. And those who made slight criticisms of them were considered iconoclasts. The three sisters were defended: 'I find strange and inadmissible,' writes Jacques d'Arnoux to Mother Agnes, 'the pretensions of those who want to know Thérèse (her character or her face) better than the Carmel of Lisieux, where God preserves for us the saint's own sisters.'[139] Fr François de Sainte-Marie does not hesitate to say: 'The sisters of the Carmel, living in a closed milieu, were subject to the influence of a literature, an imagery, in which the ideal gradually tended to supplant the real. They also influenced one another so as to arrive finally at a common vision of Thérèse which contained a large element of projection.'[140]

Free for iconolatries of thought and writing, 'prayer rises to the lips all by itself before little Thérèse as confected by our parish churches',[141] but it is at an earlier stage that we need to examine the problem raised by all the retouching of the photographs and texts of Thérèse. This problem is one of 'presentation'. Mother Agnes and Sister Geneviève want to show a 'conformist' spirituality and sanctity. In conformity to what? To their own vision, which they have cheerfully confused with Thérèse's views, her real thought, her true being. In writing this I have no desire to question their good faith or their intentions: their objective was to 'do good to souls', and with this aim they had to present a Thérèse who matched their ideas of perfection. There is something distressing, almost touching, about their desperate attempts to achieve this. Speaking of Sister Geneviève, Fr François de Sainte-Marie writes: 'Like Mother Agnes of Jesus, but in another domain, she obeyed a devouring concern for perfection which led her indefatigably to correct artistic works with which she was never satisfied, because her means were not up to her ideal.'[142] He concludes: 'There is a family characteristic here which explains why there was this perpetual retouching by the sisters of St Thérèse of the documents in their possession.'[143] Thérèse herself had given up this perfection.

The 'look', 'the presentation', the 'appearance' is the objective of the enterprises of the Martin sisters after Thérèse's death. They were blind, to the point of failing to perceive that this was diametrically opposed to Thérèse's very being, to her profound spontaneity.

Thérèse had an intense desire to see God face to face, but after her death, and above all at the end of a precise process of which she gives a good description after Easter 1896. Before that time she was still no more than a playful child who on 11 July wrote to her sister Agnes, when speaking to her of Heaven, 'What joy to see God!' Again, to Geneviève on 15 October 1896 in her Consecration to the Holy Face, for the first time she quotes two texts of John of the Cross, linking them together: 'The smallest movement of pure *Love* is more useful to the church than all other works that are achieved. So it is of the utmost importance that our souls practise *Love* a great deal, so that consuming themselves rapidly they barely stop here below and promptly come to see *Jesus Face to Face*.'

She was to take up this double text again precisely in June 1897, inscribing it on a souvenir picture intended for her three sisters by blood, who were with her at the Carmel. We can see that, while Thérèse quotes John of the Cross precisely on this souvenir picture, 'see his God Face to Face', she transforms the text in the Consecration, 'see *Jesus Face to Face*'. But the essential thing to grasp is that for her the joy of seeing 'face to face' comes only after long practice in Love. The mediation of a love which is increasingly ardent and consuming is necessary if one is to arrive at the direct, immediate vision, the face-to-face as such. Thérèse does not forget this indispensable mediation; on the contrary, she mistrusts vision and ecstasy

In her youth, faith was something clear and limpid for her. God manifested himself to her in a way which was veiled but evident: 'How *light and transparent* the veil was which hid Jesus from our gaze!'[144] Whereas after Easter 1896, 'it is no longer a veil for me, it is a wall which reaches right up to the heavens and covers the starry firmament'.[145] She then understands that if the sight of faith has been taken away from her, it is so that she can live by an even deeper faith. She had said on 21 June 1896, at the end of the Triumph of Humility, in a prayer addressed to the angels, 'Grant that we may hear your voice, but do not show yourself, so as to leave us the merit of faith.'

From Easter 1896 her lot was no longer to see. We have seen how the first pages of Manuscript C express this in June 1897. On Good Friday, Jesus gave her 'the hope of going to see Him soon in heaven';[146] she said of her faith at this moment: 'At this time I was enjoying such a living faith, such a clear faith, that the thought of heaven made up all my happiness.'[147] This clarity was taken from her at Easter; she was made completely blind, and in the most complete darkness all light disappeared; there was only 'the memory of the shining country',[148] the memory of her clear former faith. She no longer possessed anything: her situation was one of radical night and nakedness.

We should not say that she no longer thought of Heaven. 'Will I be going to see God soon?' she said a month before her death.[149] She wanted to believe in it; she hoped for it; but she no longer saw it. Around her were her religious sisters who, in keeping with their spirituality, which can be defined as a fascination with 'seeing' or a voracious passion to 'see', wanted her at any cost to 'see' again – since they needed her to recover her sight or at least to have the desire to recover it. This explains why they believed that they had seen Thérèse in ecstasy in her last moments: they wanted to state that they had actually *seen* that before her death Thérèse had rediscovered the sight of faith.

Now for Thérèse it was far more important here below not so much to see as to be, and to remain in the trial of the night, rather than to know again the 'clear' faith of before Easter 1896. Thus in contrast to her sisters Thérèse does not seek to 'have' faith anew,[150] to walk in clear light again. She has left behind all desires and particularly the desire to see; she is completely removed from an ecstasy which would drown her trial in an ocean of visibility, swallow it up in a light which, in her eyes, was no longer seasonable. She has gone beyond the time of a faith which would be evidence.

For those who lived with her, but just as much for us, this is strange at first sight: how could she not wish to possess the faith, to be illuminated by the 'luminous torch of faith'?[151] With the progress of techniques which visualize everything, our age seeks communication and revelation by sight: information and images of events which abolish all distance, short-circuit any form of intermediary, and our desire to see directly is exacerbated; we think that the real can come to us only in the 'absolute transparency' of a 'sight' that we are given.

Now faith does not have eyes which pierce through and see everything. The eyes of faith see primarily in the night. In and through her trial Thérèse renounces this 'seeing' of a faith which is still adolescent, of the kind that she had had until Easter 1896; through the obstinacy of constantly renewed acts of faith which are the response to doubt and darkness, she learns that faith always remains an act, a passion. It is always the desire of an unbeliever who believes; thus her witness joins the faith of Christians as such, those for whom doubts and darkness are daily bread. Thérèse calls this 'the bread of trial',[152] and joins her 'impious', 'unbelieving' brothers who also eat of this bread, but who have all too often not been told by Christians that they, too, know the same doubts and darkness. These Christians have often said aloud a Pharisaic prayer: 'I thank you, Lord, that I have faith, that I am fully in the light, that I do not know doubt and am in certainty.'

Because they thought that they 'had' faith, many Christians of Thérèse's century concluded that this possession counted, that it was everything, that it was sufficient. By contrast, when we look closely at Thérèse's trial, we can see that non-seeing in faith, far from laying her low, makes her ever more active in love, desiring to 'practise Love', as she says, quoting Joan of Arc.

This 'love' with which she wants to act is not an ethereal sentiment: she practises it truly in her community; and that community through mediocre acts, through certain untimely and foolish attentions, with a basic intention, insisted on showing, through Thérèse, what Mother Agnes called 'brotherly charity'.

In autumn 1896, in a small notebook into which she copied other texts, Thérèse transcribed just one scriptural text, a passage from Isaiah:[153] 'If you pour yourself out for the hungry and satisfy the desire of the afflicted, then shall your light rise in the darkness and your gloom be as the noonday.' Thus the love of those who hunger, of those who are afflicted, thenceforth became the light of her night. In this autumn 1896 she understood – and the whole of Manuscript B cries this out – that the essential thing, whether for Jesus, the church or any being, was to love. Not seeing, the night, did not matter. Her trial led her to become more and more loving to the point of wanting to desire that the very heart of Jesus would love in her.

She now knew clearly that the 'impious', 'the 'unbelievers' of whom she spoke, 'that all those who are not enlightened by the bright torch of Faith will finally see it'.[154] All those who reject God as Love will only be able to recognize him if they see the church as a burning heart of love, if they see Christians acting in their everyday life with a heart burning with love. And this warm love has to be real and become visible: 'I understand now,' she wrote in mid-June 1897, 'that perfect charity consists in bearing with the faults of others, in not being surprised at their weaknesses, in being edified by the smallest acts of charity that we see them practise.'[155]

And it is clear that this is not a matter of sentiments but of actions: 'Charity must not remain hidden in the bottom of the heart. Jesus has said: "No one lights a lamp and puts it under a bushel, but upon the lampstand, to give light to *all* in the house."'[156] She underlines 'all'. To Sister Marie of the Trinity, in a brief note on 13 June, at the very moment when she is writing these pages of Manuscript C, Thérèse speaks of 'the burning lamp of brotherly charity', the characteristic of which is to 'warm'; in Manuscript C she writes: 'The lamp represents charity which must enlighten and rejoice.'

We can see that alongside these roles of love which consist in warming and rejoicing the heart, there is that of 'enlightening', lighting up the night and those who are in the night. Thérèse can rightly say to Mother Marie de Gonzague, 'This year, dearest mother, God has given me the grace to understand what charity is.'[157]

Thérèse sensed the increasing dominance in her time, as in ours, of a culture in which God was not evident and the collapse of a Christianity in which God was evident, this Christianity to which her sisters remained desperately attached.

At the dawn of the twentieth century, which increasingly was to become the century in which seeing was to absorb all beings and events, the century of the cult of the instant image and the myth of immediate authenticity, Thérèse tells those for whom faith more and more becomes a certain fact because it is immediate – a fact that seems to be confirmed by the appearances which are so frequent in our time – that faith does not offer itself in this 'direct' glare. On the contrary, faith which has come to maturity is subject to the trial of not seeing, a trial which issues in the only outcome possible: trust. It is impossible to look at the burning bush.

Happy are those who believe without having seen. True faith does not issue from a society interested in the spectacular, nor does it resort to the subterfuges of publicity that seek to provide reassurance, nor even to miracles, cures and other illuminations. Seeing is a quest for the sunshine, a feverish desire for proofs; trust is a wager of love, in the night.

Those who have no faith

It was immediately after Easter 1987 that Thérèse learned, to her humiliation, of the trickery of Léo Taxil. He had parodied the spiritual life, playing with everything and everyone, mocking the sacraments and the whole of religion with extreme derision. Léo Taxil, who had spoken so much of Satan on the pretext of fighting against him, could not appear to her to be other than a henchman of Satan. And the example of this anticlerical figure will have made her think, along with her uncle Guérin and her cousin Dr La Néele, who fought vigorously against anticlericalism, that the 'impious' – representing for her the supreme degree of the refusal of God – were, like Léo Taxil but to an extreme degree, literally men of bad faith. They denied faith, but this denial did not really represent their deepest faith.

Now in June 1897, at the time when she learned of the trickery of Léo Taxil, Thérèse affirmed in a precise way what she had thought before Easter 1896: 'I was unable to believe there were really impious people who had no faith. I believed they were actually speaking against their own inner convictions by denying the existence of Heaven.'[158] The dénouement of the Léo Taxil affair should have made her return to this position of before Easter 1896 and reaffirm that 'the impious' were people who spoke 'against their own inner convictions', that their denial of God was a façade or a pretence, and so one could not trust what they said. Not at all. She remained rigorously faithful to the grace that she received from Jesus himself at Easter 1896: 'There are truly souls who have no faith.'[159] Was she thinking at that time of Léo Taxil? Perhaps. Or Pranzini, the nihilist of her childhood?

There is the great text on faith and nothingness: in the first pages of Manuscript C Thérèse cannot fail to speak to Mother Marie de Gonzague of the 'trial' that she considers as a 'great grace'.[160] A large number of theologians or historians who have studied Thérèse have hardly spoken of it, quite simply because they did not see its importance. Their researches were conditioned by innumerable developments which have taken place in connection with Thérèse of Lisieux's spirit of childhood. A book written by a Carmelite, which in Lisieux circles is regarded as the basic work on Thérèse's spirituality,[161] has as its subtitle 'The Genesis and Structure of the Way of Spiritual Childhood in Thérèse of Lisieux'. This theological thesis manages not to give an account of Easter 1896 and Thérèse's trial during the last eighteen months of her life. The author refers quite explicitly to the work of Fr Stéphane Piat, who has turned over the Thérèsian ground in every sense; in particular he has written *Histoire d'une famille*,[162] which extols the whole of the Martin family, and a study, *Sainte Thérèse de Lisieux à la découverte de la voie d'enfance*.[163] These books do not mention Easter 1896. 'This study,' Piat comments, 'takes its place in the great contemporary theological current which reflects on Christian hope.' But how can one 'take one's place' in this current and not at least evoke 'Easter 1896' when speaking of Thérèse's spirituality?

So we have to note that a kind of fog has enveloped these researches. Obsessed as they were by 'childhood', which is certainly an important point but secondary for Thérèse, they have omitted to do any work on 'Easter 1896' which would have changed their horizon and given a much more dynamic dimension to the 'little way'. One author, Marcel Moré, has had a flash of intuition over Easter 1896 and put it at the centre of his study on Thérèse.[164] But he was not an accepted theologian, and De Meester dismisses him by speaking quite simply of an 'outrage'.[165]

Little by little, Christians have come to perceive Thérèse's 'trial'. Just after Vatican II, in 1966, *A New Catechism. The*

Catholic Faith for Adults, made its appearance in the Netherlands. It quickly became famous under the name of *The Dutch Catechism*. In it we find: 'Thérèse of Lisieux experienced fearful doubts before her death... Her faith held up only in this ultimate abandonment: "I want to believe, help my lack of faith.".... In the midst of the great crisis of faith which her contemporaries, both intelligentsia and workers, were debating, she experienced this distress for long months with a total abandonment to love.'[166]

However, the more this 'trial' has been perceived, the more it has troubled the approved interpreters of Thérèse's thought and the commentators on it. One of these describes Easter 1896 in the following way: 'An unforeseen trial overcame her. The objections of the materialists to the existence of the beyond pressed in on her. She had the impression that nothingness awaited her after death.'[167] We have seen how the same interpreter explained Easter 1896: 'Her temptations to doubt did not relate to the existence of God but to the other world. It seemed to her that after death there is nothing.'[168] The same author takes up his idea in *Thérèse et Lisieux*.[169] He begins by describing what took place within Thérèse: 'Who knows? Might not the materialists be right? When one dies, what remains of the person? When the body disappears, can consciousness perhaps still exist?' We can ask whether Thérèse asked herself these pseudo-philosophical and very Platonizing questions in such a way. Then Descouvemont offers his conclusions: he would like to show that basically Easter 1896 is no more than an episode, that this event is purely and simply in continuity with what has gone before – and this amounts to denying what Thérèse said in speaking of this trial, affirming strongly that it was a 'grace'. 'Surprisingly, Thérèse is not distraught. For a long time she has lived in the night of faith. During her noviciate she experienced dryness in her meditation.'[170] And always the same leitmotiv: 'Her doubts were not about the existence of God but about a future life... Though her spirit was invaded by "doubts", Thérèse did not doubt.'[171]

One does not have to be a great expert in philosophy or theology to see here word-plays and sophistries which not only explain nothing but are manifestly aimed at masking and stifling reality. How can one make people understand that doubt existed in Thérèse's very faith? Is it necessary to invoke Gustave Thibone, who at the age of ninety said with much truth in his memoirs:[172] 'For me God was first person and law, then light and love, and finally absence and night'? In a conversation, he made this brief statement: 'I would say, like Gabriel Marcel, that a God who did not allow doubt would not be a true God. I constantly doubt, but I try to dominate it. It is perhaps by the quantity of doubts overcome that one measures the intensity of faith. The more I think that I am approaching God, the more I doubt him.' He ends his conversation by saying: 'I want to die in the night, dazzled, blinded by this darkness of which we do not know whether it will be succeeded by the dawn.'[173]

Let us dare to look in the face what Thérèse experienced, suddenly finding herself in a 'tunnel' in Easter 1896: her spirit was invaded by doubts. She doubted for some days, then the doubt lasted weeks, months, and did not stop. She experienced these doubts, this massive doubt; she had not looked for it; it was not a deliberate, rational questioning of her faith but a trial which befell her. What is a great example for us is that Thérèse did not become afraid in this trial, that she did not panic despite its interminable duration. Integralism, fundamentalism and fanaticism are the fruits of fear, of an inability to confront the doubts which assail one, a horrible fear of losing one's certainties, a contraction which paralyses and prevents one from becoming detached from what one believes and beginning to seek the light in a rather better way. Thérèse does not take this way at all. To affirm frenetically 'Thérèse does not doubt, she believes'[174] is to deny the reality of what Thérèse affirms. Let us say simply, 'Thérèse doubts *and* believes. And she says to God quite precisely, "I love you."'[175]

It is important to note Thérèse's reaction to the doubt that assails her;[176] her stubborn trust, her obstinate abandonment, her love and joy which remain. If this doubt does not exist, there is no trial, no Easter 1896; the last eighteen months of her life and her very death lose their meaning.

Another way of reducing Easter 1896 to nothing is to insist that this event comes from a preoccupation with contemporary unbelief and to want to make Thérèse say what suits those who are preoccupied with unbelief and unbelievers today: 'Stamped by unbelief or the lack of belief in their brothers, today's Christians are particularly sensitive to the fact that Thérèse experienced the temptation to doubt the other world. To bring her closer to the atheists of our time, people have even gone so far as to say that in the end she doubted the existence of God. The texts give the lie to such an interpretation.'[177] What does the author think of what Cardinal Sodano, pro-Secretary of State at the Vatican, wrote to Mgr Lacrampe, on 20 June 1991, for the fiftieth anniversary of the foundation of the Mission de France?[178] 'Having experienced the painful trial of religious doubt and even the night of faith, Thérèse came to be in mysterious solidarity with those who believe badly or not at all. Persuaded that every human being has the right to know that he is loved by God, she would have wanted to bring them all together.'

Let us leave aside the dubious distinctions between doubts and non-doubt. Others have understood more profoundly the real significance of doubt in a mystic like Thérèse.[179] And let us say once and for all that if a certain number of Thérèse's contemporaries and ours can think that God exists but are not at all certain that there is anything after death, this dichotomy did not exist at all in Thérèse's mind. It has been shown what Heaven meant for her – the term 'other world' never appears in her autobiographical manuscripts. It would have been unthinkable to her that one could distinguish between the existence of God and the reality of Heaven; for her 'the night of nothingness' strictly means that there is 'nothing': neither God, nor heaven nor the beyond. There is a gulf which gives her a radical vertigo, a vertigo against which she never ceases to struggle; but the call of the gulf exists, and it is a gulf.

'It is always an unbeliever who believes'

Now we have established that, one question arises for us. Here is Thérèse, aware at the deepest level 'that there really are impious people who had no faith',[180] that the darkness in which she found herself was precisely the same as the darkness experienced by those who 'reject or refuse faith'.[181] How could this

Carmelite removed from the world comprehend the unbelief which exists in this world? How could a being of faith and prayer comprehend from within what was taking place in the mind, the heart, the life of those who 'reject or refuse faith'? How could this little nun without much education thus understand, in her sphere,[182] what flooded over her time like a tidal wave and has been called 'the drama of atheistic humanism'? For Thérèse goes that far. It has been very well said that 'Thérèse of Lisieux thinks "us" and lives in the plural: she perceives that the history of the individual is not only his history, but the history of the world. The night of the individual is his night and the night of the world.'[183]

Here again it is not a matter of making some fallacious distinction. Thérèse really understood the unbelief of her time. How was she able to do that?

In confronting this question we can be helped by the introduction to a great book[184] which raises the global question 'Who knows unbelief better, the believer or the unbeliever?'[185] Daniel Pézeril, who was the confidant of Bernanos, is well qualified to raise it; here is his reply: 'It is not at all certain that it is the latter [the unbeliever], since in the end of the day how could he be aware of what he is deprived of and evaluate what is alien to him? He is certainly least authorized to speak of what he does not have.'[186]

But we need to cite the whole of Pézeril's rigorous argument. Speaking of Bernanos, he gives an admirable evocation of Thérèse's experience in her last eighteen months with a key phrase which needs to be emphasized: 'There is no person of faith who can forget that in him or her there is always an unbeliever who believes.'[187]

The disciple who progresses in faith can only discover more radically what he owes to God. He 'sees himself' better and better as he would have been yesterday, as he would be today, as he risks becoming tomorrow if left to his own resources. This clear-sighted lucidity grows, the nearer God brings himself. We find it systematically reconstructed and analysed in St John of the Cross, but no less painfully lived out by the poor Curé d'Ars or Thérèse of Lisieux. It reaches the point of vertigo in more of the faithful than one could imagine. Faith is essentially a gift of God. The faithful cannot pride themselves in it as if it were their own, as if they had acquired it through asceticism or developed it themselves. That would be to glorify themselves, but then it would be no more than a gnosis, i.e. one human thought among so many others.

No person of faith can forget that within him or her there is always an unbeliever who believes. That is a first fact. Hence the intimate communication which he or she can have not only with unbelief in general but with particular believers is often far deeper than one might imagine. It is obscured only by an inexplicable silence about oneself, one's own religious mediocrity, or sociological breaks which arise out of unfounded prejudices.[188]

The further Thérèse advanced in the faith and allowed herself to be loved by Love, the more she understood the unbelief in her and as a result the unbelief in this world, and the more she suffered, precisely because of this, the 'darkness' in which the unbeliever lives, loved by God but ignorant that he is.

It is because Bernanos descended into this domain which is too often ignored and as a novelist was given the resources to evoke it with an irresistible force that he gained such a wide audience for all his work, notably for *Monsieur Ouine*. Above all he was a believer who did not dissimulate. He was true, and that is why although the years may dull his imaginary reconstructions, for those who know how to read them, whether believers or unbelievers, they will remain a testimony to an uncommon brotherhood.[189]

Bernanos wrote a very fine passage in 1929: 'Our church is the church of the saints.' Among them 'the last, so strange, so secret saint, tortured by entrepreneurs and simoniacs, with her incomprehensible smile, is Thérèse of the Child Jesus. Would we want them [the saints] all to have been put in shrines during their lifetimes? Such kindnesses are good for the canons. They lived, they suffered like us. They were tempted like us.' Furthermore Bernanos joins up with Thérèse, for whom love is the motive force of the church (Manuscript B): 'This whole great apparatus of wisdom, of power, of flexible discipline, of magnificence and of majesty is nothing in itself if it is not animated by charity.'[190]

One might also refer to *Les Grands Cimetières sous la lune*, published in 1938, in which Bernanos meditates on the totalitarian building sites and the whole of this suicidal twentieth century, on the tragedies which have just happened and on those which he expects to come. At the heart of this torrential book is a sermon imagined by Bernanos, given in a church by an 'agnostic' on the feast of Thérèse of Lisieux, an agnostic who, he himself says, 'speaks in the capacity of an unbeliever'. The text, which is very reminiscent of Thérèse, is a hymn to the communion of saints; and this 'agnostic', seeking the causes of the dramas of this twentieth century, exclaims: 'We must seek the true cause of our misfortunes in the disincarnation of the Word.' We might say that Thérèse's spirituality is at the deepest level a mystical revolution against the monophysitism which, as Fr Congar constantly repeated, has ravaged the Roman church for centuries, in other words a revolution against spiritualities of the 'disincarnation of the Word'.

In 1897, the very year of Thérèse's death, Léon Bloy wrote of the saints – these are the last words of *La femme pauvre*: 'There is only one sadness: not to be of the saints.'

Thérèse understands the life of the unbeliever profoundly, from within. What existed in her era exists today. Her perception goes beyond space and time, beyond the vague and deceitful categories that people try to establish: bad believers, agnostics, the indifferent. She joins those who 'reject or refuse God' in whatever way; her perception is not fragmentary and random, but universal.[191]

The silence of God

The protestations of brotherly charity on the one hand and the constant invocations of God on the other which can exist in a Carmel and really did exist in the Lisieux Carmel should not hide or mask the fact that Thérèse experienced extreme solitude.

In March 1896 Mother Agnes was no longer prioress: that was the end of a double motherhood. At Easter 1896 Thérèse could enter all the more into the night since the facts allowed her to renounce the spiritual motherhood of her second mother by blood. At that time Thérèse was addressing Mother Marie de Gonzague, whom she certainly calls 'My mother', but who was primarily a representative of the law of Carmel and at the same time a being with a wide horizon who did not allow herself to be imprisoned in the letter of the law. The time of all childishness was henceforth over and the time of solitude began.

Attempts have been made to demonstrate the intensity that solitude can reach for a mystic, a lover like Thérèse, when God absents himself. Had she been a masochist she would have been engulfed in the suffering of this absence and would have been in raptures of delight. But there was nothing of that sort. From then on the absence was terrible.

Though the statement needs to be put with the utmost caution, one might be allowed to say that there is a real proximity between what Thérèse experienced, this 'agony' of solitude approaching that of Gethsemane, and what millions of human beings have experienced during this twentieth century on the threshold of which Thérèse died. One might argue that as it were prophetically, she was present in the most horrible absences of God which our era has experienced, that absence to which millions were abandoned body and soul, whether by dying on the roads, driven from their homes and their lives, or in prison, in concentration camps.

In a lecture given in 1984 a Jewish philosopher, Hans Jonas, raised the question how we can think of God after Auschwitz. How can we have faith in a deity who authorizes absolute evil? He raised the question as a philosopher and spoke of the 'concept of God' and not of the 'God of Abraham, Isaac and Jacob' invoked by Pascal; he wanted to speak on a 'purely logical level'.[192] Jonas began from the attributes conferred on God by Jewish theology: goodness, omnipotence, intelligibility. If we keep the first two we are led to renounce the third, and yet we must understand: intelligibility is at the heart of the Bible. So how does one understand the omnipotent and good God who killed himself in the genocide of the Jewish people? Jonas sacrifices omnipotence; for him God, engaged in creation, in the adventure of time and space, does not want to keep anything of himself. This renunciation attains its fullness in the birth of human beings: 'A decisive turning-point takes place, for the creation of human beings also signifies the beginning of the knowledge of freedom and from then on the possibility of the separation of good and evil, of a radical rejection of transcendence which nevertheless derives all its meaning from him.'[193] 'Human beings, created in the image of God, are from now on *responsible* for the fate of the world and, beyond that, of the deity itself.'[194]

The only possible human response is to accept our responsibility; it is the response of some whose 'holiness, often misunderstood and wounded',[195] restores a certain taste for living. Like Etty Hillesum, the young Dutch Jew who through her life communicated the idea that we can help God rather than be helped by God. In 1942 she volunteered to work in the hospital of a transit camp; one day she herself was carried off in a convoy and died in Auschwitz on 30 November 1943: 'I shall try to help You,' she said to God. 'One thing is becoming increasingly clear to me, the knowledge that You cannot help us, that we need to help You to help us. Alas, it hardly seems as if You Yourself can act on the circumstances which surround us, on our lives. I no longer hold You responsible. You cannot help us, but we can help You.'

This young girl who died in Auschwitz at the same age as Thérèse thus links Heaven and Earth by the responsibility which she assumes totally:[196] 'An infinite responsibility for the weakness of existences at the mercy of the tyranny which power exercises when it is not subordinated to any moral demand.'[197] And if we take this to the end: 'Among these existences we must count that of a sole God whose power resides in the prayer which He never ceases to address to each individual: to watch over his brother and to care for his image in creation.'[198]

Thérèse does not cease to hear this prayer of God which speaks to her of her responsibility towards every being, certainly towards the sisters of her convent and her missionary brothers, but even more towards her unbelieving or sinning brothers and sisters.

Love reified

In his work, Bernanos similarly joins 'those who reject or refuse God', to such a degree that it has been 'insinuated that the writer was ultimately a profound agnostic at odds with Catholic literature'.[199] In *Monsieur Ouine* in particular, Bernanos 'presses the counter-trial of faith to the extreme'.[200] And Albert Béguin could say of Bernanos precisely what one can say of Thérèse: 'Bernanos' universe is not divided into the good and the bad, but – and this is quite different – into the saints who have kept faith with childhood and the unfortunates who have lost it'.[201]

There is no dualism in Bernanos and no dualism in Thérèse. There are no just people and sinners of whom one hears so much in a religious culture, but, as we shall see, sinners who recognize themselves as such, throwing themselves into the Father's arms, and sinners who reject Love. Thérèse has put herself among the sinners, not the just.

For Thérèse there is no vale of tears here below which is evil, and an other world to attain. Because of Love there is a unity between Heaven and earth, so close that even after death she would like to continue to be on earth and there make Love love, that Love which unifies Heaven and earth.

Those who fear doubt, for example fanatics, are dualists: for them there is a strict Manichaeism, good and evil, faith and non-faith. At the time when Thérèse was living, Nietzsche was writing of his horror of a stubbornly dualistic thought, a thought which is buttressed by the 'antinomy of values', which separates good and evil, positive and negative, true and false. There is nothing of the dualist about Thérèse. One of the great wrongs that has been done her is to put her in the dualistic camp, indeed to see her as the very prototype of Christian dualism.

In 1937, at the time when pilgrimages to Lisieux were at their zenith, in the year in which the basilica of Lisieux was inaugurated by the papal legate Cardinal Pacelli, later to become Pius XII, a little book was published on Thérèse. It was out of keeping with all the usual hagiographical productions, and it scandalized Lisieux. Subsequently, authors who have written on

Thérèse have taken care to ignore this work, omitting to cite it. Thus in the paragraph of his article in the *Dictionnaire de spiritualité* devoted to 'Thérèse challenged',[202] Abbé Descouvemont, who seeks to reply at length to those who criticize Thérèse, for example, for her 'mawkish style', who speak of 'overrated popularity', or mock the 'avalanche of petals' or her rose-water spirituality, makes no mention[203] of this work and what seems to me to be its major objection to Thérèse.

The book looks very slim: 102 small pages. It is simply entitled *Thérèse de Lisieux*.[204] The author, Pierre Mabille, was a young doctor of thirty-three, an intern in the Paris hospitals, and an enthusiast about anthropology. In 1936 he wrote a book called *La Construction de l'homme*. His friend André Breton called him a 'man of great humanity and brotherhood'.

Why did this man who was a strict atheist want to write about Thérèse? He explains in the first lines of his book. 'This is not gratuitous entertainment on my part.' He has chosen Thérèse because in his view she represents very precisely the 'contemporary affective drama',[205] a drama arising out of the dualism which 'regards the world as formed of two opposed domains', 'which preceded the development of Christianity, and serves it in so-called lay or atheistic, even materialistic philosophies which are simply an extension of the great current of Christian ideology'.[206] 'I have chosen the example of Thérèse as a case which is particularly suitable for showing the ultimate and pernicious consequences of this dualistic interpretation of the world in the sphere of love.'[207] For him, the infatuation with Thérèse of Lisieux is 'testimony that here we have a symbol of general value... A being becomes a myth only to the degree to which he or she incarnates collective desires.'[208]

In the first chapter he seeks to relate 'objectively the facts' of Thérèse's life. The first quotation that he makes from Thérèse is this, from the *Story of a Soul*: 'I was sure that I was born to be great, and began to wonder how I should set about winning my glory; then it was revealed to me in my heart that my glory would lie in becoming a saint, though this glory would be hidden on earth.' Mabille emphasizes that Thérèse senses that her life will be short; she is 'stamped by impatience and shows an indubitable precocity. But she does not only know the duration of her life. She is aware of the value of her adventure, and she very quickly knows that she wants to become a saint.'[209] There follows the text which has just been cited, according to the *Story of a Soul*.[210] 'To achieve this,' Pierre Mabille goes on, 'she invented a new way, the "exploration of love".'[211] 'Christian faith now addresses itself to the heart. It no longer tries to prove either by reasoning or by exegesis; it wants to touch.'[212] From then on, the Church has only 'disdain for knowledge, effective knowledge'.[213]

'Thérèse will find herself engaged in the exaltation of her faith, exaltation in the form of love (contact with the heart of Jesus), lacking a link either with rational knowledge or with effective social activity.'[214] And Mabille analyses the 'masochistic form'[215] of Thérèse's love towards Jesus. He emphasizes the negation of external reality:[216] 'In Thérèse's writings one cannot find a single page in which things and beings are not done down, condemned in order to be able to exalt celestial bliss and dreams of after death. Not only is the external world thus vilified, but the whole sphere of the intelligence and of knowledge is held in contempt.' [217] 'The contemporary thrust towards a somewhat simplistic realism is in fact only a salutary reaction to this gangrene. Work, objective research, activity in the struggle to improve the human condition are immediate remedies against the invasion of these psychopathies.'[218]

The last pages of the book are devoted to 'Christianity understood as dualism in love'.[219] Thérèse experienced the separation between 'material love' and 'immaterial love' and schematizes all the damage that can be caused by 'this Catholic doctrine' which is 'far from being the love and consolation that it claims to be. What a mistake to consider it, as Jaurès does, "the song which down the centuries has cradled human pain".[220] On the contrary, and we have just noted Thérèse as a typical example, it is the monstrous agent which engenders pain, moral ruin and death.'[221]

In conclusion, Pierre Mabille asks that people of his time should 'be monistic, in other words rediscover the profound unity in themselves... guide yourselves towards the unity of your being'.[222]

How does Mabille see Easter 1896, the text of which he quotes?

'Thus in the minutes of lucid awareness Thérèse expresses this total, painful and tragic void at which she has arrived... her hope made vain since it is directed towards an inaccessible object.'[223]

One cannot reject back-handedly, in a haughty way, a text like this, the author of which is profoundly sincere and truly revolted by what he considers an immense danger to the future of civilization, this 'Christian idea' – and here he refers to Nietzsche – which is 'the infernal machine of an invading negativism'.[224] And Thérèse is taken as a significant expression of this 'infernal machine'. Such a book cannot fail to make us ask ourselves questions.

First of all, one fact cannot be denied: Mabille quotes the texts which he has at his disposal – and does so precisely – but these are the texts of the *Story of a Soul*, and not Thérèse's true texts. If we take the first text that he quotes, we shall once more discover the transformation of it made by mother Agnes.[225] Here is the true text of Manuscript A (32), in which Thérèse speaks of her admiration for Joan of Arc and says that Jesus has made her understand that there is another way: 'I considered that I was born for glory and when I searched out the means of attaining it, God inspired in me...' There is no longer any question of 'it was revealed to me in my heart', which is smug and irritating.

Here is another passage from the *Story of a Soul* quoted by Mabille, set side by side with the authentic text; this is about Thérèse being sent to boarding school at the age of eight:

Story of a Soul (Mabille, 43) Agnes	*Autobiographical manuscripts* Thérèse
It was useful for the little flower to plunge her roots often into the loved and chosen earth of the family, because only there could it find its necessary food.	The poor little flower had become accustomed to burying her fragile roots in a chosen soil made purposely for her. It seemed hard for her to see herself among flowers of all kinds with roots frequently indelicate; and she had to find in this common soil the food necessary for her sustenance (A,22).

From the text which he has before him, Mabille concludes that it would have been impossible for Thérèse to 'adapt herself to an active social life',[226] and we can understand him, whereas in the true text Thérèse simply says that it was 'hard' for her to be transplanted to the boarding school and to have to find nourishment there in a different milieu from that of the family.

Mother Agnes travesties the text completely: she shows a Thérèse incapable of adapting socially and offers an almost totalitarian eulogy of the 'family'. Now happily Thérèse had these five years in the boarding school: otherwise she would have been truly asocial; for even if she suffered during them, these years were beneficial.[227]

A third and last example – so as not to give too many – relates to a quotation from the end of Manuscript B:

Story of a Soul (Mabille, 56) *Agnes*	*Autobiographical manuscripts* *Thérèse*
For as long as you wish, I will stay with my eyes fixed on you, longing to be *fascinated* by your divine gaze,[228] longing to be the prey of your love. One day, I hope,[229] you will swoop upon me and, carrying me off to the hearth of love, will at last plunge me into its glowing abyss, that I may become for ever the happy victim (Chapter XI).	As long as you desire it, O my Beloved, your little bird will remain without strength and without wings and will always stay with its gaze fixed on you. It wants to be *fascinated* by your divine look; it wants to become the *prey* of your Love. One day I hope that you, Adored Eagle, will come to fetch me, Your little bird, and ascending with it to the hearth of Love, you will plunge it for all eternity into the burning Abyss of This Love to which it has offered itself as victim (B,5).

Mabille is confronted with Mother Agnes' text, which eliminates the allegory of the Eagle and the little bird and at the same time emphasizes the word 'prey' on which God is going to 'swoop';

this is a movement when God comes like a thunderbolt to carry Thérèse off to the 'Fire of Love'. Faced with this transformed and travestied text, Mabille is right to speak of 'vulgar expressions' and 'an exalted masochism'![230]

It will be noted that Mother Agnes has suppressed 'God' in the first text in favour of an impersonal revelation; that she has suppressed the school and Thérèse's confrontation with the other children of her time in the second; that she has suppressed the 'O my Beloved', which is so expressive, and the very symbolic 'Adored Eagle' in the third text. God becomes impersonal and thus appears sadistic.

In a few words, Mother Agnes's universe unfolds and unveils itself before our eyes: flight from the world, withdrawal into the cocoon of the family, a reification of love contrary to what it really is, namely verve and freedom, fire and joy. In the name of this universe she sets out to transform Thérèse's text in ways which some want at all costs to regard as benign, but which are serious and so significant.

It was under the priorate and the impulse of Mother Agnes in the three years leading up to March 1896 that Thérèse wrote Manuscript A, essentially her childhood memories. During this priorate the forty-six letters which Thérèse wrote were restricted to the family. Mother Agnes unconsciously wanted to confine Thérèse to her family and the spirituality which was that of the Martin family. When she corrected Manuscript A, she did so in the name of this universe of hers, in the name of a conception of hidden life which was synonymous with being closed in on oneself, in the name of a theology of redemption which emphasized asceticism and reparation for the faults of sinners, in other words for those outside the family circle, the family of the 'saved'. She went further still in her transformations, which affect not only words and phrases, but the very structure of the text; since this is a history, one can rightly wonder about the dualism implied by the *Story of a Soul*. History is forgotten, the soul is no longer in history, or rather history becomes the account of what takes place in a closed world, a world in which, for example, no one goes to school. Instead of history, instead of giving us Thérèse's writings in the sequence in which they were written, in the *Story of a Soul* Mother Agnes gives us, after

Manuscript A, Manuscript C which is dated June 1897 and only then Manuscript B, which dates from September 1896. This is a significant reversal of order. We must not forget the structure of *Story of a Soul* as Mother Agnes has constructed it: eleven chapters, with titles and sub-titles which enclose and reduce. The two last subtitles of Chapter II are eloquent: 'Sublime childhood', 'Call to all little souls'. Thus Mother Agnes is profoundly logical with herself; faithful to the human and spiritual education which she had received, she keeps the faith. She brings Thérèse to the world and shows her to the world in her own way: she makes her sister an example against the world, an example which she brandishes and will not cease to brandish until her death; but what she thus shows is above all herself and her own spirituality.

It must be emphasized again that we have seen the difference between the period of the priorate of mother Agnes and the last eighteen months of Thérèse's life, under the priorate of Mother Marie de Gonzague. One sign is that of the eighty-one letters which Thérèse wrote then, during precisely sixteen months, half are sent outside the family circle. It is the new prioress who brings out this verve, this openness to the world; she is the source of the new style and content of what Thérèse writes, and what is to become Manuscripts B and C.

However, this was only a very brief parenthesis, little more than a year. After her death Thérèse was taken up again by the family circle, which put all its energies into making her its affair, which again imprisoned her in the maternal bosom of Mother Agnes and her spirituality.

Pierre Mabille wrote in 1937, forty years after Thérèse's death, forty years of a Thérèsian desert methodically organized by Agnes's universe. Silence. A child was killed. Like Mabille, Bernanos was well aware of this. The love to which Thérèse bears witness, a blazing love, inventive, open to all, a passionate love for those who think and live otherwise, a love which expresses itself through brotherly charity, full of humour towards everyone in the narrow convent in which she lived, this love was proclaimed to the world but was given so pale and false an image that it lost all its savour and all its truth.

The sinners

Among the sinners there was Loyson. On 19 August 1897, the day on which Thérèse took communion for the last time, there was a festival at the Carmel for St Hyacinth, and this name could not fail to evoke or suggest Hyacinth Loyson, since he occupied a great place in the history of the nineteenth-century Carmel.

Fr Loyson, a Carmelite, had become preacher at Notre-Dame in 1864 at the age of thirty-seven and was tremendously success-ful. Superior of the Paris Carmel, he was sent to London by his order; he met Newman there and thought that nothing was to be expected from the Vatican Council which was about to open. The church needed to reform itself, and so did the Carmelites: 'The reformers went out of the order to found another order alongside,' he wrote. 'That is a law. I do not think that one can reform the Roman church while remaining within it.' He was soon attacked for his positions by the Carmelites, who were Ultramontanists. He left his order to a great uproar in 1869; people talked about a 'new Luther'.

Loyson married in 1872 and founded a Gallican Catholic Church in which he proposed the election of bishops by the faithful, mass in the national language, and the marriage of priests. A great idealist and a very religious soul, he favoured peace: 'The victory will go to the one who has the least hatred and the most love.' 'I love the church while fighting it, and I fight it because I love it.' In 1893 *Le Figaro* published the programme of his 'new religion'. He constantly travelled all over France to give lectures, at which he encountered hostility and gained supporters.

Loyson had a son who, like Thérèse, was born in 1873. This son left all religion and his father was desperate at seeing him 'in the camp of the impious'.

The Carmel regarded Loyson as an apostate for whom they never ceased to pray. 'Perhaps there never was an apostate for whose conversion Carmelites offered so many prayers, fasts and macerations', wrote his biographer,[231] who speaks of Sister Thérèse of the Child Jesus. The Lisieux Carmel in fact sent a copy of the *Story of a Soul* to Loyson, saying that it had 'offered its prayers and its sufferings to God' for his 'conversion'. Loyson, thanking the Carmel for sending the book, picked up the word, saying, 'What is called "my conversion" means my submission to teachings imposed by the Pope on consciences which abdicate into his hands.'

So Thérèse knew Loyson. She speaks at length of him, for example in a letter to Céline on 8 July 1891; she gives details of a lecture that he has just given in Caen:[232] 'Céline, he is really culpable, more culpable than any other sinner ever was who was converted.' She says that her 'only desire is to save a soul which seems to be lost for ever'.

In *Un prêtre marié*, Barbey d'Aurevilly had described the life of one of these men, who at this time were the object of immense reprobation. This married priest ultimately committed suicide; for the novelist, in these cases for which divine vengeance was inexorable, repentance itself was impossible.

Thérèse is in quite a different position: Jesus is the master of the impossible. Even if Loyson is the greatest sinner imaginable, 'Cannot Jesus do once what He has not yet ever done?', she asks Céline.

What is very important is to see that while Loyson is a great sinner in Thérèse's eyes, she never speaks of divine vengeance, nor does she despair of his conversion. Better, she continues to call him 'our brother', and finally and above all, after she uses this the term which indicates 'the table of sinners' at which she will take her place, calling them her 'brothers', there is a tiny phrase which avoids all the Pharisaisms: 'No one knows whether he is just or a sinner.'

This is the one for whom she offers her communion, which will be her last communion, on 19 August. It is as if Jesus was taking her at her word: this suffering, thereafter, of no longer being able to take communion, this extreme void and lack, is offered to Thérèse to experience for the man who in her eyes is so to speak the prototype of sinners, of her 'brothers'. One might think that to the end, as in the case of Pranzini, Thérèse hoped that Loyson would leave his uncompromising position and open himself to the heart of God.[233] But was he not already open? For who is a sinner and who is righteous? Thérèse recognized that she herself was in the camp of the sinners, and none of the eulogies made of her virtues changed that conviction in any way. In this communion, as Sister Marie of the Eucharist has testified, she physically 'suffered martyrdom'. Perhaps she also experienced another suffering thinking of Loyson, her proud, stubborn brother. But perhaps Thérèse, who was in process of suffering the just around her, also had compassion and brotherly tenderness for Hyacinth Loyson, who himself had had to suffer at the hands of a church of the just and was in revolt against it.

'The bliss of Heaven is not what attracts me'

The last letter which Thérèse wrote before her death is dated 10 August: it is addressed to Abbé Bellière. Two months earlier, on 9 June, she had sent him quite a long letter: it was a 'farewell' because she thought she would die soon.

Between 9 June and 10 August, a period during which Thérèse wrote several short notes to her novices or her family, we have only one long letter to the family, to M. and Mme Guérin on 16 July. The other important letters were addressed to Fr Roulland and Abbé Bellière who, like Pranzini, Taxil or Loyson, were also her 'brothers'. It seems that Thérèse used her last strength to write them; they occupy a very important place in her life up to the end and, as we shall see, she entrusted last confidences to them. Both were 'missionaries'. Abbé Bellière, a year younger than she, was still a seminarian; he was to embark at Marseilles for Algiers and the noviciate of the White Fathers on 29 September 1897, the eve of Thérèse's death. Fr Roulland was three years older than Thérèse: a priest of the Foreign Missions, he embarked in September 1896 for China. It was Mother Agnes, then prioress, who had designated Abbé Bellière a spiritual brother for Thérèse, but it was in October 1896, under the priorate of Mother Marie de Gonzague, that a correspondence began between them; and it was Mother Marie de Gonzague who gave Thérèse a second brother, Fr Roulland. This brought her a very lively joy and 'filled' her desire 'in an unexpected way'.[234]

Abbé Belliére had spoken of his 'beautiful years wasted' and of his sins. On 21 June Thérèse brushes all that aside. Is he a sinner? 'Ah! Brother, like me you can sing the mercies of the Lord', and she evokes Mary Magdalene in the same terms as those she uses of her right at the end of her black notebook: '*her heart* has understood the abysses of love and mercy of the *Heart of Jesus*'. 'The remembrance of my faults humbles me,' she confides, 'but this remembrance speaks to me of mercy and love.' She then locates her way: 'I know that there are some saints who spent their life in the practice of astonishing mortifications to expiate their sins, but what of it? "There are many mansions in the house of my heavenly Father," Jesus has said, and it is because of this that I follow the way He is tracing out for me. I try to be no longer occupied with myself in anything, and I abandon myself to what Jesus sees fit to do in my soul, for I have not chosen an austere life to expiate my faults but those of others.' There is no turning in on herself: her act of abandonment goes even so far as to leave her faults to God.

Will not Abbé Bellière have been perplexed on reading these lines? 'I have just read over my note, and I wonder whether you are going to understand me,' she goes on to write, 'for I have expressed myself very poorly. Do not think that I condemn the repentance you have for your faults and your desire to expiate them.' But she is there to expiate his faults for him. 'Above all,' she concludes, 'I hope that one day Jesus will make you walk by the same way as myself.'

We have seen the links which became established with, as she told Mother Marie de Gonzague, 'your dear spiritual sons who are my brothers',[235] 'my brothers who now have such a large place in my life',[236] as she writes in her notebook in the middle of June 1897. What is the nature of these links? 'See how I am spiritually united to the apostles whom Jesus has given me as brothers: all that I have, each of them has.'[237] What does she mean? That the love with which Jesus has set her on fire is communicated to them. And that this 'communion of saints' will continue even beyond death, so that they may make Love known better.

This is in fact an extremely powerful desire on the part of this young Carmelite in process of dying: to continue to work on earth after her death.[238] She does not envisage heaven as a refuge and a rest, but as a place where an action, a flow of love to earth, can continue. She expresses this clearly. Sister Geneviève has passed on her thought to us precisely in a letter to Mme Guérin dated 22 July 1897: 'The other day I was reading her a passage on the bliss of Heaven when she interrupted me to say, "That's not what attracts me." "Then what does?" "Oh, love, to love, to be loved and to return to earth."'[239]

'Return to earth': to Fr Roulland, to whom she wrote for the last time on 14 July – 'When you receive this letter, no doubt I shall have left this earth' – she indicates what she is going to do in Heaven when Jesus has opened his kingdom to her: 'I shall be able to draw from his treasures in order to lavish them on the souls who are dear to me. Believe, Brother, that your little sister will hold to her promises, and her soul, freed from the weight of the mortal envelope, will joyfully fly towards the distant regions that you are evangelizing. Ah! Brother, I feel it, I shall be more useful to you in Heaven than on earth.' It is certain that Jesus will give her 'the means of helping' her brother 'more effectively' in his apostolic works': 'I really count on not remaining inactive in heaven. My desire is to work still for the church and for souls. I am asking God for this and I am certain He will hear me.'

On 9 June she had affirmed to Abbé Bellière – and this is a way of 'returning to earth' – 'All that I cannot say to you here below, I will make you understand from the heights of heaven.' When she tells him on 21 June, 'You know, now we are *two*, the work will be done more quickly', she is thinking that her 'way', as she says, abandonment to Love, a different 'manner' from that of Abbé Bellière, who is still entangled in fear and mortifications, is more effective:[240] 'I with *my way* will do more than you.' She will continue to do this work with him after death. She repeats this on 13 July: 'I shall do more than write to my dear little Brother, more even than speak to him in the fatiguing language of this earth. I shall *be very close* to him, I shall see all that is necessary for him and I shall give God no rest if He does not give me all I want' (viz., for you). 'When my dear little Brother leaves for Africa, I shall no longer follow him by thought, by prayer; my soul will be always with him... *to the last day of his life.*' This is certainly an echo of the saying of Jesus when he sends his disciples on their mission after the resurrection: 'I am with you always, even to the end of the world.'[241] Since she will be with Jesus, with him she will be close to her missionary brother.

Thérèse is well aware of having made almost excessive statements, and she puts herself in the Abbé's place on reading this letter: 'all these promises, Brother, may perhaps appear to you somewhat chimerical'. But she persists, and she signs the letter. What are her arguments? Jesus 'has always made me desire what he wanted to give me. Will he begin then in heaven not to carry out my desires any more? Truly, I cannot believe it, and I say: "Soon, little Brother, I shall be near you."'

Poor Abbé Bellière does not understand her. An orphan who has attached himself to Thérèse, he is on the point of losing her: 'What a blow to my poor heart. It was so little prepared, do not ask of it this joy you feel at the approach of bliss... no mother, no family, it was concentrating on its sister's love, confident in being sustained,' he replies to her on 17 August, in a letter which shows how lost he feels without her. When she received this letter, Thérèse replied to it – on the 18th. What he has understood of her joy at the approach of heaven has particularly attracted her attention; she explains herself by taking up what she had said to Sister Geneviève about the 'bliss of heaven' and her lack of interest; at the same time she hints at what she feels: 'The thought of heavenly bliss... does not cause me any joy[242]... it is the thought alone of accomplishing the Lord's will that makes up all my joy.' She had already written on 14 July to Fr Roulland: 'If I am already leaving the battlefield it is not with the selfish desire of taking my rest. The thought of eternal bliss hardly thrills my heart.'[243] This is the echo that we find again in her letter of 22 July to Sister Geneviève. And we may remember the important letter of 19 March to Fr Roulland, in which she exclaims: 'I would like to save souls and forget myself for them; I would like to save them even after my death.' It is this action to be realized in heaven which interests her, and not bliss.

We should note that between March and July she has advanced to a further stage; in March, when death was more uncertain, she said, 'I would be happy to work and suffer a long time for him.' But His will is to be done: 'Whether to love Him by suffering or to go to rejoice in Him in Heaven.' Now that death is evident, she is hesitant about the aspect of 'going to rejoice in him in Heaven'.

The profound reason for this is that Thérèse, a realist for whom everything is grist to her mill, has become so to speak adapted to suffering, to suffering born of spiritual trial, since Easter 1896, and to the physical suffering which has been added for the first time for some months now.[244] She has learned to cope with this twofold suffering; she has literally made it her heaven. 'Suffering,' she tells Fr Roulland on 14 July, 'has become my Heaven here below.' And she takes up the saying of St John of the Cross which she had quoted on 19 March to Fr Roulland: 'When you find suffering sweet and when you love it for the love of Jesus Christ, you will have found Paradise on earth.' She adds: 'This paradise is really that of the missionary and the Carmelite... The works and sufferings are a very sweet reality, a foretaste of the happiness of Heaven.' But if in March she experienced suffering as a 'foretaste of the happiness of heaven', now she is disconcerted, since in heaven there will be neither works nor sufferings: 'I really have trouble,' she says to Fr Roulland on 14 July, 'in conceiving how I shall be able to acclimatize myself in a country where joy reigns without any admixture of sadness. Jesus will have to transform my soul and give it the capacity to rejoice, otherwise I shall not be able to put up with eternal delights.' 'I sometimes ask myself,' she writes to Abbé Bellière on 18 July, 'how it will be possible to be happy without suffering.' So she is disconcerted by the unmingled joy which will be the delight of heaven; she then thinks that it will be for Jesus to adapt her to this. Since she cannot see for a moment how she will be able to do it, she abandons himself to Him up there as well. But she tells herself that if, in heaven, there will no longer be these 'sufferings'[245] which she now knows well, there will always be 'works' – which she desires and asks firmly for from Jesus. She can describe to Fr Roulland the twofold face of Heaven which attracts her: 'The hope of loving Him finally as I have so much desired to love Him, and the thought that I shall be able to make him loved by a multitude of souls, who will bless him eternally.'

So her desire is not for 'the bliss of Heaven', but for love; to meet Him whom she loves and to continue to make him loved.

This is what she tells Sister Geneviève on 22 July as a programme for heaven: 'To love, to be loved and to return to earth.'
On 9 June she had written that 'the thought of Heaven', 'up till
then so sweet', was no longer anything but 'the cause of struggle
and torment'[246] for her; that 'now this trial' had taken away
'everything that could be a natural satisfaction in [her] desire for
heaven'.[247] And on 13 July she told Abbé Bellière the only
reason which made her happy to die: she felt that 'this is the will
of God'. But she does not speak to him in any way of the
happiness of Heaven; for the moment, that remains a void for
her. The 'dear little brother' did not understand at all,[248] and
with good reason: 'Ah,' she tells him on the 18th, 'if you could
read my soul for a few minutes, how surprised you would be!'
He is in fact far from thinking that she is in darkness. And who
could think it, seeing her happy at the thought of dying? Who
could imagine that the clouds of the 'night of nothingness' were
continuing to pass over her, this night which she described so
recently, on 9 June, to Mother Marie de Gonzague? We must
remind ourselves again of this night, for it did not cease to exist,
even while Thérèse was writing these pages to her two brothers.
It was this night which constantly led her to 'recognize her
nothingness' before God, as she writes to Abbé Bellière on 26
July.

The fruits of Easter 1896

Here we can ask an important question. What did that night of
Easter 1896 produce in Thérèse?

First of all there is an answer that we can certainly give. Her
trial, by taking from her all her natural desire for heaven, led her
to be involved in, to throw herself into, the 'present moment' – a
moment composed only of love. She no longer desired anything
other than to love as much as possible, to love day after day and
ultimately to die of love. She says this on 9 June: 'I no longer
have any great desires except that of loving to the point of dying
of love.' Thus it is the impossibility of escaping upwards,
banging herself against a wall and a closed horizon, which, one
might say, leads her to fall back with realism and intensity on
what remains to her: to love there, 'now' – this word which she

constantly repeats in her black notebook – and finally to die, but to die of love, death still being a 'now' of love.

But in connection with this question of Easter 1896 there is another perspective which we must consider, at least as a hypothesis. This kind of petrification of her great desires for Heaven produced by Easter 1896, which led her to stop thinking of eternity and to live in the here and now of everyday love, also led her to renounce the 'happiness of heaven' to the point of wanting 'to return to earth', to the point of wanting to make her life after death not 'the eternal possession of the Creator',[249] but an action of love here below.

Let us review the stages:

– before Easter 1896 the thought of Heaven was all her happiness: she rejoiced in heaven on earth;

– at Easter 1896, Heaven became blurred. How did she react? 'I tell Him, Jesus, that I am happy not to enjoy this beautiful heaven on this earth.'[250] To what end? 'So that He will open it for all eternity to poor unbelievers.' And she makes the suffering of her trial her Heaven on earth;

– when she knows that this life on earth, this life in the night, in suffering, is soon going to end, she asks herself questions. She has become accustomed to this suffering which she has made her Heaven on earth, but she does not see what the life of Heaven could be:

– a new reaction, a new step forward is to say: in the Heaven where I shall be, in the Heaven where I shall finally be able to know all the love of Jesus, I do not want to forget earth and turn my back on it. It is impossible for me to be shut up in eternal bliss; I want to 'return to earth', to work – there is work to be done – so that Love may be better known and loved.

This development confirms the hypothesis that Easter 1896 drives her to want to 'return to earth'. Thus this is not only night but a light in the night, a ray in the darkness.

What work, in Heaven, does she want to do on earth? She repeats this on 18 July: 'When I am in port, I shall teach you, dear little brother of my soul, how you must sail the stormy sea of the world with the abandonment and the love of a child who knows that his Father loves him.' 'I shall help you a lot to walk by this way,' she adds.

'But why speak to you of the life of trust and love? I explain myself so poorly that I must wait for heaven in order to converse with you about this happy life. What I wanted to do today was to console you.' 'I must bear with myself such as I am with all my imperfections,' she had written at the beginning of June 1897, 'but I want to seek out a means of going to heaven by a little way, a way that is very straight, very short, and totally new. We are living now in an age of inventions, and we no longer have to take the trouble of climbing stairs, for, in the homes of the rich, an elevator has replaced these very successfully. I wanted to find an elevator which would raise me to Jesus, for I am too small to climb the rough stairway of perfection.'²⁵¹ She will reveal – they will be the very last words of Manuscript C – that 'I raise myself to Him by trust and love.'²⁵² Clearly this is her way, and no other.²⁵³

She says again at the end of her letter: 'My soul will not cease to *smile* at you when it is near you.' And she signs it: 'To my *dear and much loved* brother, believe that I shall be for all eternity *your true* little sister.'

Mother Marie de Gonzague sent Abbé Bellière a photograph of Thérèse taken on 7 June. The Abbé found what he had 'won': 'This is no longer strictly abstract, it is you now,' he wrote to Thérèse on 21 July. 'You have given me this joy of possessing you almost really near me, always with me.' He agrees that Thérèse's soul can smile on him from Heaven, but he is happy to have this photograph, which is very concrete.²⁵⁴ He has understood what Thérèse wrote to him, about the 'work' done together: 'We shall leave for the desert, we shall be missionaries,' he tells her. In part he has got over the suffering of her imminent death. Above all he has grasped Thérèse's thought and desire to 'enter into love and trust'.

'How much your letter pleased me!' Thérèse replied to him on 26 July. In fact he was entering on this way which she had traced out for him in her letter of 21 June: we may remember what she had written to him: 'I hope that one day Jesus will make you walk by the same way as myself.' That had happened. She is happy if her 'exile' has been 'prolonged' to allow her to help him enter into the 'life of trust and love'. Returning to the questions of the faults that he has brought up again: 'You cannot know me very well if you fear that a detailed account of your faults may diminish the tenderness I have for your soul!' 'Jesus,' she assures him, 'has long forgotten your infidelities.' Finally she promises him once again that she will continue to be close to him: 'I promise to have you taste after my departure for eternal life the happiness one can find in feeling a friendly soul next to oneself.' And she is happy about the way that he is choosing. 'Ah! Brother, how little known are the *goodness, the merciful love* of Jesus...The way of simple and loving trust is well made for you.' 'I hope to write to you again if the trembling of my hand does not increase, for I was obliged to write my letter in several stages.'

'The brotherly tenderness of the Blessed'

He replied to her on Thursday 5 August. Clearly he had not yet properly grasped the way of trust and love. However, on 26 July, having said to him, 'He [Jesus] has long forgotten your infidelities', she had told him with authority: 'I have noted, more so than in your other letters, that you are *forbidden* to go to Heaven by any other way than that of your little sister.' He has retrogressed, and one passage of his letter literally makes Thérèse jump. This has given us a text – Thérèse's last long text, which sums her up admirably – a kind of extraordinary testament which contains all her thought on justice and love. In it she proclaims the tenderness of God towards human beings; and since the saints participate in this divine tenderness, they have only 'fraternal tenderness' for those who are still on earth. This text is in direct line with what Thérèse had written two months earlier in her black notebook on the subject of the 'inexpressible tenderness'[255] which Jesus showed to his disciples at the Last Supper.[256] He wants us to love others with this tenderness – and Thérèse dared to say, simply, to Mother Marie de Gonzague: 'My beloved Mother, it is this tenderness with which I love you, and I love my sisters.'[257]

Here is this text with all its verve and vigour, a text written at the heart of a long agony, as a last burst, written by someone who had difficulty in holding her pencil,[258] exhausted by suffering, a text of immense theological significance.

I tell you, little brother, that we do not understand Heaven in the same way. It seems to you that sharing in the justice, in the holiness of God, I would be unable as on earth to excuse your faults. Are you forgetting, then, that I shall be sharing also in the *infinite mercy* of the Lord? I believe that the Blessed have great compassion on our miseries; they remember, being weak and mortal like us, that they committed the same faults, sustained the same combats, and their fraternal tenderness becomes greater than it was when they were on earth, and for this reason, they never cease protecting us and praying for us.[259]

This text is truly Thérèse's last text, her 'last words'.

I do not want to say anything about Thérèse's last days,[260] or about her death; this took place on Thursday 30 September a little after 7 p.m., while the rain was falling on Lisieux.

Mother Agnes immediately sent word to Léonie and to M. and Mme Guérin: 'Our Angel is in heaven. She gave her last sigh at seven o'clock, pressing her crucifix to her heart and saying, "Oh! I love you!" She had just lifted her eyes to heaven; what was she seeing!!!!'[261]

She was buried on 4 October in the town cemetery, in a plot which Uncle Guérin had just bought for the Carmel. Léonie led the mourning.

On 10 October Sister Geneviève wrote to Brother Simeon: 'Before giving her last sigh she seemed to be in ecstasy. The sisters believe that at that time she caught a glimpse of a little corner of Paradise.'

On 29 October Mother Marie de Gonzague wrote to Fr Madelaine: 'The last events which have taken place here have left me almost lifeless: I don't know where I am or where I'm going. The death of our angel has left a void in me which will never be filled.'

On 11 November the prioress wrote to Fr Roulland: 'The dear treasure left us on 30 September in a surge of love after three months of great suffering and several days of a painful agony... Her smile, which she kept to the last moment, was ravishing, never a complaint. On the last day she said to me:

"Mother, my cup is full and I cannot take any more – But what if Jesus wants it to overflow? I want that too, I want it too."'

Notes

Method

1. Paris: Saint-Paul 1950.
2. It is surely another personal projection on the part of Mother Agnes when she says to Thérèse on 15 August: 'How I sense your agony! And yet it's a month ago that you were saying such beautiful things about the death of love' (LC, 148). Mother Agnes 'senses'; she interprets and knows, while Thérèse keeps quiet.
3. B, 4.
4. B, 3.
5. B, 5.
6. Maurice Viller, 'Abandon', *Dictionnaire de spiritualité I*, Paris: Beauchesne, col.21.
7. Jacques Le Brun, *Esprit*, August-September 1985, 107.
8. Ibid., 108.
9. Ibid. (cf. M.de Certeau and his studies on Surin).
10. Ibid.
11. Ibid.
12. Cf. Jean-Francois Six, *Thérèse de Lisieux au Carmel*, Paris: Seuil 1973 (Chapter IV: 'Le Carmel de France au XIXe siècle').
13. Ibid., 122.
14. Louis-Marie, 'Thérèse de Jésus', *Dictionnaire de spiritualité* (n.6), col.658.
15. Ibid.
16. Ibid., col.659.
17. Ibid., col.660.
18. Yellow Notebook, 10 July 1897, LC, 85.
19. B, 5.
20. B, 3.
21. Yellow Notebook, 15 May 1897, LC, 43.
22. Yellow Notebook, 23 June 1897, LC, 67.
23. Paris: Beauchesne 1973.

24. One proof, among others, is that in the Yellow Notebook, under the date of 20 August 1897 (LC, 159), with an additional text dated 21 August (LC, 161f.), we have a long discourse made up of words 'spoken' by Thérèse. The commentator (Père Gaucher?) in the French edition is inevitably bothered about what he calls 'this long exposition' (p.574), since he has to recall that 'in this period of August, Thérèse was quite incapable of speaking at such length' (574). Then instead of acknowledging that it was all constructed by Mother Agnes – who moreover made two attempts – the commentator evades the problem by saying that it is 'the date' of these unwarranted developments which is 'without doubt fictitious' (574). What date? What proof? It is the text as such, presented as coming from Thérèse, that is fictitious: it is a 'Mother Agnes fiction'.

25. Nouvelle Édition du centenaire, Paris: Cerf-DDB 1992.

26. A note in the French edition of the *Last Conversations* (p.51) tells us in connection with Mother Marie de Gonzague: 'A complete exploration of the archives of the Carmel and documents of the period will certainly allow us to discover the truth even more closely.' It is ninety years since Mother Marie de Gonzague was slandered. It is high time to bring out these documents to do her at least a degree of justice.

1. A Faith on Trial

1. C, 4.
2. Ibid.
3. A, 45.
4. A, 82 and 83.
5. Ibid.
6. Ibid.
7. Ibid.
8. C, 5.
9. A, 14.
10. A, 17.
11. A, 36.
12. C, 4 and 5.
13. C, 5.
14. Ibid.
15. Ibid.

16. A, 80.
17. Ibid.
18. P.Descouvemont (DLTH, 182) builds a somewhat confused romance on this. Mother Agnes firmly suppressed this important episode of the confession to Père Alexis from *Story of a Soul*.
19. A, 80.
20. Cf. Jean-François Six, *Thérèse de Lisieux au carmel*, Paris: Seuil 1973, Ch.IV, 113–36.
21. Mother Agnes has attested that at this moment 'fear of offending God poisoned her life' (PO, 157). Mother Agnes neither saw nor understood that in fact Thérèse was under the constraints of customary spirituality at the Carmel and that she aspired to go beyond it, to live out quite a different spirituality.
22. C, 5.
23. Ibid.
24. Ibid.
25. *Story of a Soul*, Chapter 9.
26. Here is an example of this evasion: in 1990 the *Dictionnaire de spiritualité*, Paris: Beauchesne, published an article on 'Thérèse de l'Enfant Jésus et de la Sainte-Face' signed by Abbé Pierre Descouvemont (who is also the author of the texts in the volume of '600 documentary photographs', *Thérèse et Lisieux*, published by Éditions du Cerf in 1990). This article speaks essentially of the 'little way' of Thérèse of Lisieux. It is enough here to quote some lines from the review by L.Tudeau in *Vie thérésienne* (July 1990, 187–8), a journal to which Abbé Descouvement frequently contributes. Having spoken of the 'copious development along the little way', Tudeau writes: 'In the biography the author makes very brief mention of the *trial of faith* offered for unbelievers. One is surprised that this thought is not taken up in the spiritual synthesis.' So are we. Tudeau adds that this question of the trial of faith 'returns, however, in the part on "Influence", but this is above all in connection with a new summary on the question of doubt. If Thérèse had the temptation to doubt the world to come, that does not mean that she really doubted it. One cannot accuse Thérèse of having really doubted the existence of God, contrary to the texts, on the pretext of bringing her close to unbelievers.' Tudeau here expounds the thesis of Abbé Descouvemont, who writes text by text (and therefore not in Section III of his article entitled 'Spiritual Synthesis', but only in Section V, entitled 'In-

fluence'): 'Thérèse knew the *spiritual night* in the last eighteen months of her life. Stamped by the unbelief or the perverse belief of their brothers, Christians today are particularly sensitive to the fact that Thérèse experienced the temptation to doubt the other world. To bring her nearer to the atheists of our time, people have even gone so far as to say that at the end of her life she doubted the existence of God. The texts give the lie to such an interpretation. Her temptations to doubt never related to the existence of God but to the other world.' Abbé Descouvemont concludes from this that Thérèse experienced 'no real doubt' (col.605). L.Tudeau discreetly writes of this amazing statement by his colleague: 'All the same let us say that on this point one remains curious.' So do we.

The reader will have noted in particular the toing and froing between the 'existence of God' and the 'other world'. For Thérèse, the 'impious who have no faith' are the same as those who 'deny the existence of Heaven' (C, 5, 241).

27. C, 5.
28. For the one and only time to our knowledge (but in the very complete 'Table of quotations' of the *Manuscrits autobiographiques*, Office central de Lisieux 1956, the term 'impious' has curiously been forgotten!).
29. C, 5.
30. Ibid.
31. Ibid.
32. C, 36.
33. C, 15.
34. Ibid.
35. Matt.12.31.
36. John 12.46.
37. C, 5 and 6.
38. John 1.5; 3.19; 9.41.
39. This is the only time she uses the word 'discouragement'.
40. She does not say' the trial of faith', as Guy Gaucher (MA, 333, 342, etc.) states; he also speaks (403) of the 'trial against faith'.
41. C, 5.
42. C, 7.
43. Ibid.
44. MA, 342.
45. B, 2.

46. C, 5.
47. Ibid.
48. Ibid.
49. C, 6.
50. Ibid.
51. Ibid.
52. C,7.
53. *L'Aventure du politique*, Paris: Critérion 1981, 91.
54. R. Laurentin has replied in *Thérèse de Lisieux* (cf. René Laurentin and Jean-François Six, *Verse et Controverse*, Paris: Beauchesne 1973, 113): 'You attacked one of my articles in *Le Figaro* dated 3 January 1972, saying: "The statement made by René Laurentin when he said that after 1896 Thérèse was inwardly seized by a radical atheism is a mistake on the historical level and nonsense on the theological level" (p.256 of your second volume and p.155 of your lecture to the Catho... in which you speak of "serious nonsense"). I grant that I used a deliberately ambiguous formula... You know the limits of journalism, in which one has to convey a mass of information in two pages.'
55. C, 11.
56. P. Descouvement, in the disturbing article on Thérèse de Lisieux in the *Dictionnaire de spiritualité*, writes of Thérèse's trial: 'Her spirit invaded by objections and "doubts", Thérèse does not doubt' (col.582). Similarly Paul Poupard: 'Thérèse enters the deep night of doubt... the nocturnal struggle in which love and the doubt of faith come face to face' (*Vie thérésienne*, February 1994, 11).
57. *Thérèse de Lisieux*, Paris 1973, 406.
58. Ibid., 409.
59. Letter of 26 April 1983, published by *Vie thérésienne* 127, 447–8.
60. In a lecture given in 1973, H.U.von Balthasar thought that it was Thérèse's 'constant need to return to herself... which perhaps deprived her of the possibility of being introduced by God to the true dark night' (special number of *Nouvelles de l'Institut catholique de Paris* on Thérèse of Lisieux, May 1973, 119–20). According to this conception, it would be a certain capacity of introspection – in which Thérèse is certainly a contemporary of Freud – that will have prevented her from welcoming 'the real dark night' sent by God. Our contemporaries, and those advanced in the

human sciences, would thus be deprived of the grace of the most profound mysticism by letting themselves be lured into this world of depth psychology... We cannot agree.'

61. 'Nuit', in J.Chevalier and A.Gheerbrant, *Dictionnaire de symboles*, Paris: Laffont 1969, 545.

62. C.A.Bernard, *Le Dieu des mystiques*, Paris: Cerf 1994, 519 (cf. here 'La nuit', 517–70). Cf. id., 'L'Amour sauveur dans la vie de sainte Thérèse de Lisieux', *Revue d'ascétique et de mystique*, July-September and October-December 1956.

63. And this confidence of Père Congar speaking of one of the three elements of the 'genius of Thérèse of Lisieux': 'For those who have genius, their profound perception of things *lasts*, whereas it is only transient among ordinary mortals. Without doubt I have been Thérèse of the Child Jesus for ten or fifteen minutes, feeling a disjunction of the soul like hers. But for her that lasted!' (*Annales de Thérèse de Lisieux*, May 1990, 4).

64. 'The symbol of night accompanies the movement of annihilation which ends up in the glorious resurrection'; cf. Bernard, *Dieu des Mystiques* (n.62), 521.

65. C, 1 to 7.

66. Yellow Notebook, 11 August 1897 (LC, 146).

67. B, 1.

68. Schopenhauerian pessimism seized this last quarter of the nineteenth century in which Thérèse lived and put its stamp on the whole of the twentieth century; Schopenhauer's work 'indeed originates in tragic existential philosophy; it is the source not only of the philosophy of Nietzsche and Wagner's librettos but also of the pessimism of Heidegger and the doctrines of the absurd' (Robert Misrahl, 'Schopenhauer', *Encyclopedia universalis*, 740). 'For us the last word of wisdom,' Schopenhauer will say, 'will henceforth consist in plunging ourselves in nothingness.' The French thinkers of the end of the nineteenth century show Schopenhauer's nihilism, his negative doctrine of the void of existence, and his constant way of preferring nothingness to being.

69. The book dates from 1873, the year of Thérèse's birth.

70. By contrast, when one ceases to militate against belief, one finds oneself in a state described by the *Grand Dictionnaire*, quoting Bonald: 'Indifference is the weariness of impiety.'

71. Jean-Pierre Rioux, *Chronique d'une fin de siècle, 1889–1900*, Paris: Seuil, 169.

72. Freemasonry had just been condemned by the Pope in the encyclical *Humanum Genus* (20 April 1884).
73. Isidore Guérin is violently antisemitic and anti-masonic in his articles in *Le Normand* (cf. J.-F. Six, *Vie de Thérèse de Lisieux*, Paris: Seuil 1975, 80–102).
74. E.Renault, 'Thérèse et l'affaire Léo Taxil', *Vie thérésienne* 116, October 1989, 212.
75. She was declared 'venerable' on 27 January 1894 (a great ceremony had taken place this same Tuesday, 8 May 1894, in the cathedral of Saint-Pierre de Lisieux in honour of Joan of Arc).
76. *Le Normand*, 6 September 1892.
77. Ibid., 13 December 1892.
78. 1 January 1894.
79. A, 28. In 1883 Isidore Guérin had been certain of that.
80. Ibid.
81. A, 76.
82. Ibid.
83. Ibid.
84. Ibid.
85. Ibid.
86. C,5.
87. Cf. Eugen Weber, *Satan franc-maçon. La Mystification de Léo Taxil*, Paris: Juillard 1964.
88. In C, 11.
89. Mother Agnes wanted to sanction this version, doubtless to tone down the bad effect given by the fact that the saint had allowed herself to be laughed at; she then declares (to the PO, 1910): 'The servant of God, who was primarily interested in these revelations, did not wait for the deluded official to pronounce that they do not deserve any credit. Now she based her reprobation on the sole fact that on one of these pages the supposed Diana Vaughan was speaking against the authority of a bishop.' This is edifying, but contrived and wrong: Thérèse believed to the end.
90. P.381.
91. Ibid., 215.
92. Rioux, *Chronique* (n. 71), 169.
93. Renault, 'Thérèse et Taxil' (n.74), 212.
94. Ibid., 215.
95. Ibid.
96. OE II, 471–2 (Renault, 'Thérèse et Taxil' [n.74], 215). This is a

text about which I have the greatest reservations; it would seem to be pure Mother Agnes and not Thérèse; for example, Thérèse would never have written the pejorative 'worst'.

97. In criticism of my *La Veritable Enfance de Thérèse de Lisieux*, published in 1972 (Paris: Seuil), a good Carmelite father, Conrad De Meester (*Ephemerides Carmeliticae* 1977, no.1), said that he doubted that 'the social and political life' of Lisieux was 'an important thing for the interpretation of Thérèse' (108). And he reproached me in particular for having drawn only 'a few quotations from the anti-clerical journal *Le Lexovien*', while I had produced 'a pile of extracts from the extreme right-wing journal *Le Normand*' (107). The reason why I quoted *Le Normand* so much was because it was edited by Thérèse's uncle Isidore Guérin, whose thought it was important to make known. But De Meester wants above all to emphasize that I have shown the anti-masonic (and anti-Jewish) virulence of *Le Normand* without exposing the anti-clerical virulence of the Republican *Lexovien*. Why not recognize that the anti-clerical virulence was in cahoots with the other?

98. Rioux, *Chronique* (n.71), 169.

99. C, 31.

100. For the festival of Joan of Arc at Lisieux on 8 May 1894, Céline and her cousin Marie Guérin put together twelve immense white streamers sewn with fleurs-de-lis (Joan of Arc and Thérèse both died young and only a few miles apart, in Normandy).

101. A, 32.

102. Ibid.

103. Ibid.

104. Ibid.

105. A, 84.

106. Ibid.

107. Ibid.

108. Ibid.

109. Ibid.

110. C, 7.

111. C, 6.

112. C, 7.

113. Note also how the text has been watered down by Mother Agnes: for Thérèse, her 'enemies' *come* to provoke her, in direct action; Mother Agnes speaks of the demon who *wants* to provoke

her. [Unfortunately Mother Agnes still dominates the translation of the text in the 'Critical Edition' which does not reproduce what Thérèse actually says.] At the Apostolic Process (1915–1917, 151), in her testimony she would say that Thérèse had confided to her: 'If you knew what terrible thoughts obsess me! Pray for me so that I do not hear the demon who wants to persuade me of so many lies.'

114. MA, note p.341.
115. Ibid.
116. C, 7.
117. As remarked by the commentator in the *Manuscrits autobiographiques* (note, p.256).
118. C, 11.
119. J.Ratzinger, 'Substitution', *Encyclopédie de la foi*, Paris: Cerf 1967, 273. Ratzinger concludes his article: 'The idea of substitution is one of the primitive facts of the biblical testimony, the rediscovery of which in today's world can help Christianity to renew and deepen in a decisive way the conception it has of itself' (cf. J.F.Six, 'De la prière à la compassion et à l'action', in *Présence de Louis Massignon*, Paris: Maisonneuve 1987, and J.-F.Six, *L'Aventure de l'amour de Dieu*, Paris: Seuil 1993, chapter 'La Badaliya', 277ff.). 'The term which characterizes the existence of Jesus Christ most centrally is that of substitution'; cf. H.Urs von Balthasar, 'Catholicisme et communion des saints', *Communio*, January-February 1988, 22. (According to Didier Anzieu, *Nouvelle Revue de psychoanalyse* 22, autumn 1980, 159, the Christian religion 'is the only one to speak of a mystical body'.)
120. B, 3.
121. Ibid.
122. She cites the same text of John of the Cross in B,4.
123. C,6.
124. Ibid.
125. Ibid.
126. C,12, [The English translation disastrously has 'fishermen' (*pêcheurs*) for Thérèse's 'sinners' (*pécheurs*)].
127. C,6.
128. Ibid.
129. Ibid.
130. As Mother Agnes indicates by transforming the text and adding: 'She sits for your love.' There, too, there is commiseration.

132. C, 6.

133. Mother Agnes transforms this by speaking of the 'bread of tears', which obliterates an important fact.

134. 'She reacted with the magnanimity of a saint, by forgiving' (E.Renault, 'Thérèse et Taxil' [n.74], 215). One cannot see where Thérèse pardoned Leo Taxil; she entered into brotherhood with him, so that God would pardon unbelievers, including Léo Taxil.

135. Renault, 'Thérèse et Taxil' (n.74), 215.

136. Ibid., 214.

137. This is underlined by the author of the article, but not in the text itself.

138. Ibid., 214–15.

139. B,4. In the notes on the Yellow Notebook (DE, 482), we are told: 'For Thérèse's demand for truth, her rejection of illusions, her taste for the real, cf...' There follows a whole series of references, all taken from the *Last Conversations*! The only certain quotation, B,4, is not given!

140. We find again in Fr Renault the fantastic distinction that Abbé Descouvemont had made in the *Dictionnaire de spiritualité*: 'Her temptations to doubt do not relate to the existence of God but to the other world' (one might also ask: what is a 'temptation to doubt'?).

141. C, 6.

142. A, 81.

143. Writing on the same day, 20 February, to Mother Agnes, Thérèse spoke of a 'veil' cast over this day.

144. Being a novice, Thérèse was not present at the turbulent election; her title of sub-mistress of novices was purely nominal; she was simply the 'doyenne' of the novices.

145. Letter 190 (GC 2, 958f.).

146. Céline entered the Carmel in 1894, when Mother Agnes, her sister, was prioress. She was enthusiastic about photography and was given permission to being her camera in. From 1894 to 1897 there are forty-one negatives on which Thérèse appears either in a community group or alone. Céline – Sister Geneviève – was also a painter; but her training had been very mediocre; she did not paint any portrait of Thérèse while Thérèse was alive. However, in 1899, when *Story of a Soul* became a success, since it was necessary to have a portrait of Thérèse as a frontispiece, Sister

Notes

Geneviève painted one in charcoal, making it as angelic as possible. Other drawings followed, millions of copies of which spread all over the world: 'As a result of this retouching, Thérèse appeared less in command of herself, much more dependent on those around her, on external injunctions: a little girl who wants to give pleasure, to be very good. By losing their differentiation the features no longer have that reflection of intelligence which lights up the photographs.' So writes Fr François de Sainte-Marie (in *Visage de Thérèse de Lisieux*, Office central de Lisieux, 37), who finally, in 1961, more than sixty years after the death of Thérèse, presented the real photographs taken at the Carmel. 'In the last century,' Fr François de Sainte-Marie also says (33, 41), 'the work of art appeared far more as the necessary idealization of reality...The sisters of the Carmel, living in a closed milieu, were influenced by a literature and an imagery in which the ideal tended gradually to supplant the real.' Mother Agnes and Sister Geneviève did not resist the temptation to be fully of their century and of the world; and they certainly did not think that this way of doing things would rapidly become a swindle which allowed thousands of churches all over the planet to be populated with what Claudel called 'standardized St Thérèses'.

147. MA, 218 (cf. *Oeuvres complètes*, 1266).
148. Written in bold characters. Thérèse later claimed that she was very severe to the novices (C, 23). She had been to a good school.
149. A, 70.
150. A, 26.
151. C,1.
152. Ibid.
153. Quoted by de Sainte-Marie, *Visage* (n.146), 14 n.10.
154. PA, 376.
155. PA, 2897.
156. C,4.
157. PA, 592 ('beloved [*bien-aimée*] mother' recurs thirty-nine times in manuscript C and 'dearest [*chérie*] mother' twenty-one times; the English translation confines itself to 'dear' for both).
158. Guy Gaucher, *The Passion of Thérèse de Lisieux* (1973), Homebush: Australia: St Paul Publications 1989, 25.
159. Thérèse writes in the first line of the manuscript in January 1895: 'To you who are twice my mother.'
160. Gaucher, *Passion* (n.158), 25.

161. Jean Vinatier, *Mère Agnès de Jésus*, Paris: Cerf 1993.
162. Thérèse relates how her sister Marie of the Trinity comes to tell her of a dream that she has had; she was with one of her sisters, Anna, whom she wanted to 'detach from all the vanities she loves so much' (C, 24); the religious thinks that 'God perhaps willed [her] to give Him this soul' (ibid.), and she says that the best thing would be to write to her to tell her this dream; Thérèse listens and replies 'that she could try' (ibid.), but adds that first she must ask permission from Mother Marie de Gonzague, who is novice mistress; she replies that it is 'not through letters that Carmelites must save souls but through prayer'.
163. For the commentator on the poems *(Poésies*, Nouvelle edition du centénaire, 158), 'between the child and the old person, between the novice on her knees with a malicious smile and the prioress seated, marked by the "irremediable outrage" of the passing years, Thérèse stands upright like a sweet and strong mediator, serene and grave'. Mother Marie de Gonzague had just turned sixty-two; she is not looking at the lens but is leaning forward; one has the impression that she does not like being photographed at all.
164. Sister Marie of the Trinity later boasted about this friendship with Thérèse and of the spiritual help which Thérèse lavished on her. And at the apostolic process she was to be particularly on the side of Mother Agnes, teaming up with her to attack Mother Marie de Gonzague, whom she did not like (we can understand how Mother Marie de Gonzague, faced with the criticisms of Sister Marie of the Trinity, could have wanted to send her to the Saigon Carmel with Mother Agnes and Sister Geneviève). The commentator on the *Manuscrits autobiographiques* is obliged to write (p.397, on C,28): 'It is regrettable that certain depositions of Thérèse's own sisters or of Marie of the Trinity, particularly at the apostolic process, could have suggested that apart from the Martin sisters the Carmelites of Lisieux were on the whole narrow-minded or lax. This romanticizing has been engaged in by Maxence Van der Meersch in *La Petite Sainte Thérèse*. Such Manicheanism must be shown up.'
165. We know that during the winter of 1947–1948 Bernanos, just before he died, was inspired by this event to write his *Dialogue of the Carmelites*, in which Christ's anguish and agony are evoked ceaselessly; thus, for example:
  ' – On the Mount of Olives, Christ is no longer master of

anything. Human anguish has never mounted so high, and it will never reach this level again. It had concealed everything in Him, except this extreme point of the soul in which the divine acceptance was consummated.

– He was afraid of death. So many martyrs have no fear of death...

– The martyrs were supported by Christ, but Christ had no help from anyone.'

166. C, 31. Her parents had very much wanted to have a son who would be a priest; two boys were born to them, but both died in infancy.

167. C, 32.

168. Ibid.

169. Ibid. Thérèse is mistaken here.

170. C, 10.

171. Ibid. The superiors of Mother Marie de Gonzague had prevented her in 1862 from going to replace the sisters of the Saigon Carmel who were exhausted by the heat and by adaptation.

172. C, 33.

173. Ibid. In *Story of a Soul*, Mother Agnes adds an 's' and transforms it into 'embrace'. [So does the English translation of Manuscript C!.]

174. Ibid.

175. Letter from Thérèse to Fr Roulland, 19 March 1897.

176. Thérèse pays attention, since the letter that Léonie addresses to her has first been read by her three elder sisters and she does not want her reply, which will also be read, to disturb Mother Agnes.

177. Song of Songs 4.9.

178. She had frequent bronchitis.

179. C, 9.

180. Ibid.

181. 'You understood their aspirations since you had asked in your own youthful days to go to Saigon. It is thus that the desires of mothers find an echo in the soul of their children' (C, 9–10). Mother Agnes will have been thirty-five on 7 September 1896. Marie de Gonzague had asked to leave for Saigon in 1862.

182. C, 10.

183. Ibid.

184. Ibid. It was with the same desire for exile of the heart that Charles de Foucauld left his people on 15 January 1890 to lose

himself in a poor priory founded in Syria by the Trappist Notre-Dame des Neiges; like Thérèse, he wanted to live unknown and in strict poverty.

185. C, 7.

186. M.Martin, Marie, Léonie, Céline and Thérèse were enrolled in the Confraternity of the Holy Face on 26 April 1885. In the garden of the house of Les Buissonets, M.Martin had installed an arbour which he christened the 'hermitage of the Holy Face'. When he was in the mental hospital of the Good Shepherd at Caen, the arbour was given to the Carmel. It was made to back on the avenue of chestnut trees; Thérèse put a painting on linen in it which she had painted from the model in Tours.

187. Letter to Mother Agnes, July-August 1889.

188. Sister Marie of St Peter joined in the movement for atoning devotion. Along this line, M.Martin had offered himself as a victim ('Victimal', *Dictionnaire de spiritualité*, col.543: 'The essential element by which the victim is acceptable to God is the offering of love... The antithesis "victim of justice/victim of love" no longer has any meaning; it is an opposition typical of past spirituality caused by the projection on to God of our human conception of justice, expiation and reparation... The victim is always the victim of love. This is the happy intuition of Thérèse of the Child Jesus who offers herself as a victim to "merciful love".').

189. The nine children of the Martin couple.

190. A, 71.

191. Letter of 14 July 1897 to Fr Roulland.

192. The Transfiguration is one of the main festivals of the Confraternity of the Holy Face.

193. Marie Guérin had entered the Lisieux Carmel on 15 September 1895 at the age of twenty-five. Thérèse reproached her cousin and novice for having been attached to her parents for too long; on 15 August 1896, at the end of the poem 'Jesus Alone', which she wrote for her, Thérèse discreetly reproached her: she insisted on the need to prove to Jesus the love one had for him, and to that end to surrender everything to him, including those one loved, family affections. The poem ends with the lines:

> And those whom I love, my Spouse, my King
> I do not want to love more than you.

Thérèse was not wrong in making this reproach. When we read, for example, the letters of Sister Marie of the Eucharist to her parents between July and October (published in *Vie Thérésienne* 127, July-October 1992), we can only be astounded at their emotionalism and sentimentality; thus on 29 July (her parents had sent her chocolate): 'Last night's little packet of chocolate gave me great pleasure; this little surprise touched me a great deal. I could have wept. You are too kind, and often tears come to my eyes', and so on.

194. Spiritual Canticle B, annotation on strophe XXIX. This quotation would soon be taken up on 8 September in Manuscript B, 4, but in quotation marks. It would be sent, in a letter to Fr Roulland, on 19 March 1897, with an indication of the author, St John of the Cross.

195. *The Living Flame of Love*, strophe 1, explanation of v.6. Thérèse does not quote these last three lines in manuscript B, but she spoke of 'the science of love' (B,1) and of the desire to consume her life (B, 4).

196. This is something that Mother Agnes did not understand at all: she kept solely to the Face of the Crucified. At the apostolic process, she still said: 'The devotion to the Holy Face was the special attraction for the servant of God. Tender though her devotion was to the Child Jesus, it could not be compared with her devotion to the Holy Face. It was at the Carmel, at the moments of our great trials over the mental illness of our father, that she became more attached to the mystery of the Passion' (PA, 580). Thérèse did not restrict herself either to this family reduction or solely to Veronica's Veil.

197. The face is important for Thérèse (cf. her father's face, A, 20, p.101). It would be interesting to study this element in her work and that of the look in connection with the theme of the face in the thought of Emmanuel Levinas (cf. David Banon, 'Résistance du visage et renoncement au sacrifice', in *Cahier de l'Herne Emmanuel Levinas*, 399–407). In his reading of the sacrifice of Abraham, Banon shows the place and the significance of the trial in the life of the patriarchs, particularly in the life of Abraham. The face, Levinas says, is a 'pure experience, an experience without concept', cf. *En découvrant l'existence avec Husserl et Heidegger*, Paris: Vrin 1967, 177.

198. Song of Songs 5.2.

199. Doubtless her two sisters will have asked her for some explana-

tion of this.

200. We shall soon find in Manuscript B this thirst for the love of Jesus.

201. NEC, *Récreations pieuses, Prières*. This is one of the four prayers found in her breviary after her death.

202. 'Kiss of your Mouth' is clearly a reference to Song of Songs 1.2. Similarly 'enflame' and 'consume' (cf. the Consecration to the Holy Face, in which the two verses already exist), which refer to the divine Furnace at the end of the Song of Songs. The commentator has systematically removed the reference to the Song of Songs, even at the cost of twisting words. Why?

2. The Song of Love

1. Furthermore, in *Story of a Soul*, Mother Agnes suppressed lines 1 to 20, and lines 29 to 43 in B,1, along with other lines in B, 2 to 5, not to mention modifying the texts themselves.

2. One might have thought that Fr François de Sainte-Marie – who died prematurely – would have admitted that he was wrong in 1956 and would have been driven to this true solution.

3. Almost, at some moments, her stupidity.

4. This word is repeated three times in this paragraph of fourteen lines.

5. Ibid.

6. Ibid.

7. Ibid.

8. Ibid.

9. Ibid.

10. Ibid.

11. Ibid.

12. A gesture of benediction.

13. B, 2.

14. Ibid.

15. Ibid.

16. Ibid.

17. Ibid.

18. Ibid.

19. C,7.

20. So one can only challenge the statement of the commentator on the *Manuscrits autobiographiques* (292): 'This dream strengthens

Thérèse in the assurance that there is a Heaven, the object of the piercing doubt of her last eighteen months.' This is no way an 'assurance' (!); it is hardly even a slight sign, and very uncertain.

21. C, 7.
22. As the same commentary again says (292). Can there be a personal experience which is not lived out? 'Feel' is one of the words used most frequently by Thérèse: 138 times in the *Manuscrits autobiographiques*.
23. C, 7.
24. A, 48.
25. B, 2.
26. B,5.
27. Ibid.
28. One might recall Fr Congar's remark on Thérèse's genius and duration (Chapter I, n.63).
29. B, 5.
30. Ibid.
31. She had begun this text with the exclamation 'O Jesus, my Beloved', and each of the essential parts also began with a similar address to Jesus, either 'O my Beloved' (twice), 'O Jesus' (seven times), 'O my Jesus' (three times) or more simply 'Jesus' (four times).
32. B, 2 (224). We know that the Act of Oblation to Merciful Love, of 9 June 1895, and therefore written under the priorate of Mother Agnes and sent to her, was submitted by Mother Agnes to the ecclesiastical authorities. According to her they required a correction of the Act: in place of 'I feel in myself *infinite* desires', which Thérèse had written, they wanted her to say 'I feel in myself *immense* desires'. When Thérèse writes, here in September 1896, 'my desires which... touch on the infinite', she cannot fail to have remembered the correction which was required of her for the Act; with her precise style, she gets round the difficulty by writing this formula: 'my desires... which touch on the infinite'. (In the list of quotations by Fr François de Sainte-Marie, the word' infinite' applies essentially to God: 'infinite splendour', 'infinite mercy'). Thérèse would discreetly recall this incident – since the request for this change hurt her – in a passage of a letter to Mother Agnes on 28 May 1897: 'Yes, the Lord will do for us marvels that will infinitely surpass our *immense* desires.' Here too she surreptitiously introduces the word 'infinite'.

33. B, 2.
34. Ibid.
35. B,3.
36. Ibid.
37. Ibid.
38. Ibid.
39. This is quite a different response to that of the commentator on the *Manuscrits autobiographiques* (notes on pp.294–7 of NEC). He would like to prove to us that Thérèse was all that: 'Thérèse always had a warlike and chivalrous fibre... she liked using military vocabulary'. 'Missionary' is 'one of the vocations that she realized in fullness since she was to be proclaimed patron of missions'. Martyr: like John of Arc who died murmuring 'Jesus, Jesus', Thérèse would die stammering, 'My God, I love you', gripping her crucifix, i.e. Jesus, and looking at it, and so on.
40. B, 3.
41. Ibid.
42. Ibid.
43. A, 60.
44. John 20.11–12.
45. B,4. 'Love only pays itself by love'; cf. St John of the Cross, *Explanation of the Spiritual Canticle*, strophe IX.
46. C, 35.
47. B,4.
48. Commentary on the *Manuscrits autobiographiques*, 306.
49. LC, 205.
50. B,1.
51. 8.7.
52. Ibid., 3.1.
53. B, 3.
54. P.297.
55. C, 6.
56. P.297. Mother Agnes again suppresses the capital here.
57. B, 3.
58. Ibid.
59. At the beginning of manuscript A, a year earlier, Thérèse had written: 'The characteristic of Love being to stoop' (A, 2), but in what is obviously a far less powerful paragraph.
60. Ibid. Mother Agnes transcribes: 'As a victim to your love, O Jesus.'

61. And not, as the commentator on the *Manuscrits autobiographiques* would have it, on the 'Song of the Three Hebrews (Daniel 3)' (283).
62. Twenty lines which have been suppressed in *Story of a Soul*.
63. A, 85. Also suppressed by Mother Agnes.
64. B,3.
65. B,5.
66. Ibid.
67. A, 84.
68. B, 5 for the three texts quoted.
69. Ibid., Thérèse develops a parable at length in B, 4 and 5; she contrasts 'the great souls, the Eagles' with the 'little souls' represented by the 'little bird', namely herself. Marcel Moré has made a close study of this text (*Dieu vivant* 24, 48–53). He has shown definitively the serious alterations made here by the *Story of a Soul*, alterations which he bluntly calls 'treason' (p.48). 'The hand of the editors has been pleased not only to massacre one of the finest texts of mystical literature but has also made Thérèse write precisely the opposite of what she had said, and said on essential points' (p.346).
70. Ibid. The last twenty lines of the manuscript have been particularly toned down by Mother Agnes, who has robbed her of her breathless style, her rhythm and her power. In this connection we must quote once and for all the remark by Marcel Moré (*Dieu vivant* 24, 45). 'In altering the text, the editors (Mother Agnes and her consorts) have not only hindered an understanding of the passages which have been retouched but have stifled the mysterious resonances which spread through the pages of a writer who is seeking to deliver up her most secret depths.'
71. B, 3 for all the texts cited.
72. Ibid. Just afterwards, she takes herself up and corrects herself: 'Why speak of a delirious joy? No, this expression is not correct, for it was rather the calm and serene peace of the navigator perceiving the beacon which must lead him to the port.' We have seen that this was Jesus, the 'luminous Beacon of love'.
73. Three times in A, not at all in C.
74. B,1.
75. Ibid.
76. The verb is in the present.
77. Ibid. (p.220). On 'divine furnace' the commentator of the

Manuscrits autobiographiques indicates (283) that the origin of this word is 'in the Song of the three Hebrews (Daniel 3)'. No, the word takes up the last verse of the Song of Songs (moreover Thérèse, three lines before, speaks of the 'bride of the sacred Canticles').

78. B, 1.
79. Ibid.
80. Ibid.
81. Ibid.
82. B, 3.
83. He had already preached the community retreat in 1882 and 1890 (this retreat generally preceded 15 October, the feast of St Teresa of Avila). He had also preached the triduum of 22–24 June 1895. He would revise *Story of a Soul* with Mother Agnes and give it a preface (1898).
84. For example, when she accuses herself of falling asleep during prayer.
85. II, 923–4. It has to be said that she was helped by the Guérin family, which was the principal source of provisions for the Carmel. Marie Guérin – Sister Marie of the Eucharist – thanks her parents at length in October 1896: 'If I had to say enough thank-yous for the jars of jam, figs, dried pears, peaches and other things, I think it would take me all day... Yesterday evening and this morning the cases filled the refectory and we counted as far as possible all the content of these fine cases' (at the end of the meal the porter read out the gifts received from benefactors; the Mother then had a Pater and an Ave said in silence for the donors). Another letter from Marie Guérin to her parents on 24 or 25 November 1896: 'The other day in the refectory the list of alms was read out, as happens at festivals. When they got to M. and Mme Guérin the list of vegetables, cakes etc. was so long that in the middle of the list there was a great burst of laughter; everyone laughed. In the end they finished the list by saying, "and lastly they have given all kinds of cakes".' Marie's letters often contain requests; thus on 28 February 1897 for pieces of linen: 'At present we are excessively poor in this respect...; we drag the devil by the tail and I fear that one of these fine days we shall be left with it in our hands.' We learn from this letter that as well as the dowry for his daughter, M.Guérin gave 1500 francs a year to the Carmel.

86. Nouvelle Edition du centenaire, Paris, Cerf-DDB.
87. We are given only 'extracts' from this letter. Why?
88. As we shall see later, she explains herself in Manuscript C.
89. The vesicatory plasters often used at this time almost all contained extracts of cantharis which irritated the skin; they produced a discharge of fluid under the skin. This was fixed with appropriate bandages (cf. *Grand Larousse du XIXe siècle*, articles 'Vésication' and 'Vésicatoire'). Dr Francis La Néele, husband of Jeanne Guérin, sister of Marie and cousin of Thérèse, was a doctor; he specialized in chest problems. Marie Guérin had written to Céline on 21 October 1894 to recommend him to the Carmel, since at that time Thérèse was suffering from throat pains. He visited Thérèse three times confidentially in August and September in dramatized circumstances, as we shall see.
90. A,45.
91. Cf. ' Since that night I have never been defeated in any combat, but rather walked from victory to victory' (A,44).
92. Later, we shall see the poem 'My arms', written on 25 March 1897, which ends:

> And in your arms, my divine Spouse,
> singing I shall die on the battlefield,
> arms in hand.

93. Cf. 'O Divine Word... coming into this land of exile, You willed to suffer and to die in order to draw souls to the bosom of the Eternal Hearth of the Blessed Trinity. Ascending once again to the inaccessible Light, henceforth Your abode, you remain still in this valley of tears' (B,5). The last member of the phrase is precise: the Word is *still* at work on earth and that is why Thérèse writes 'you leave' (which Mother Agnes changes into 'you left').
94. B,4.
95. Ibid.
96. Jean Vinatier, *Mère Agnes de Jesus*, Paris: Cerf 1993, 98.
97. The Martin family and the Carmel regularly used Brother Simeon to obtain either the relics of saints or 'apostolic benedictions' from the Pope (thus the one addressed to Thérèse and M.Martin on 29 August 1890: text in *Correspondance générale*, Vol. 1, 562).
98. Proof that she was not as discontented with her talents or as horrified at Thérèse's 'pride' as Mother Agnes claims.

99. In 1895 he became Curé of Saint-Jacques de Lisieux, where he replaced his cousin, Canon Delatroëtte; at the same time he became superior of the Carmel.
100. Thérèse knew this saint: on her entry into the Carmel she was given the cell dedicated to St Stanislas.
101. By A.M.Blanche, who suggests in his work 'making sanctity seem something less accessible, shall I say something easy, simple' (8).
102. *Way of Perfection*, Ch.III.
103. *Thérèse de Lisieux*, 1991, 296.
104. Ibid.
105. P.478. The same commentator notes (p.479) some contradictions in which Mother Agnes gets lost.
106. A, 80.
107. A, 81.
108. In the Yellow Notebook, Mother Agnes makes Thérèse say on 13 July 1897: 'I think of all the good I would like to do after my death... but first console my little sisters' (LC, 95).
109. Seven volumes would be published between 1907 and 1925, the date of the canonization of Thérèse, which describe in detail, as more or less miraculous or extraordinary facts, all that has been obtained by the intercession of Thérèse; these volumes are called *Showers of Roses*.
110. A, 17.
111. A detail, but a significant one. Thérèse wrote: 'But one simply throws away the unpetalled rose.' Mother Agnes corrects this and writes 'unpetalling'. Whereas Thérèse wants to indicate that she is allowing herself to lose her leaves, Mother Agnes wants to show an active Thérèse. Thérèse writes the verse 'Unpetalled I want...' only after she has allowed Jesus to throw her to the winds.
112. PO, 1644.
113. PA, 2337.
114. Abbé Descouvemont (p.290) romances a little more: 'After the meal in the room adjacent to the refectory, Thérèse, her elbow resting on a piece of furniture, declared very seriously to her godmother: "I, too, after my death will rain roses."' 'Adjoin', 'elbow resting': that makes it seem more authentic.
115. Eph.6.11; it is in the rule of the Carmel.
116. Matt.11.12.
117. Matt.10.34; Luke 12.49.
118. Letter of 17 or 18 April 1897.

Notes

119. Cf. 'An Unpetalled Rose':

> Lord, on your altars more than one fresh rose
> loves to shine
> It gives itself to you... but I dream of something else, to lose my
> petals.

120. Cf. J.F.Six, *Thérèse de Lisieux au Carmel*, Paris: Seuil 1973, especially Chapter IV, 'Le carmel de France au XIXe siecle'.

121. In the book *Je choisis tout*, Paris: CLD 1992 – which *Vie thérésienne* (April 1992, 393–5) described as 'heavy, very heavy, sometimes overwhelming! Heavy with theological thoughts and spiritual references' – Fr Molinié makes a useful distinction between 'the justice which condemns, punishes and sometimes curses' and 'the justice which excuses, pardons, blesses'; between 'vindictive justice' and 'the justice of Love' (116). 'The divine desire to give itself,' the author writes in an excellent passage, 'respects freedom: this respect is the very Justice of Love. When the creature says no to this invitation, to some degree it makes use of its "right", it makes use of Justice against Love – if you like, of Love in so far as it respects against Love and in so far as it gives itself and asks the creature to give itself' (117.). 'This rejection,' he adds, 'is sin *par excellence*... an incredible violence imposed on the desires of God' (118). And he says this, which is very illuminating: 'Thérèse certainly wants to offer herself as a victim to console the merciful Love wounded by the rejection of creatures, but not to appease vindictive Justice' (120). At the beginning of the conclusion, Fr Molinié writes: 'Thérèse's perception underlying the act of oblation comprises two levels of depth:

> 1. To offer herself to the wound of Love to console him for the rejection of sinners and above all the incredulous.
>
> 2. To communicate at the chalice of the pain of Love faced with this rejection' (223).

122. G.Gaucher, *The Passion of Thérèse of Lisieux* (1973), Homebush, Australia: St Paul Publications 1989, 71: 'To write a biography of Sister Thérèse of the Child Jesus and of the Holy Face beginning in April 1897 consists mainly in following the stages of her illness.' I find this scandalous.

123. The commentator (*Correspondance générale* XI, 990) rightly comments on this letter: 'The adjective "little" recurs fourteen

times in this letter. It is no less frequent in the following letters. This fact is worth noting to the degree that it influences the vocabulary of the *Last Conversations* ("little" figures 374 times in the Yellow Notebook). Mother Agnes could have introduced it into her transcriptions of sayings of Jesus beyond Thérèse's own real usage.' To that point everything is fine: Thérèse uses 'little' only 54 times in Manuscript C. But the commentator adds: 'At all events, Thérèse adapted her language to that of her "little" Mother.' This is to fail to understand Thérèse and her basic independence, despite her protestations of obedience to Mother Agnes.

124. Sic. The use of the verb in the absolute and not the pronominal sense well expresses what is meant.

125. Against Mother Marie de Gonzague?

126. 'Little' again. However, it is the last adjective that could be applied to her character. She had a character which seemed very strong, and basically a great affective vulnerability; but perhaps it is from this that she forged a carapace for herself...

127. 'Try to' is more active than 'attempt to' or 'make an attempt at'. In connection with this usage Littré quotes one of Pascal's *Pensées*: 'It is the greatest subject of the happiness of the condition of kings, that which people try ceaselessly to divert them from by all sorts of pleasures.'

128. Sub-prioress from 1866 to 1872; she was then elected prioress six times, making her priorate twenty-one years in all.

129. 17 September 1910.

130. It is she who is doing things in her eyes; she seems to forget that the prioress ordered Thérèse to write, out of obedience.

131. Gaucher, *Passion* (n.122), 184.

132. Ibid.

133. At the apostolic process in 1915, Sister Geneviève took over from Mother Agnes, saying that Thérèse, in writing her book, 'envisaged, I believe, not that someone would edit these notes as such but would use them, retouching them, to publish a book which would show by what way she had gone to God'.

134. *Manuscrits autobiographiques*, I, 70.

135. Ibid., 67.

136. No passage from which has been published (*Correspondance generale* II, 1007).

137. We know the influence on Charles de Foucauld of a remark that Abbé Huvelin made in a sermon in 1888: 'Jesus took last place in

such a way that no one could ever snatch it from him.' 'This is a saying so inviolably engraved on my soul', Charles de Foucauld was to say (cf. J.-F.Six, *Itinéraire spirituel de Charles de Foucauld*, Paris: Seuil 1958. In this book, twenty-four texts by Thérèse of Lisieux have been cited, showing the very significant points of correspondence with similar texts by Charles de Foucauld in the same period, 1890–1897.).

138. Fr François de Sainte-Marie, *Manuscrits autobiographiques*, Carmel de Lisieux 1956, introduction, 48.

139. The garden, the trees and shrubs where she was in the afternoon.

140. As this notebook was written out of obedience, she wants to tell the prioress that she is taking her seriously.

141. C, 17.

142. Ibid. Saint-Louis de Gonzague, 21 June.

143. Henri Bremond, who was very reticent about the *Story of a Soul*, nevertheless wrote in 1909 (*L'Inquiétude religieuse*, Paris: Perrin 1909, 386): 'What a splendid chapter I would give myself to write in the history of the Carmel today if I summed up in fifty pages the large volume that has recently been devoted to a young sister, who died in the odour of sanctity. Some letters from this charming soul, some intimate notes have an incomparable youth, grace and charity.' Now Abbé Bremond had the version of the *Story of a Soul* by Mother Agnes. What would he have said had he had the true text?

144. Fr François de Sainte-Marie, *Manuscrits autobiographiques* (n.138), 52–3.

145. Or again the 'brute art' which Jean Dubuffet defined as 'productions with a spontaneous character', owing as little as possible to customary art or cultural stereotypes, with obscure figures as authors, alien to professional artistic milieus. Or again 'popular art', paintings with a story: like the *ex-voto* sailors who present the earth and the skies, the unleashing of the elements and the miracle which has preserved them from shipwreck.

146. Léonie wrote to Céline on 18 July: 'If you can put down all she said in writing, it would be a consolation to me to have it all, since I don't have the happiness of being with my dear sister, like you, my beloved little sisters.'

147. Cf. the letter of January 1897 to Sister Marie of St Joseph. 'I, like a poor little sparrow, sigh in my corner, singing like the wander-

ing Jew. "Death can do nothing for me, I can well see."' 'The Complaint of the Wandering Jew', very famous in the nineteenth century – it was sold in the squares and market places – was sung to country people in Thérèse's childhood; it began with these verses:

> Is there anything on earth
> which is more surprising
> than the great misery
> of the poor wandering Jew?

Here is the twenty-second couplet, to which Thérèse seems to be referring:

> Jesus, your very goodness,
> says to me with a sigh:
> You will go with me
> for more than a thousand years.
> The last judgment
> will end your torment.

The couplets say that for centuries the wandering Jew has gone through battles and epidemics without ever being affected by them; hence the two verses (from the fifteenth couplet) quoted to Sister Marie of St Joseph.

148. C,1 (Ps.88.2). Mother Agnes removed this first page in the *Story of a Soul*.
149. DE, general introduction, 43.
150. C,1.
151. C, 6.
152. C, 18.
153. C, 32–3.
154. C, 11.
155. We saw earlier how the commentator on the *Manuscrits autobiographiques* (p.353) made use of this text to suggest a curious obedience, full of formalism.
156. C,11. ('You will see, dearest Mother, in the exercise book containing my childhood memories,' she told her earlier [C,1], 'what I think of the *strong* and maternal education I received from you.')

157. C,1.
158. 'The intimacy desired by Mother Agnes became more demanding. Persuaded of the imminent death of her sister, she did not hesitate to question her time and again. This insistence on provoking reactions and responses – sometimes almost aggravating – will have had the advantage of leading the saint to make her thought more precise and take a position' (DE, General Intention, 45). Is it certain that this questioning helped Thérèse to make her thought precise? What proof could be advanced of this? When we think how after Thérèse's death Mother Agnes would transform and travesty her thought....!
159. Let us note that, another forty years later, Mother Agnes thought that Thérèse had shaped her memories to what she, Mother Agnes, had wanted.
160. *Annales de sainte Thérèse de Lisieux*, no.662, November 1987.
161. This list does not seem to come from Mother Agnes but from Fr Gaucher.
162. This is a typical turn of phrase in Thérèse: the use of this 'to' of movement: 'I would prefer to keep quiet rather than to try in vain to sing what is going on in my little soul'; cf. the letter to Mother Agnes, 1 June 1897, already cited.
163. NPPA, 'Her faith'.
164. A,12. [The English translation with its first person totally distorts this.]
165. A, 31.
166. A, 35.
167. A, 44.
168. A, 48.
169. A, 49 and 53. Quoted rather differently on p.53 and without quotation marks: 'Resting in the shade of the One whom I have so ardently desired.'
170. A, 61.
171. A, 67 and 68.
172. Letter of 30–31 August 1890. The most frequent quotations from the Song of Songs can be found in the correspondence between Thérèse and Céline – Sister Geneviève. Why? The explanation of this is simple: both read this text. In fact, when Céline entered the Carmel on 14 September 1894, she brought with her – quite apart from her photographic equipment – a small notebook into which she had copied a certain number of extracts

from the Bible; the young Carmelites did not have permission to read a complete Bible including the Old Testament: 'St Thérèse of the Child Jesus made enthusiastic use of this notebook and could not be separated from it,' writes C.de Meester in his *Dynamic de la Confiance*, Paris: Cerf 1969, 79, presenting these sources in his research. Now in these pages in which he speaks of 'Céline's notebook', the author evokes several Old Testament texts, Proverbs, Isaiah, etc., but succeeds in not saying a word about the Song of Songs, which holds pride of place in this notebook and which is transcribed almost in its entirety: Chapter 1 in its entirety except for vv.2b and 3a; Chapter 2 in its entirety; Chapter 3.1–6; Chapter 4 in its entirety except for v.5; Chapter 5 in its entirety, except for v.15; Chapter 6 in its entirety; Chapter 7 in its entirety except for vv.4, 8b, 9b, 13b; Chapter 8 in its entirety except for vv.5b, 10a, 11b, 12 [Thérèse writes 'spread' in the singular instead of the plural].

173. Thirteen quotations.

174. Six quotations.

175. 2. 14.

176. RP, 2.5 (2.11–14 and the last verse of the Song of Songs: 'The flame of love', 8.7).

177. Lecture at Notre-Dame de Paris for the centenary of the birth of Thérèse of Lisieux, *Revue de l'Institut catholique*, May 1973, 111–12.

178. Others continue not to see it, despite the passing years. One is bewildered by the fact that the article on Thérèse in the venerable – and admirable – *Dictionnaire de spiritualité* does not indicate this 'centre' of Thérèse's mysticism in any way and that the Song of Songs is not cited even in Section IV of this article, on Thérèse's scriptural sources. We are compelled to note that the author of the article, Abbé Descouvement, the duty thurifer, is a great specialist in the insipid and stale incense which people constantly burn before Thérèse in contempt of history and the truth.

170. Cf. Mme Guérin's letter to her daughter Jeanne La Néelle, 6 June 1897, asking her to join in this novena: 'The Carmelites are very disturbed. They are finding that the sickness is progressing rapidly. She is hardly eating and has become excessively weak; moreover she has very sharp pains in her side. She has changed a great deal this week; she has fits of coughing, sometimes vomits her meals and eats almost nothing.' Madame Guérin adds that

'Thérèse is very well looked after' and that Mother Marie de Gonzague is 'taking great care of her'. In a letter to M. and Mme Guérin on 7 June, Mother Agnes wrote of Mother Marie de Gonzague: 'This poor Mother began to weep hot tears when she began the *Salve Regina* on Saturday. It is true that on that day our poor little angel was *very sick*.'

180. C, 34–37. Thérèse stops on the recto of folio 37, which she has hardly begun.

181. C, 34.

182. C, 35.

183. If she speaks of her missionary brothers, it is because in fact she is addressing Mother Louis de Gonzague, the only one who knew of the existence of Fr Roulland and the correspondence with him.

184. C, 36.

185. I am following the text in the precise reproduction of Thérèse's black notebook as given by Fr François de Sainte-Marie, inviting readers to refer to it if possible.

186. Thus 'captivate', used twice on these pages, which is never used elsewhere in any of the manuscripts, A, B and C.

187. C,35.

188. We should remember that she said of the Song of Songs: 'I have discovered in this book such profound things about the union of the soul with its Beloved.'

189. G.Gaucher gives a resumé of this text which one cannot but find flat and reductive, not very enthusiastic, and somewhat mawkish: 'We find ourselves in the presence of a discovery about contemplative-apostolic prayer which is so important at Carmel... and for all Christian life', cf. *Annales* (n.160), 7.

190. On 7 July Sister Geneviève writes to Brother Simeon, the friend of the Martin family, to whom on the previous 11 February she had sent Thérèse's poem 'Live by Love', that Thérèse 'is dying'. 'Her sickness is love. She has none other than that dying of Love as she had so desired.'

191. C, 35.

192. She attests her experience to her and she cannot imagine a greater: 'Here below, I cannot conceive a greater immensity of love than that which it has pleased you to lavish on me freely, without any merit on my part.'

193. B, 5.

194. It is impossible to exaggerate the perplexity into which some

commentators plunge us. Thus for this passage (C,35) the word 'abyss' is used only to denote God himself, Love, the Abyss. How can anyone suggest a passage from the Psalms which has nothing to do with it? Here is the text (MA, 414 note): 'Perhaps a recollection of Ps.41.8: "Abyss calls to abyss" suggested by Thérèse's formula, "Love attracts love."' Now the Latin expression *abyssus abyssum invocat* has passed into French in a proverb, 'The abyss attracts the abyss', in the sense of 'one misfortune brings on another' or 'one crime provokes another'. I cannot see the connection with Thérèse's text.

195. B,4.
196. C,34.
197. C,35.
198. Ibid.
199. John 6.44
200. Cf. the article 'Feu' in the *Dictionnaire de spiritualité*.
201. C,35–36. The text of Abbé d'Arminjon (*Fin du monde présent et Mystères de la vie future*, 200) by which Thérèse is inspired has nothing of Thérèse's rhythm, and above all it omits the 'seems simply to make one with him', the importance of which we shall see. Thérèse is inspired by this text and transforms it; Mother Agnes takes Thérèse's texts and disfigures them. Here is Arminjon's text: 'It must be the soul of their soul, penetrate them and steep them in my divinity, as the fire steeps iron.'
202. C,36.
203. 'Divine furnace'; cf. the end of the Song of the Songs.
204. The commentator of MA writes, along the same lines as Mother Agnes: 'Prayer is Thérèse's last word, because it is the means of fusion with God' (418).
205. *Thérèse de Lisieux au Carmel*, Paris: Seuil 1972, 367.
206. Without wanting to provoke sensitive souls, in connection with Thérèse's text and to evoke her loving passion, one could quote a passage from A.Pieyre de Mandiargues, *Le Lis de mer*, Folio, 140–1: 'Vanina recalled (she could not have said from what depths this emerged) a fragment of a letter of Merimée, about an attractive girl he met in Madrid. This young person, when asked, "Does he maltreat you?", fiercely replied: "If one loves a man, even if he had a red-hot iron one would not feel pain." Then Vanina thought that she had been wrong to get perpetually mixed up in cultural matters and that it would be a good thing for her to

become a brute, like Juliette. But she did not cry when she felt the burning fire.'

3. Faced with the Silence of God

1. B, 1.
2. C,36.
3. Ibid.
4. As the commentator remarks (MA, 418), what Thérèse confided to Mother Marie de Gonzague has already been emphasized: 'Beloved mother, this is my prayer: I ask Jesus to draw me into the flames of his love.'
5. C, 36.
6. Ibid.
7. B, 3.
8. The church militant: the church which is still on earth, the church triumphant being that of the saints in heaven.
9. C, 36 (perhaps today we would say 'motor' rather than 'lever').
10. B, 3.
11. Ibid.
12. C, 36.
13. C, 34.
14. Ibid.
15. C, 36.
16. C, 6.
17. C,36.
18. C,34.
19. C,36.
20. Ibid. A text from the *Last Conversations* is cited to give this somewhat surprising conclusion: the perfume is the tangible consolation which Thérèse gives herself from the poetry of language, basing herself on the Song of Songs (and thus in an irreproachable way as far as 'religious discipline' is concerned). Commentary on MA, 410 (cf. commentary MA, 339: 'In Thérèse perfume far surpasses its sensual value').
21. Cf. Song of Songs 1.3.
22. Thérèse uses the word only twice in MA: 'divine substance' (B,5) and 'burning substance' (C, 36).
23. C, 34.
24. Ibid.

25. John 17.4–24.
26. C, 34; cf. C, 36, the last lines of Manuscript C, in which this time she is the Prodigal Son: 'I imitate the conduct of Magdalene; her loving audacity which charms the Heart of Jesus seduces mine. Yes, I feel it; even though I had on my conscience all the sins that can be committed I would go, my heart broken with repentance, to throw myself into the arms of Jesus, for I know how much he cherishes the prodigal child who returns to Him.'
27. C,35. There is a terrible mistake in the English translation, cf. 207 n.126 above.
28. C, 12.
29. Ibid.
30. C,11. This phrase has been suppressed by Mother Agnes in the *Story of a Soul,* where we only find: 'At the Last Supper, he gave his new commandment.' And it is Mother Agnes who underlines the word 'commandment'.
31. When they thus have an 'ardent love' towards Jesus, the apostles are like the church, since the church has a 'Heart burning with love' (B,3); and it then discovers its vocation, which is that of Magdalene (B,3). Magdalene has a 'heart set on fire with love' as she listens to the 'sweet and burning' words of Jesus (C,36). We might recall Thérèse's remark in connection with the journey to Rome in 1887, about the rejection of women in certain places: 'Don't enter here! Don't enter there, you will be excommunicated!' (Mother Agnes has suppressed the passage in question in *Story of a Soul* [why? one asks] and also the one which follows: 'Ah! poor women, how they are misunderstood! and yet they love God in much larger numbers than men do and during the Passion of Our Lord, women had more courage than the apostles since they braved the insults of the soldiers and dared to wipe the adorable Face of Jesus. It is undoubtedly because of this that he allows misunderstanding to be their lot on earth, since he chose it for himself. In heaven, he will then show that his thoughts are not men's thoughts, for then the last will be first' [A,66]). The commentator (MA, 205) admires this: 'Here Thérèse shows with verve her "feminism", which is very remarkable for her time and place.' This is a quite radical misunderstanding; Thérèse is not putting herself on this level and is not a 'feminist' before her time; she wants to emphasize the ardour of the love of Mary Magdalene, Veronica and the others, and their greater courage than that of the apostles during the passion.

32. C,12.
33. Ibid.
34. C, 11. Mother Agnes transcribes this, suppressing 'Dearest Mother', as follows: 'Among the numberless graces that I have received this year, I think not the least that which has granted me to understand the precept of charity in all its extent.' This really leads us up the garden path: Thérèse with a very precise, immense grace.
35. Cf. the story of Sister St Peter (C, 28–29), which would have delighted Henri Bremond.
36. Thus C,13: 'There is in the community a Sister who has the faculty of displeasing me in everything...' Mother Marie de Gonzague cannot fail to understand from the portrait which sister this is.
37. C 13 to 15 is a hymn rejoicing in 'desertion': '*My last means* of not being defeated in combats... and it has always succeeded perfectly with me' (C,14). We have seen that these are the same means that she uses in her trial in connection with faith, faced with the darkness which assails her.
38. C, 28.
39. C, 36.
40. C, 37.
41. B, 3. Cf. the letter of 7 June 1897 to Sister Geneviève: 'When he sees we are very much convinced of our nothingness, he extends His hand to us.'
42. C.De Meester, *Dynamique de la confiance*, Paris: Cerf 1969, reprinted 1995, 291.
43. C,15.
44. C,1.
45. C,2.
46. 'This is the moment of *perfect joy* for the *poor little* weak creature', B,5.
47. C, 2.
48. C,15.
49. Ibid.
50. A.Combes, *Introduction à la spiritualité de sainte Thérèse de l'Enfant-Jésus*, Paris: Vrin, 294–5.
51. A verse never cited in MA (where, however, there are many passages from the psalms) nor in her correspondence.
52. P.1160.

53. *Last Conversations*, p. 59, no.8 (the quotations which follows are quoted similarly by page and number).
54. 62, no.2.
55. 71f., no.3.
56. 72, no.5.
57. 73, no.3.
58. 77, no.4.
59. 84, no.2.
60. 88, no.3
61. 90, no.9.
62. 92, no.7.
63. 103, no.1 (July 19).
64. 103, no.1 (July 20).
65. 106, no.3.
66. 119, no.8
67. 119, no.2.
68. 114, no.1.
69. 143, no.4.
70. 143, no.2 (10 August).
71. A, 40.
72. Ibid.
73. In a 1973 lecture *(Nouvelles de l'Institut catholique*, May 1973, 174–5), G.Gaucher noted 'the extreme discretion of [Thérèse] over her inner sufferings. Even with Mother Agnes, who now knew of their existence, she remained very reserved.' However, it is clear that faced with the questions raised by Mother Agnes about her 'trial', Thérèse saw that her sister did not understand, and so she did not persist.
74. Isidore Guérin and his niece Mother Agnes had always been very close. They felt the same way about Thérèse's imminent death: Isidore Guérin wrote to his daughter, Sister Marie of the Eucharist, on 9 July: 'This eventuality which makes us sad is the dawn of a triumph.' By contrast Céline suffered terribly, like Mother Marie de Gonzague; she writes to her cousin Jeanne on 12 July; 'I am so upset! It is my little companion, my dearest sister, my friend, my dear little other half who's going away.' Marie, Sister Marie of the Sacred Heart, was on the 'Mother Agnes' side. On 14 July she wrote to Mme Guérin, her aunt: 'Like you, I think one has the right to be proud to have such an angel in the family; it is a grace of privilege.' One day the posthumous life of Thérèse of

Lisieux as constructed by her three sisters and particularly by Mother Agnes should be written. Guy Gaucher, in an article in *La Vie thérésienne* (April 1993), has quoted the dedication which Bernanos had planned for his *Jeanne relapse et sainte* (Plon 1934): 'To the dear and august memory of the one who was, with Joan, the most heroic of the saints of our race, a true little French knight, Thérèse of the Child Jesus, sold by her sisters.'

75. She does not say, as before, 'twice my mother'.

76. Mother Marie de Gonzague.

77. At least this relieved Thérèse of a weight!

78. According to Sister Marie of the Eucharist (letter of 30 July to her father), Mother Agnes 'has not eaten for a long time and I fear that after all her emotions her health will suffer, because she is very weak'. This way of reacting to Thérèse's situation could only accentuate the exaltation: there are anorexias which cause over-excitement.

79. Interested readers can refer to G.Gaucher, *The Passion of Thérèse of Lisieux* (1973), Homebush: Australia, St Paul Publications 1989, 79ff., who has tried to establish as meticulously as possible the number of times blood was coughed up in the month of July (he adds: 'this is certainly below the real figure'). Gaucher gives a detailed count. The whole book contains other medical information.

80. Similarly, again to her father, three weeks later, on 28 July: 'The illness is following its course. Once again she has twice coughed up blood: this tires her and drags her down a great deal, but she can still make jokes with us from time to time.'

81. For Thérèse's humour in these weeks see J.-F.Six, *Thérèse de Lisieux*, Paris: Seuil 1975, 300f.

82. Dr Cornière, who had long hair and whom she calls 'M.Clodion' (letter of April-May 1897) after 'Clodion le Chevelu', a king of France whom she had noted down in one of her school books.

83. At that time she was taking only milk.

84. Sister Mary of the Eucharist, to Mme Guérin, on 25 July: 'She is also calm and happy to die, but she is not there yet.'

85. 'Circumstances', 'events': the terms also recur frequently in Charles de Foucauld, of whom his bishop would say in December 1904: 'Like those who are guided by the Spirit of God, he knows marvellously how to appreciate the circumstances.'

86. The photographs show a 'beautiful plant' (1.62m tall, the tallest

of the Martin sisters), with a full face, determined, prominent chin (which has been retouched in the arranged reproductions).

87. *Thérèse de Lisieux au Carmel*, Paris: Seuil 1972, 310f.

88. Among these poor figures is Bernadette Soubirous, who died of tuberculosis in 1879 at the age of thirty-five, and who had begun to cough in October 1859, eighteen months after the first appearance at Lourdes.

89. Alphonsine Duplessis, Alexandre Dumas's *La Dame aux camélias* and the Violetta of Verdi's *La Traviata*, was born like Thérèse in Normandy; having lost her mother at ten, she launched herself into the Parisian demi-monde and became Marie Duplessis, beyond question the most adulated courtesan of the nineteenth century. She passed from lover to lover and burned herself out; at one point she was the mistress of Liszt, who would say of her that she was 'the most absolute incarnation of woman that ever existed'. She died at the age of twenty-three (cf. M.Boudet, *La Fleur du Mal*, Paris: Albin Michel 1994). Thérèse's consumption would be very long-drawn-out.

90. Letter of Sister Marie of the Eucharist to her father on 8 July; Sister Geneviève had spoken to Brother Simeon (letter of 25 April 1897) of 'illness of the chest'.

91. The legend that Thérèse was uncared-for during her illness has now been discredited. There was also the legend of Mother Marie de Gonzague persecuting Thérèse throughout her religious life. This legend was taken up again by Maxence Van der Meersch; after his book appeared a substantial collective work was published entitled *La petite soeur Thérèse de Lisieux de M.Van der Meersch devant la critique et devant les textes:* Paris, Editions Saint-Paul 1950, in which ten specialists combined to confound the romancer. Because I had as spiritual director Mgr Tiberghien, who had known Van der Meersch well – he blessed his tomb at Mouvaux cemetery, since the romancer had refused to be buried at the church – I have been given a few stories about the affair. G.Gaucher writes: 'While recognizing the errors committed by Van der Meersch... we regret the way in which ten eminent specialists treated this author. The search for truth and the value of their arguments do not justify a certain tone and constant slating of a Christian brother who is mistaken. These acrid polemics abount Thérèse do not appear today to be in conformity with the spirit of Vatican II, and above all with the spirit

of the saint herself' *(Passion* [n.79], 241 n.a). But by what testimonies was the romancer inspired, among other things, to fall upon Mother Marie de Gonzague, if not those which came from Lisieux itself and from Thérèse's sisters – Mother Agnes and Sister Genevieve? Poor Maxence, who trusted Lisieux and then paid the price! As for 'the spirit of the saint herself' to which Lisieux boasts that it is faithful, I would quietly like to give my own personal testimony: for more than twenty years, silence has been maintained on all my works on Thérèse. They have been boycotted and pilloried by Lisieux. This is no longer the method of savaging but that of gagging, which is much more serious. Is this method in keeping with the spirit of Thérèse?

92. Doubtless in the month of May.

93. Polemic about this seems quite vain, and I do not share the arguments of Fr Noché against Dr de Cornière in *La petite soeur Thérèse de Lisieux* (n.91), as I did in 1975 *(Thérèse de Lisieux* [n.87], 293). Dr de Cornière – he was then sixty-five – was of the old school and prescribed the treatment used with tuberculosis patients at that time; Dr La Néele was of another generation.

94. Letter of Sister Marie of the Eucharist to her father, 8 July 1897.

95. PO, p.1101.

96. Cahier noir, 1908, 81.

97. In appendix II of his book *(Passion* [n.79], 241–6), Gaucher has examined this question ('Was Thérèse well cared for?'). In particular he studies the attitude of Mother Marie de Gonzague. These pages do not prove very satisfactory.

98. There is the same indication in the letter of Mother Agnes to the Guérins, on 5 August.

99. Sister Marie of the Eucharist to M.Guérin, 17 August.

100. Ibid.

101. Ibid.

102. From Vichy, where she was with her husband, having received news of the visit of her son-in-law to Thérèse on 17 August, Mme Guérin writes on 20 August: 'I did not dare to hope, although Marie had told us that this was possible in the absence of the doctor.'

103. 'She had little sympathy for Thérèse's young outspoken and frank cousin, who hardly troubled himself to ask for permissions',

writes Gaucher *(Passion*, 243). Let us say that he was impetuous and believed that he was allowed to do anything.

104. That is to say when he came on 17 August.

105. Letter of Mme Guérin to her husband (who was taking a cure at Vichy), on the evening of 30 August.

106. Had not Dr La Néele been 'worked up' against the prioress by Mother Agnes and Céline?

107. The doctor having slept at Mme Guérin's home on the evening of 30 September.

108. He had returned the previous evening.

109. Doubtless to say something to Dr La Néele on the 17th.

110. Thus in this affair, and at the very moment it was taking place, Isidore Guérin clearly takes sides with Mother Marie de Gonzague. Why does Guy Gaucher follow the very much later indications of Mother Agnes and affirm the contrary without hesitation: 'The changing character of Mother Marie de Gonzague provoked scenes for which Thérèse paid the price'? (Cf. *Histoire d'une âme*, Paris: Cerf 1993, 208.)

111. As we have seen, the two letters from Mme Guérin to her daughter (27 August and 1 September) are of the utmost importance: clear, above suspicion, true. Why does the edition of the *Derniers Entretiens* (760–1) give only extracts from the letter of 27 August, without any explanation?

112. Cahiers verts, 30 August, cf. *Dernières Paroles*, 350.

113. Ibid.

114. Guy Gaucher *(Passion* [n.79], 111) does not hesitate to cite Mother Agnes's text as such without the least critical commentary to accredit this testimony. How can one follow him?

115. PA, 2377, *Derniers Entretiens*, 555.

116. 'Mother Agnes, who thought that the end was near, questioned her often and asked for more precise details' (Gaucher, *Passion* [n.79], 84). For Mother Agnes, Thérèse, who is dying, is especially a subject of edification for the community; on 5 August she writes to the Guérins, speaking of their daughter, Sister Marie of the Eucharist: '[She] is in process of becoming very good, and the sickness of her (novice) mistress is very profitable for her. There is so much to admire and imitate. This is a memory for a lifetime.'

117. DE, 8 August 1897, 327.

118. H.Urs von Balthasar, lecture, 119.

119. It was thought that she would not last the night.
120. At this time the rules and customs relating to communion strictly forbade it if there was the least danger that the host might be seen to be rejected, for example by vomiting. This prescription was applied to Thérèse. Guy Gauchet makes two comments in this connection: 'She was deprived of the eucharist because she was unable to fulfil the conditions necessary for the reception of this sacrament. (They were very strict at that time.)' (86). Later on, he speaks of 'her not being able to receive communion', which was 'a very severe trial to her. And it must have been all the more so since it was due rather to her extreme weakness than to the very strict canonical legislation of the time: she was not able to endure the long ceremonial involved in taking communion' (118). But if this was the main reason, was it not possible to shorten what was only a ceremonial and in this way allow her the communion that she desired so much?
121. Hence 19 August.
122. Thérèse puts 'éclair' in the feminine.
123. Letter, LC, 291.
124. And in *Novissima Verba* she speaks of the 'ecstasy of the last moment. The face of our saint took on the tint of the lily which it had when she was in full health, her eyes were fixed on high, radiant and expressing a happiness which surpassed all her hopes.'
125. Quoted in François de Sainte-Marie, *Visages de Thérèse de Lisieux*, Office central de Lisieux 1981, 18.
126. Ibid., 19.
127. Ibid., 20.
128. 'The way in which the photographs were retouched' (ibid., 31f.).
129. Sister Geneviève, ibid., 24.
130. Mother Agnes would be prioress from 19 April 1902 until her death on 28 July 1951, with the exception of eighteen months (the priorate of Mother Marie-Ange of the Child Jesus, from 8 May 1908 until her death on 11 November 1909). Mother Agnes was to be confirmed in her charge for life on 31 May 1923 by Pope Pius XI. That was contrary to the constitutions of the Carmel.
131. François de Sainte-Marie, *Visages* (n.125), 25f.
132. Ibid., 27.
133. Ibid.
134. Quoted, 23.

135. Ibid., 35.
136. Does Fr François de Sainte-Marie know that Gide's *Nourritures terrestres* date from 1895?
137. François de Sainte-Marie, *Visages* (n.125), 36: 'The impression of determination and power which comes out of the photographic documents is destroyed by the retouching' (ibid.).
138. Ibid., 37. It was this portrait (of which more than 8 million copies were printed in France alone between 1898 and 1913) which would produce faith: 'During the 1914–1918 war,' writes Fr François de Sainte-Marie, 'there were numerous soldiers – among them the least devout – who carried on their persons the image, in vivid colours, of this seductive virgin, the friend and rival of Joan of Arc' (ibid., 42).
139. Ibid., 40.
140. Ibid., 41.
141. A.Frossard, *Les Greniers du Vatican*, Paris: Fayard 1930, 144.
142. Ibid., 33.
143. Ibid.
144. A, 48.
145. C, 7.
146. C, 4.
147. C, 5.
148. C, 6.
149. Letter from Dr La Néele to M.Guérin, 26 August 1897.
150. 'The abyss which the religious man looks out for is the desire to confiscate God as an assured possession', says A.Vergote in *La Mort rédemptrice du Christ à la lumière de l'anthropologie*, Brussels: Editions Saint-Louis 1976, 80.
151. C, 6.
152. Ibid.
153. 58.10.
154. C, 6.
155. C, 12.
156. Ibid.
157. C,11.
158. C,5.
159. Ibid.
160. 'Beloved mother, you know about this trial; however, I am going to speak to you about it, for I consider it as a great grace I received during your blessed Priorate' (C, 4). It has to be said again here

that if Thérèse can speak about it to her prioress, it is because she thinks that the latter could understand.

161. De Meester, *Dynamique de la confiance* (n.42).

162. Central office of Lisieux 1948. He also wrote biographies of Léonie Martin, Céline, Marie Martin, Marie Guérin and so on.

163. Paris 1964. In his book Conrad de Meester says that he wants 'to insert himself' into the work of Fr Piat, 'to complete it' (21).

164. Marcel Moré, 'Crime et sainteté', *Dieu vivant* 14, 1949, 37–71, and above all 'La table des pécheurs', *Dieu vivant* 24, 1953, 13–103. Marcel Moré based himself especially upon the pioneering works of Abbé Combes, which are indispensable; e.g. his *Introduction à la spiritualité de Thérèse de Lisieux*, Paris: Vrin 1948. But Abbé Combes was rapidly removed from the Carmel archives by Mother Agnes. In his book, Conrad De Meester often repeats that he 'parts company' with Abbé Combes. Indeed the two writers do not adopt the same perspective. Fr De Meester succeeds in speaking at length of Thérèse's text of September 1896 (Manuscript B) which he calls 'the manifesto', a 'major document of the way of spiritual childhood', a 'real map of the way of spiritual childhood' (231), making only a brief and purely descriptive illusion to Easter 1896 (232).

165. Contrary to Moré, De Meester thinks that 'neither Thérèse's person nor her doctrine have been distorted by the brotherly censorship to which her autobiographical writings had been subjected' (19). However, he is compelled to agree 'that there is no exhaustive comparative study of the two texts which enables us to put forward precise conclusions' (ibid.). On the evidence, we can now judge that M.Moré was completely right.

166. *A New Catechism, The Catholic Faith for Adults*, Burns & Oates 1967.

167. Abbé Descouvemont, *Dictionnaire de spiritualité*, cols.581–2

168. Ibid., col.605. It seems that Abbé Descouvemont is taking up here an idea put forward by Guy Gaucher in his lecture cited above (80), but expressed with far more precautions: 'She herself says that the trial related "to Heaven", that is to say to the existence of a future life, the possibility of eternal bliss; that death appeared to her as the passage to nothingness. Did she really doubt the existence of God? There is nothing in her *Writings* which might suggest that. Was she tempted to doubt his love? It seems so.' These commentators should be referred to their dear

studies, to Ia, IIae 91 to 95 of the *Summa theologiae*, for example, on Heaven and blessedness. We have seen that if Thérèse, after the manner of Teresa of Avila, is ready to renounce the enjoyment of bliss – of Love as such – in order to work to make it known more on earth, it is because she does not separate Heaven from the risen Jesus. Abbé Descouvemont had also put forward the same idea in an article in *Christus* (no.109, January 1981), 'L'espérance du ciel chez Thérèse de Lisieux': 'The doubts do not relate to the existence of God but to the existence of a future life' (p.111). Thérèse could not separate one from the other, and in Christian faith one cannot separate one from the other: the whole of this issue of *Christus*, on Heaven, says so. 'I believe in God... I believe in the resurrection,' says the Creed.

169. P.258.
170. Ibid.
171. Ibid.
172. *Au soir de ma vie*, Paris: Plon 1993.
173. Statements collected by B.Révillon, *La Vie*, 18 March 1993 (on another level one might perhaps quote Nietzsche: 'It is not doubt but certainty that makes one mad').
174. *Thérèse et Lisieux*, 258.
175. 'Basically, *to be a believer is to want to be a believer*. Seeking to give an account of her faith, to the faith of her life, Thérèse of Lisieux called herself a Christian because she "wanted to believe", a term which she underlined as essential... This will is not a matter of a voluntarism but of a "first passion"' (Michel de Certeau, *La Faiblesse de croire*, Paris: Seuil 1987, 295).
176. A happy trial: 'I believe I have made more acts of faith in this past year than throughout my whole life,' she confides to Mother Marie de Gonzague (C,7).
177. *Dictionnaire de spiritualité*, col.605 ('People have even gone...') Does Descouvemont perhaps include *The Dutch Catechism*? Or Cardinal Poupard?
178. A foundation established at Lisieux.
179. The *Nouvel Observateur* of 20–26 May 1993 published an article by E.Schemla entitled 'Verbatim: les fausses confidences. Jacques Attali accusé de plagier un livre de Mitterand et Wiesel'. Schemla illustrates his article with the facsimile of a page of *Verbatim* (501, dated 13 September 1983) and the facsimile of a passage of *Entretiens du président avec Élie Wiesel*, 6 January

1988, in the chapter 'La foi' (6–8). On both sides, the president indicates that in faith there is 'a great heroism of the spirit' in continuing 'to look for it when one has already found it'. Then the president (taking the Wiesel version) speaks of the two Thérèses: Teresa of Avila, 'who is a great mystic', and Thérèse of Lisieux, 'who is a little religious without much culture, without any culture at all. Among the great mystiques, that is that. Basically they will have spent half their lives doubting, but they have an internalized faith of such a kind that it allows them constantly to have a point of reference: "I doubt, I am in the desert, it is absolute dryness, God is absent and precisely because of that I continue to believe in Him."'

180. C, 5.

181. Cf. Marie-Dominique Molinié, *Je Choisis tout*, Paris: CLD 1992, 153ff.: 'We must not be blind: this text does not consider believers who sin mortally (and moreover risk losing faith by the abuse of grace) – far less the lukewarm, far less feeble and imperfect souls, or even the desperate: it is solely about those who reject or refuse the faith' (157).

182. Thus on 25 April, Sister Geneviève wrote to Fr Simeon: 'We are privileged and God has put us in a hothouse; our exile passes with chosen souls. Oh! the religious vocation is a great grace. What fine examples we have always!'

183. Georges Morel, *Le Sens de l'existence selon saint Jean de la Croix*, Paris: Aubier 1960, II, 345.

184. *Cahiers de 'Monsieur Ouine' de Georges Bernanos*, présenté par Daniel Pézéril, Paris: Seuil 1991.

185. Ibid., p.11.

186. Ibid. In a fine testimony entitled 'Thérèse de la Nuit' (*Annales de Lisieux*, October 1992, 13–14), Didier Decoin writes: 'Converts – of whom I am one – are often hybrid beings, divided between the joy of bedazzlement which has made them reel and the anxiety which makes them think that this marvellous light is about to be eclipsed: I have never had such fear of losing God as I have had since I found him.' And later: 'The faith of Thérèse of the night is no longer credulity, it is no longer reflection, it is no longer mysticism, no longer intellect; it is trust towards and against everything, an obstinate trust like a revolt.'

187. In an article entitled 'Bernanos et l'incroyance' (*La Croix*, 23 May 1992), Emile Poulat has expressed two basic disagreements with the position of Daniel Pézéril: 'Can one understand the

mystics if one is not mystical oneself?' is his definition of his first disagreement. The second concerns 'a way of reducing the other to oneself... at the same time denying him in his otherness: "My brothers, unbelievers, in your own way you are believers like us."' For Émile Poulat, in the end of the day there is a strict dualism in a binary hermetical categorization (even a reductive dualism, for example, in his own account of the evolution of Christianity: 'We have gone from a world filled with God to a word which has departed from God', *Paris-Match*, 23 August 1994). Daniel Pézeril has responded to him (*La Croix*, 16 June 1992): 'I will say simply that I am very surprised that M.Poulat has not mentioned the interpretation which motivated my introduction to the *Cahiers de 'Monsieur Ouine'*. It would have prevented such seriously disparaging comments'; and Daniel Pézeril emphasizes the primordial conviction expressed in his introduction, a conviction, he says that '[he has] summed up in [his] text by this phrase – which M.Poulat has not quoted: "No believer can ever forget that within him is always an unbeliever who believes."'

188. Ibid., 11–12. The author then applies this analysis to Bernanos.
189. Ibid., 12.
190. Cf. also Bernanos' 1947 lecture 'Nos amis les saints' in *La liberté, pour quoi faire?*, Paris: Folio Essais 1995, 210–30.
191. It is quite amazing to see that Thérèse is utilized to attenuate contemporary unbelief. In a lecture entitled 'Sainte Thérèse de l'Enfant-Jesus, docteur de l'Amour, et le monde de l'incroyance' (19 July 1990, published by *Vie thérésienne*, April-July 1991), Cardinal Poupard, President of the Pontifical Council for Dialogue with Non-Believers and the Pontifical Council of Culture, begins by saying that among the 'marvels that God did through Thérèse, there is an astonishing and extraordinary one, her relationship with unbelief' (69). The cardinal states firmly that Thérèse experienced 'the trial of faith in the midst of a world assailed by unbelief' (ibid.), that she entered the 'dense night of doubt' (73). 'Thérèse's painful experience is undeniably linked to the awareness of the concrete existence of atheism' (79). 'Does it not seem that she is already experiencing the drama of atheistic humanism: "Does God exist?"' (78). 'Thérèse dared to look in the face what Jesus made her see in faith: unbelief exists' (81). Contrary to a number of her contemporaries for whom unbelief was a sign of intellectual weakness or of more or less hidden

immorality, Thérèse takes seriously the drama of human freedom which has the power to deny God within the very heart of its reason' (82).

To that point I can only agree, all the more so since Cardinal Poupard is taking up almost word for word a text 'Thérèse de Lisieux et les incroyants' which I wrote for *Les Nouvelles de l'Institut catholique de Paris* (May 1973, 151–65), an institute of which he was the rector (in his lecture, in the midst of numerous quotations, my name was not mentioned once, but never mind!).

Where the shoe pinches is that Cardinal Poupard, having spoken of unbelief in the time of Thérèse, makes this astonishing statement: 'The non-believers of today are no longer those of Thérèse's time. They are often those who believe badly, more often still agnostics and those who are apparently indifferent... An inversion of tendency between her age and ours has come about. Whereas the scientism and rationalism of the end of the nineteenth century encouraged unbelief, today scholars, having become seekers, are on the whole more modest. A number of non-believers are discovering the emptiness of atheistic philosophical systems. The social and cultural, political and economic catastrophe of Marxism-Leninism has engendered an immense frustration, a void and a call.' Now Thérèse went to the depth of unbelief and a rejection of God which has not varied for a century, an unbelief which is certainly even stronger today!

192. Hans Jonas, *Der Gottesbegriff nach Auschwitz*, Tübingen 1984. [The author refers to this as quoted by another source, in French.]

193. Ibid.

194. Ibid.

195. Ibid.

196. Thérèse said that in a way God in Heaven is impotent to save souls, that this comes about through hearts burning with his love which works on earth; she also thought that when she was in heaven she would continue, through a heart burning with love, to work on earth, helping those who work to make God known.

197. Jonas, *Der Gottesbegriff nach Auschwitz* (n.192).

198. Ibid.

199. A statement made to Daniel Pézeril, *Cahiers de 'Monsieur Ouine'* (n.184),11.

200. Ibid., 10.

201. *Bernanos par lui-meme*, Paris: Seuil 1957, 41.
202. *Dictionnaire de spiritualité*, cols.606–8.
203. And not a word in the bibliography.
204. Paris: José Corti 1937 (reissued Paris: Editions Denoël-Gonthier 1078). On the cover of the book is the usual Thérèse, flower of Lisieux, with her crucifix in her arms, from which a shower of roses is falling in pure Sulpician style.
205. Ibid., 101.
206. Ibid., 11.
207. Ibid., 12.
208. Ibid., 14.
209. Ibid., 22.
210. Chapter IV.
211. Mabille, *Thérèse de Lisieux* (n.204), 27.
212. Ibid., 32.
213. Ibid.
214. Ibid., 33.
215. Ibid., 65.
216. Ibid., 73.
217. Ibid., 31.
218. Ibid., 74.
219. Ibid., 81.
220. Ibid., 101.
221. Ibid., 80.
222. Ibid., 102.
223. Ibid., 77.
224. Ibid., 78.
225. And Mother Agnes substitutes 'never', which is absolute, for 'not', which is relative.
226. Ibid., 43.
227. The phrase 'The five years that I spent there were the saddest of my life' (A.22), which Abbé Descouvemont puts at the head of his text and which he emphasizes (*Thérèse et Lisieux*, 42), is curiously suppressed by Mother Agnes (*Story of a Soul*, Chapter III).
228. 'Longing... gaze' omitted by Mabille.
229. 'I hope' also omitted by Mabille.
230. Mabille, *Thérèse de Lisieux*, 56.
231. Cf. J.-F.Six, *Thérèse de Lisieux au carmel*, 106–12, 123–4.
232. Four extracts of issues of *La Croix du Calvados* of this date have

been found among Thérèse's papers: the articles virulently attack the 'renegade monk'.

233. One might recall the last words of Manuscript C in which she portrays sin in the extreme to indicate abandonment in the extreme, in trust in the hands of God: 'Even if I had on my conscience all the sins that can be committed, I would go, my heart broken with sorrow, and throw myself into Jesus' arms' (C, 36).

234. C, 32.

235. C, 35.

236. C, 33.

237. Ibid., 280.

238. Jean Guitton has his distinctive way of putting it: 'Thérèse still counts on being active in glory and working effectively. She has no desire to enter into the rest that we would wish for the dead. It is not the *requiem aeternam* but, on the contrary if one might put it that way, the *actionem aeternam dona nobis domine* that she would pronounce. "My God, give me power to act eternally with you"' (*Nouvelles de l'Institut catholique de Paris*, May 1973, 35).

239. To this text, written later, has been added 'to make love love'. Note 148 of the *Derniers Entretiens* (721–3) gives an excellent example of the amplification and transformation ('amplification', says Gaucher modestly, *Passion* [n.79], 247), which texts of Thérèse have been subjected. On 19 March 1950, Sister Geneviève explained that the gloss 'to make love love' added in the *Story of a Soul* had been very successful and that she had not lied to the process: 'The judge of the tribunal knew this phrase by heart, and I found myself led to take it up, and at that point I did not think it a good thing to re-establish the precise formula. In other circumstances these gentlemen made me accept such and such an expression without my daring to protest indefinitely and to impose my thought.' Unfortunately Sister Geneviève does not indicate these 'other circumstances', and it is a pity that she did not defend truth more. Mother Agnes kept the gloss in *Novissima Verba* (1927), and would not budge until her death (28 July 1951), despite the correction made by Sister Geneviève.

240. She would say on 18 July that her soul was 'called to raise itself to God by the ELEVATOR of love and not to climb the rough stairway of fear'.

241. Matthew 28.20.
242. Cf. C, 7.
243. To Fr Roulland.
244. Sister Marie passes on to her father on 27 August, at the time when Thérèse was suffering most, one of her sayings: 'Happily I did not ask for suffering, for if I had asked for it I would be afraid of not having the patience to bear it, while since it comes from the pure will of the good God, He cannot refuse me the patience and grace necessary to bear it.'
245. How can one not find jarring, in so many books about Thérèse, the continual emphasis on the physical suffering that she underwent? One would say this was a ploy to attract pity. How many others have experienced such suffering and in much more uncomfortable material and sanitary conditions! 'I suffer, I suffer', appears in large capitals in Abbé Descouvemont's *Thérèse et Lisieux* (288, 289), and he sets out in large capitals (294) a saying from the *Last Conversations* which does not seem to come from Thérèse, because it is so pretentious: 'I have suffered much here below; souls should be made to know this' (31 August 1897).
246. C,5.
247. C,7.
248. On 5 August, Mother Agnes wrote to M. and Mme Guérin – and I am citing the testimony here because it was written at the time and has not been retouched: 'The other day she aroused my pity; she looked at me with such a suffering little air and I said to her, "Oh! my poor darling, you have difficulty in seeing that Heaven is not for tomorrow, don't you?" She immediately replied, "Little mother, don't you know yet?"' In fact Mother Agnes did not understand her, simply did not understand, like Abbé Bellière. But Mother Agnes had always been near her; she should have understood.
249. C, 6 (cf. 'the eternal possession of God').
250. C,7.
251. C, 2–3. It is the only time in the autobiographical manuscripts that she talks of the 'little way'.
252. C, 36–37.
253. Speaking of Thérèse's genius, Fr Congar writes: 'This genius is also the fact of an original and profound intuition which is pushed to the limit of its consequences. The person of genius does not see things superficially, but sees them in their depth and draws the absolute consequences. This is what Thérèse did with her intui-

tions about the Love of God and the "little way" of going to him'
(4).

254. Abbé Bellière prefigures all those who will want to 'see'.

255. C, 11.

256. She had already spoken of this text to Abbé Belliere on 18 July,
writing 'the last scene'.

257. C, 12.

258. On 5 August Mother Agnes wrote to M. and Mme Guérin, who
had sent a letter to Thérèse: 'She keenly wanted to reply to it:
immediately she wanted to be given her pencil, but she was too
tired. It would not have been prudent.' Fortunately Mother Agnes
could not prevent her from writing to Abbé Bellière on 10 August.

259. There are some orthographical mistakes, errors and abbrevia-
tions in her text.

260. There is the black notebook, Manuscript C, addressed to Mother
Marie de Gonzague, written in June and at the beginning of July;
and there is Thérèse's correspondence which stops on August 10.
I am keeping strictly to that (I have explained why in the
introduction, 'Method').

261. Again, with Mother Agnes, we have the itch to 'see'.